# OCCUPATION AND PAY IN GREAT BRITAIN 1906–79

## Guy Routh

*Reader in Economics*
*University of Sussex*

First edition (entitled *Occupation and Pay in Great Britain 1906–60* and published for the National Institute of Economic and Social Research by Cambridge University Press) 1965
Second edition (published by Macmillan) 1980

THE MACMILLAN PRESS LTD
*London and Basingstoke*
*Companies and representatives*
*throughout the world*

*Printed in Hong Kong*


British Library Cataloguing in Publication Data

Routh, Guy
  Occupation and pay in Great Britain, 1906–79
  – 2nd ed.
  1. Wages – Great Britain – History – 20th century
  2. Great Britain – Occupations
  I. Title
  331.2'8          HD5015

ISBN 0–333–28417–8
ISBN 0–333–28653–7 (Paper)

# Contents

# List of Tables and Figures

## TABLES

vi

FIGURES

# Preface to the Second Edition

The first edition of this book was compiled over a period of five years by a small team of people working at the National Institute of Economic and Social Research. The Institute has now kindly given me permission to bring out a second edition, extending the story of occupation and pay in Great Britain from 1960 (where the first edition ended) to 1979. In the late fifties and early sixties, there was a dearth of data and we had to collect much of it ourselves, a requirement not without advantages for it entailed interviewing people to whom the data applied and thus gave insight into what the material actually meant. Today, the researcher suffers from an embarrassment of riches, which brings with it problems of its own relating to interpretation and reconciliation. Each new accession of data knocks out old theories and calls for new hypotheses to enter the ring.

The process of rethinking has been much aided by a series of seminars at which I was able to present ideas and harvest those of the people who attended. They were held at the Institute of Manpower Studies at the University of Sussex; the New York School of Industrial and Labor Relations at Cornell University, kindly arranged by Robert L. Aronson; the Oxford Institute of Economics and Statistics, to which Derek Robinson gathered a small group of eminent people; the National Institute of Economic and Social Research; the Labour Studies Graduate Division of the University of Sussex. It was rewarding, too, at the invitation of Laurie Hunter, to address the British Universities Industrial Relations Association at their conference at the University of Edinburgh this year, and present my problems to seventy labour specialists. Those who remain dissatisfied with the results should consider what they would have been like had they not been tempered in these intellectual fires.

I am grateful to the Institute of Manpower Studies for funds that they provided for assistance in the research for the new edition. Edward Fordyce did sterling work in the incorporation in the occupation tables of the data from the Population Census of 1971, a process demanding considerable patience and accuracy. Alison Mitchell collected data and wrote a memorandum on managers' pay in the 1970s, which helped me in the difficult task of reconciling the old data with the new.

I was able to gather useful material at the Institute of Industrial Relations at the University of California, Berkeley, where I benefited from the advice of Lloyd Ulman. At the Sussex European Research Centre, I have enjoyed the counsel of Christopher Saunders and David Marsden who have been engaged with problems similar to those treated in this book, but on a European scale. I have been helped, too, by discussions with Stuart Rusby of the New Earnings Survey, James Scullion and Gay Wenban-Smith of the staff of the Royal Commission on the Distribution of Income and Wealth, S. D. Margolis of the Engineering Employers' Federation, Jay Gershuny of the Science Policy Research Unit, and T. H. R. who checked the statistics with saint-like fortitude.

The literature, especially on the subject of pay, is now enormous, and quite beyond the compass of any one person, despite the feat of George Bain and Gillian Woolven of cataloguing it, for Britain, in their *Bibliography of British Industrial Relations*. I am sure I must have missed many papers and books relevant to the topics here considered. I apologise to their authors, to whom I should be grateful for offprints or references.

Guy Routh

University of Sussex
November 1979

# Preface to the First Edition

The project from which this book has come was designed originally by Mr W. A. B. Hopkin when he was Director of the National Institute of Economic and Social Research. With funds from the Nuffield Foundation, the Institute appointed me to begin research in September 1957, and I was joined soon after by Miss Beryl Swift and later by Miss Pam Peachey.

Our brief was to investigate the changing economic fortunes of the principal 'Common Interest Groups' of which society is composed. Source of income was suggested as the criterion by which common interest should be defined and since, for the economically active population, occupation is the main determinant of income, it followed that our concern should be with the fortunes of people following similar occupations. For most occupations there are professional institutions, associations or trade unions whose function is to protect and promote the interests of the group they represent. Here, we have tried to measure the growth or decline in numbers of these groups and in their relative income between the years immediately preceding the First World War and 1960. The income data cover the major groups of employees and, in addition, some of those in independent practice in the professions, but other self-employed people, proprietors and employers, are omitted. Ideally, we should have included these too, as well as those whose income is derived from property, but an extension of our research into these fields would have yielded dubious results for much labour and we did not even attempt it.

In the event, we found the shifts in occupational distribution much smaller than we had anticipated. General characteristics in 1951 (and in 1959, as far as we could judge) were similar to those of 1911: the bulk of the labour force was still engaged in manual work, while the higher professional class remained numerically insignificant. Managers and working proprietors were an almost constant proportion of the total and though skilled manual workers fell as a proportion, they remained almost constant in numbers. Of the seven classes into which we divided the labour force, only clerical workers rose substantially both in numbers and as a proportion of the whole. As another measure of the extent of quantitative change in the labour force, we estimated time spent in vocational training, over and above minimum school-leaving requirements: this rose from 16·1 years per hundred persons employed in 1911 to 18·3 years in 1959. The rise occasioned considerable effort, but registered as little more than an additional week per occupied person.

Judged by their social and political correlates, these occupational changes have been small; but the *technical* effect of even a small change in proportions may be very great. The work of doctors, engineers and scientists is of profound importance; it is their presence that distinguishes the present from previous epochs. Yet, in 1951, the census showed only 62,000 doctors, 138,000 engineers, surveyors and architects, and 49,000 scientists. In 1911, however, there were only 36,000 doctors, 25,000 engineers and 5,000 scientists. Their numbers have almost quadrupled, though the increase represents only three-quarters of one per cent of the labour force.

In pay structure, again, the most impressive finding was the rigidity of the inter-class and inter-occupational relationships. According to our calculations, the average for semi-skilled men was 86 per cent of the all-class average in 1913 and 85 per cent in 1960; for unskilled men, the percentage was the same in both years. The women's average was 63 per cent of the all-class average in 1913 and 64 per cent in 1960.

For manual workers in manufacturing and building, there were moderate changes in the dispersion of earnings, as measured by the relationship between median and quartiles, between 1906, 1938 and 1960; but much of this change is eliminated when adjustments are made for the changed proportions of skilled, semi-skilled and unskilled manual workers. For men in manufacturing, the semi-skilled median is 75·7 per cent of the average for foremen and skilled workers in 1906 and 73·3 per cent in 1960; for unskilled men it is 61·9 per cent in both years.

Over the whole range of occupations, however, there have been some striking changes: specifically, in the reduced relative pay of professional workers, both higher and lower, and of male clerical workers. There has been some reduction, too, in the relative pay of skilled manual-working men. These changes have led some people to believe in an inherent tendency for inequalities of pay to diminish with economic advance. When one traces the course of relative pay over time, however, the interesting fact emerges that these reductions have not occurred gradually, as a result of a general tendency, but suddenly, within short periods and owing to an extraordinary conjuncture of circumstances. In intervening periods, egalitarian tendencies have disappeared or been reversed. It is the medieval doctrine of the Just Wage that asserts itself, while the neo-classic doctrine of marginal productivity or even the broader classical doctrine of demand and supply are but dimly discerned.

In the course of our investigations we consulted many individuals and organizations. With few exceptions, they answered our questions with patience and candour.* Particular thanks must go to the Ministry of Labour, whose officials were generous with advice and information, and the Committee of London Clearing Bankers, who conducted a special inquiry to give us information that could be compared with pre-war data.

Individuals to whom particular thanks are due for general guidance or help on special problems are Professors E. H. Phelps Brown, B. C. Roberts, Alec Nove and Joan Robinson; Mr Bernard Benjamin of the General Register Office; Mr G. Paine of the Inland Revenue; Mr V. Peschanski of the Institute of World Economy, Moscow; Mr Joseph S. Zeisel of the United States Department of Labor; and my one-time fellow-students of the London School of Economics, Dr Stefan Nedzynski (now Assistant General Secretary of the International Confederation of Free Trade Unions) and Mr J. Simmons (now of the Israel Institute of Productivity). Still more particularly, I should like to thank Lady Wootton, who read and commented on various drafts of the present book and greatly encouraged our efforts; Mr Ernest Kettley who, as Education Officer of the Institute of Personnel Management, collaborated with me in organizing a series of conferences on pay and employment; Mr Christopher Saunders, at that time Director of the National Institute of Economic and Social Research, and Mrs Anne Jackson, the Institute's Executive Secretary. To Mr Saunders, my debt is profound. He worked through my pages with immense patience; his suggestions have made the book much more intelligible than it would otherwise have been. Miss Jane Harington, the Institute's Librarian, had the task of preparing the manuscript for the press—in the course of which it was greatly improved. The secretarial work was performed with calm efficiency by Miss Ivy Aird.

The labour of collecting and interpreting the data was shared with Miss Swift and Miss Peachey; this was a truly co-operative effort, though the final responsibility for the presentation and interpretation, with all their imperfections, is my own.

---

* The most notable exception being the national newspapers, who declined to reveal the pay of their editors, now or in days gone by.

Finally, I must thank the Nuffield Foundation who so generously financed this enterprise and Mr W. A. B. Hopkin on whose initiative it was begun.

GUY ROUTH

University of Sussex,
April 1965

# List of Abbreviations

| | |
|---|---|
| Cmd. | Command Paper |
| DEP | Department of Employment, previously Ministry of Labour |
| HMSO | Her/His Majesty's Stationery Office |
| n.e.c. | Not elsewhere classified |
| n.e.s. | Not elsewhere specified |
| NES | New Earnings Survey |

## SYMBOLS USED IN TABLES

| | |
|---|---|
| .. | not available or not applicable |
| — | nil or negligible |
| n.d. | not distinguished |
| ( ) | doubtful, or not completely distinguished |

# Introduction

For the fifty years between leaving school and retirement, man's central activity is work. His work creates the wealth of society and entitles him to a share of that wealth; and the sort of work that he does is a major determinant of the size of his share. On this basic economic relationship of production and distribution, a complex of other relationships exists, for occupation is itself an important (though by no means the only) determinant of differences in morbidity, mortality, fertility, social outlook and political allegiance, while the occupation of the father, again, partly determines the occupations of his children and, in turn, his children's children.[1] It is to be expected, then, that those who follow a particular occupation should have common interests and a common destiny and should be drawn together to protect and promote those interests.

The British Medical Association was established in 1832, the National Union of Teachers in 1870,[2] and somewhere in between there grew the associations of skilled craftsmen that formed the basis of the modern trade union movement. In the 1890s there followed the large-scale organisation of unskilled workers, on the one hand, and non-manual workers on the other. Later, we shall consider the role of these organisations in determining changes in pay, but here we may note that, in origin, they were associations of people following the same occupations (or closely related occupations) and that, even today when trade unions sometimes attempt to embrace all the occupations in a particular industry, rates of pay are fixed by occupation, with other features, such as personal qualities, industry or place, as secondary considerations.

This book is concerned with the changing size of occupational classes and with their concomitant pay structure in Great Britain in the years 1906 to 1979.[3] Comparisons of occupational structure in a country at different times (or different countries at the same time) are significant indicators of social differences because each occupation consists of a bundle of attributes: literacy, theoretical knowledge or manual skill; earning and productive capacity; fertility, mortality and social outlook.

Occupational patterns change with technical advance and capital

1

accumulation, which require a growth of investment in people no less than in machines. Rising living standards themselves call new services into being, thus causing further occupational change. Technical advance requires a more highly educated work force; and this itself speeds the rate of advance.

Pay structure, too, is indicative of a country's stage of development, a large rural and small urban population going with great inequalities of pay between unskilled labourers and craftsmen and between manual workers in general and professional, administrative and clerical workers. Later, with diversification of the labour force and the spread of literacy, the gulf is narrowed, though what happens in subsequent stages of development is more obscure. Some writers claim to have discovered an inherent tendency for inequalities to disappear as industrial societies mature; others dispute their claims.

The basic assumption of economic theory is that changes in one or more of the variables demand, supply and price will produce such changes in the other or others as to restore (or tend to restore) the equilibrium of the system. But Adam Smith, Mill, Cairnes, Wicksteed and Marshall all gave prominence to warnings of the institutional and psychological impediments to the achievement of this ideal. In latter-day economics, these aspects have tended to be obscured by a controversy about the role of trade unions in the pay-fixing process, some attributing to them almost unlimited power to raise pay whilst others regard them as simple underwriters of market decisions that would have been arrived at anyway. Concurrently, the question of social stratification has become a major preoccupation of sociologists, whose findings have great relevance to the understanding of the labour market.

The questions thus raised are fundamental to an understanding of the society in which we live. To answer them, even tentatively, we need to know a good deal about the changing quantity and price of the occupational units of which the labour market is composed and the demand-supply relationships with which they are associated. In what follows, the quantity aspect (occupational class structure) is considered in Chapter 1; price (or pay structure) in Chapter 2; the time and circumstance of pay changes in Chapter 3. Finally, in Chapter 4 we consider the nature of the society that has given rise to these relationships and changes, and the relevance to it of the dominant theories of economics and sociology.

# 1 Occupational Class Structure

## 1. OCCUPATIONAL CLASSIFICATION

Occupation is what a worker does; industry is defined by the final product. The occupations of fitter, clerk, typographer and packer, for example, are followed in a multitude of different industries. The two main agencies for the compilation of manpower data are the Department of Employment and the Office of Population Censuses and Surveys (in conjunction with the General Register Office, Edinburgh). The Department of Employment collects data from employers, on a monthly or annual basis, the Census Office from heads of households in the decennial census of population.

The census occupational tables classify the occupied population (including those seeking work) according to 'the kind of work done and the nature of the operation performed'. Each heading describes a group of closely related jobs, performed by people of the same sort of skill, using similar materials and techniques in the same sort of environment. The advantage of this method is its flexibility; the parts are small enough to be manoeuvrable but not so small as to overwhelm with detail. They are susceptible to classification into larger groups, whose limits are defined by the purpose of the particular study.

The census occupational tables reached their apogee in 1951 when they distinguished 584 job-groups.[1] In 1961, prudence or parsimony resulted in their reduction to 201 categories.[2] This pattern was followed, with only minor amendments, in 1966 and 1971. Some 'illusions of accuracy' have doubtless been eliminated, but against this must be set the pain and suffering of those of us who like to make comparisons over the years to find out what is going on. To us the Registrar General tersely remarks, 'Comparison of occupation figures for 1951 and 1961 is very difficult as the occupation classification has been completely revised.'[3]

For present purposes, the problem is not insuperable. We had posted

3

the 584 occupations of the 1951 census to seven classes, two of which were subdivided:

Class 1A. Higher professional
     B. Lower professional
   2A. Employers and proprietors
     B. Managers and administrators
    3. Clerical workers
    4. Foremen, inspectors, supervisors
       *Manual workers*
    5. Skilled
    6. Semi-skilled
    7. Unskilled

We refer to these groups as *occupational classes* to distinguish them from the social classes and socio-economic groups used in the census. They are essentially an adaptation of these census groupings, with certain modifications of detail. Their composition is shown in Appendix A.

Between 1861 and 1961, census reports for England and Wales, on the one hand, and Scotland, on the other, were published separately, though the count was held on the same day; here the numbers have been combined. There was no great difficulty in reconciling the classification of 1921 and 1931 with 1951, though the status divisions of 1931 caused trouble, for employers and managers were combined under the title 'managerial'; where other guides were not available, these were subdivided in the 1921 ratio.[4] For 1911, a number of other sources were used to supplement the census: for mining and railways, current reports; for process workers in manufacturing, the Board of Trade *Report of an Enquiry . . . into Earnings and Hours of Labour of Workpeople in the United Kingdom in 1906*, 8 parts (London: HMSO, 1909–13). Where estimates have been based on inadequate information, numbers in the ensuing tables have been put in brackets.

In 1961 and 1966, the census again did curious things with the status categories: in 1961, employers and managers in the detailed tables were pooled in the manner of 1931, but divided between 'large establishments' (comprising twenty-five or more persons) and 'small establishments', while summary tables were presented showing employers and managers separately; in 1966, for a change, employers and self-employed were combined under the heading 'self-employed with and without employees'. In 1971, there was, happily, a return to the style of 1951.

The revised, and much condensed, classification introduced in 1961 has caused difficulty in the allocation of manual workers to classes 5, 6 and 7: skilled, semi-skilled and unskilled manual workers. Where occupations that in 1951 fell into different classes have been combined for 1961 and subsequent years, the allocation of the census social classes or socio-economic groups has been followed,[5] or (where stated in the text) the 1971 totals have been split in the proportions of 1951, or some other means used to disaggregate them.

## 2. DISTRIBUTION BY OCCUPATIONAL CLASS

The Year 1911 appears remote when viewed from the modern age. We look back, over wars and revolutions, to a world of gaslight, music-halls and hansom cabs, which seems vastly different from our own. We should expect these differences to be reflected in the occupational groupings of the labour force, and yet the dominant fact, then and now, is the preponderance of manual workers. The professionals, though their proportion has more than doubled, remain quite a small minority of the whole, their growth having been exceeded by that of the clerks. Numbers and proportions for six census years are shown in Table 1.1. The grand changes may be summarised thus:[6]

|  | *Percentages* | | | | | |
|---|---|---|---|---|---|---|
|  | *1911* | *1921* | *1931* | *1951* | *1961* | *1971* |
| 1. Professional | 4·05 | 4·53 | 4·60 | 6·63 | 9·00 | 11·07 |
| 2. Employers, managers | 10·14 | 10·46 | 10·36 | 10·50 | 10·10 | 12·43 |
| 3. Clerical | 4·84 | 6·72 | 6·97 | 10·68 | 12·70 | 13·90 |
| 4–7. Foremen and manual | 80·97 | 78·29 | 78·07 | 72·19 | 68·10 | 62·60 |
| Total | 100·00 | 100·00 | 100·00 | 100·00 | 100·00 | 100·00 |

Over the sixty years, classes 4–7 have lost nearly twenty percentage points; of these, 6·5 have gone to the professionals, 2·5 to employers and managers, and 9·0 to the clerks. Figure 1·1 illustrates the change in configuration that these have brought about. The bulk of the cake is still composed of a mixture of classes 4–7, but the three layers of icing have become a good deal thicker. Of course, the constituents of classes 4–7

TABLE 1.1 Occupational class and industrial status of the gainfully occupied population in Great Britain, 1911, 1921, 1931, 1951, 1971: numbers in thousands

| | All | | | | | Males | | | | | Females | | | | |
|---|---|---|---|---|---|---|---|---|---|---|---|---|---|---|---|
| | 1911 | 1921 | 1931 | 1951 | 1971 | 1911 | 1921 | 1931 | 1951 | 1971 | 1911 | 1921 | 1931 | 1951 | 1971 |
| **1. Professional** | | | | | | | | | | | | | | | |
| **A. Higher** | | | | | | | | | | | | | | | |
| Employers | .. | 25 | 38 | 34 | 79 | .. | 25 | 37 | 33 | 75 | .. | — | — | 1 | 4 |
| Own account | .. | 36 | 44 | 44 | 59 | .. | 35 | 41 | 40 | 53 | .. | 2 | 3 | 4 | 7 |
| Employees | .. | 134 | 158 | 356 | 687 | .. | 126 | 144 | 326 | 646 | .. | 8 | 15 | 31 | 40 |
| All | 184 | 195 | 240 | 434 | 824 | 173 | 186 | 222 | 399 | 774 | 11 | 10 | 18 | 36 | 50 |
| % | 1·00 | 1·01 | 1·14 | 1·93 | 3·29 | 1·34 | 1·36 | 1·50 | 2·56 | 4·87 | 0·20 | 0·18 | 0·29 | 0·52 | 0·55 |
| **B. Lower** | | | | | | | | | | | | | | | |
| Employers | .. | 18 | 15 | 10 | 25 | .. | 14 | 8 | 7 | 17 | .. | 4 | 7 | 3 | 7 |
| Own account | .. | 62 | 70 | 42 | 59 | .. | 20 | 22 | 22 | 37 | .. | 42 | 48 | 20 | 22 |
| Employees | .. | 600 | 643 | 1007 | 1863 | .. | 242 | 270 | 463 | 892 | .. | 357 | 373 | 544 | 971 |
| All | 560 | 680 | 728 | 1059 | 1946 | 208 | 276 | 300 | 492 | 946 | 352 | 403 | 428 | 567 | 1000 |
| % | 3·05 | 3·52 | 3·46 | 4·70 | 7·78 | 1·61 | 2·02 | 2·03 | 3·16 | 5·95 | 6·49 | 7·07 | 6·83 | 8·18 | 10·95 |
| **2. Employers, administrators, managers** | | | | | | | | | | | | | | | |
| **A. Employers and proprietors** | | | | | | | | | | | | | | | |
| Employers | 763 | 692 | 727 | 457 | 621 | 661 | 613 | 646 | 400 | 485 | 102 | 79 | 82 | 56 | 136 |
| Own account | 469 | 626 | 682 | 661 | 435 | 339 | 435 | 483 | 494 | 320 | 130 | 191 | 196 | 167 | 115 |
| All | 1232 | 1318 | 1409 | 1118 | 1056 | 1000 | 1048 | 1129 | 894 | 805 | 232 | 270 | 278 | 223 | 251 |
| % | 6·71 | 6·82 | 6·70 | 4·97 | 4·22 | 7·74 | 7·69 | 7·65 | 5·74 | 5·07 | 4·28 | 4·74 | 4·44 | 3·22 | 2·75 |
| **B. Managers and administrators** | | | | | | | | | | | | | | | |
| Own account | 21 | 29 | 30 | 31 | 46 | 20 | 27 | 28 | 27 | 35 | 2 | 2 | 2 | 3 | 11 |
| Employees | 608 | 675 | 740 | 1215 | 2008 | 486 | 557 | 642 | 1029 | 1698 | 123 | 118 | 98 | 186 | 310 |
| All | 629 | 704 | 770 | 1246 | 2054 | 506 | 584 | 670 | 1056 | 1733 | 125 | 120 | 100 | 189 | 321 |
| % | 3·43 | 3·64 | 3·66 | 5·53 | 8·21 | 3·91 | 4·28 | 4·54 | 6·78 | 10·91 | 2·30 | 2·11 | 1·60 | 2·73 | 3·51 |

|  | | | | | | | | | | | | | | | |
|---|---|---|---|---|---|---|---|---|---|---|---|---|---|---|---|
| **3. Clerical workers** | | | | | | | | | | | | | | | |
| Own account | — | 1 | 2 | 3 | 22 | — | 1 | 2 | 2 | 5 | — | — | — | 1 | 17 |
| Employees | 887 | 1299 | 1463 | 2401 | 3457 | 708 | 735 | 815 | 988 | 1008 | 179 | 564 | 648 | 1413 | 2449 |
| All | 887 | 1300 | 1465 | 2404 | 3479 | 708 | 736 | 817 | 990 | 1013 | 179 | 564 | 648 | 1414 | 2466 |
| % | 4·84 | 6·72 | 6·97 | 10·68 | 13·90 | 5·48 | 5·40 | 5·53 | 6·35 | 6·38 | 3·30 | 9·90 | 10·34 | 20·41 | 27·00 |
| **4. Foremen, inspectors supervisors** | | | | | | | | | | | | | | | |
| Employees | 236 | 279 | 323 | 590 | 968 | 227 | 261 | 295 | 511 | 801 | 10 | 18 | 28 | 79 | 168 |
| % | 1·29 | 1·44 | 1·54 | 2·62 | 3·87 | 1·75 | 1·91 | 2·00 | 3·28 | 5·04 | 0·18 | 0·32 | 0·45 | 1·14 | 1·84 |
| *Manual workers* | | | | | | | | | | | | | | | |
| **5. Skilled** | | | | | | | | | | | | | | | |
| Own account | 329 | 293 | 268 | 251 | 349 | 170 | 205 | 200 | 214 | 324 | 159 | 88 | 68 | 37 | 25 |
| Employees | 5279 | 5280 | 5351 | 5365 | 5045 | 4094 | 4200 | 4223 | 4519 | 4295 | 1185 | 1080 | 1128 | 847 | 750 |
| All | 5608 | 5573 | 5619 | 5616 | 5394 | 4264 | 4405 | 4423 | 4733 | 4619 | 1344 | 1168 | 1196 | 884 | 775 |
| % | 30·56 | 28·83 | 26·72 | 24·95 | 21·56 | 32·99 | 32·30 | 29·96 | 30·36 | 29·08 | 24·78 | 20·50 | 19·09 | 12·75 | 8·48 |
| **6. Semi-skilled** | | | | | | | | | | | | | | | |
| Own account | 71 | 98 | 96 | 82 | 53 | 41 | 70 | 78 | 73 | 35 | 30 | 28 | 17 | 10 | 18 |
| Employees | 7173 | 6446 | 7264 | 7256 | 6258 | 4305 | 3789 | 4181 | 4279 | 3272 | 2868 | 2656 | 3084 | 2978 | 2986 |
| All | 7244 | 6544 | 7360 | 7338 | 6312 | 4346 | 3859 | 4259 | 4352 | 3307 | 2898 | 2684 | 3101 | 2988 | 3005 |
| % | 39·48 | 33·85 | 35·00 | 32·60 | 25·23 | 33·63 | 28·30 | 28·85 | 27·92 | 20·82 | 53·42 | 47·11 | 49·51 | 43·12 | 32·90 |
| **7. Unskilled** | | | | | | | | | | | | | | | |
| Own account | 47 | 62 | 78 | 33 | 92 | 38 | 48 | 65 | 29 | 86 | 9 | 14 | 13 | 3 | 6 |
| Employees | 1720 | 2678 | 3034 | 2676 | 2895 | 1455 | 2232 | 2580 | 2129 | 1803 | 265 | 446 | 454 | 547 | 1092 |
| All | 1767 | 2740 | 3115 | 2709 | 2987 | 1493 | 2280 | 2645 | 2158 | 1889 | 274 | 460 | 467 | 550 | 1098 |
| % | 9·63 | 14·17 | 14·81 | 12·03 | 11·94 | 11·55 | 16·72 | 17·92 | 13·84 | 11·89 | 5·05 | 8·07 | 7·45 | 7·94 | 12·02 |
| **All** | 18,347 | 19,333 | 21,029 | 22,514 | 25,021 | 12,925 | 13,636 | 14,761 | 15,584 | 15,884 | 5425 | 5697 | 6264 | 6930 | 9138 |
| % | 100·00 | 100·00 | 100·00 | 100·00 | 100·00 | 100·00 | 100·00 | 100·00 | 100·00 | 100·00 | 100·00 | 100·00 | 100·00 | 100·00 | 100·00 |

Note: Because numbers are rounded to the nearest thousand, totals may not equal the sum of their parts.

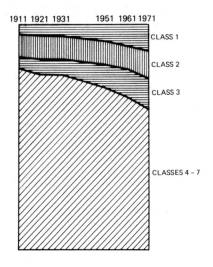

FIGURE 1.1 Occupational distribution, 1911–71

have themselves changed. The proportion of foremen within this group has increased from 1·6 to 6·2 per cent; that of skilled workers has fallen from 37·75 to 34·4; the semi-skilled are down from 48·8 to 40·3, while unskilled proportions have risen from 11·9 to 19·1.

The proportion of skilled manual workers drifted down while their numbers, until 1951, fluctuated about 5·6 million. By 1971, they were down to 5·4 million. By contrast, the number of higher professionals rose from 184,000 to 824,000, a factor of 4·5. The factor for lower professionals was 3·5 and for clerical workers 3·9. A change of 1 per cent in the overall distribution in 1971, it must be noted, represents the transfer of 250,000 people from one class to another.

Not only are there great differences in the rate of increase of various classes; these rates have varied considerably over time. This is best shown by comparing the average annual compound percentage rates of increase in the different periods:

|                          | 1911–21 | 1921–31 | 1931–51 | 1951–61 | 1961–71 |
|--------------------------|---------|---------|---------|---------|---------|
| IA. Higher professional  | 0·5     | 2·1     | 3·0     | 5·2     | 1·4     |
| IB. Lower professional   | 1·9     | 0·7     | 1·9     | 2·9     | 3·1     |
| 3. Clerks                | 3·9     | 1·2     | 2·5     | 2·2     | 1·5     |

The class changes are the net result of various effects: the rise or fall of the occupations of which each class is composed, which themselves are in part the result of changes in industrial distribution, in part the result of changes in techniques of production within each industry. These will be considered later in this chapter, after an examination of the constituents and changes within each class.

## 3. INTERNATIONAL COMPARISONS

We have had a preliminary look at the way occupational class distribution changed in Britain over time: before going on to examine the changes in more detail, it will be interesting to see where that puts the country in a wider spectrum. Table 1.2 gives data for a selection of countries, with the percentage distribution of the labour force in six groups.[7] The first group, professional, technical and related workers, approximates closely to our occupational class 1, but for the other groups there are some important differences.[8] The important point, for the purposes of Table 1.2, is that the composition of the groups is consistent between countries.

According to the United Nations *Yearbook of National Accounts Statistics*, Sweden had the highest *per capita* income of the countries listed in Table 1.2, fifty-five times that of India. The first three columns accounted for 38·6 per cent of its labour force and only 6·4 per cent of that of India. The United States, next in wealth to Sweden, had 38·4 per cent in the first three columns. As one moves down the scale of wealth, so the proportion of professional and clerical workers falls, while that of farmers etc. (agricultural, animal husbandry and forestry workers, fishermen and hunters) rises. But there is much inconsistency: judging by its proportions of professionals, managers and clerks, the United Kingdom should be richer than France and Germany and much richer than Japan; but it is poorer than all three. It is strange that Germany and Japan, two of the world's most successful industrial nations, should get along with a comparatively low proportion of professional and technical workers, and that Czechoslovakia, somewhat low on the wealth scale, should have so many. This, and the fact that they have so few clerks, no doubt characterises advanced, centrally planned economies. In the first edition of this book it was noted that in 1959 clerks accounted for 12 per cent of the occupied population in Britain and 2·8 per cent in the USSR, and that Professor Alec Nove had commented, 'there are remarkably few clerks in the Soviet civil service, and this, one

TABLE 1.2 Percentage distribution of labour force in six groups, various countries, *circa* 1970

| | | Professional, technical and related | Admin. and managerial | Clerical and related | Sales | Farmers etc. | Others |
|---|---|---|---|---|---|---|---|
| Czechoslovakia | 1970 | 19·4 | 2.4 | 7·4 | 7·0 | 12·0 | 51·8 |
| Sweden | 1970 | 19·2 | 2·3 | 17·1 | 9·0 | 8·0 | 44·4 |
| New Zealand | 1976 | 14·4 | 3·4 | 16·2 | 10·0 | 10·2 | 45·8 |
| United States | 1970 | 13·8 | 7·8 | 16·8 | 6·6 | 2·9 | 52·1 |
| Canada | 1971 | 12·4 | 4·2 | 15·6 | 9·3 | 6·9 | 51·6 |
| France | 1968 | 11·4 | 2·7 | 11·7 | 7·6 | 15·3 | 51·3 |
| United Kingdom | 1971 | 11·1 | 3·7 | 17·9 | 9·0 | 3·0 | 55·3 |
| USSR | 1970 | 10·4 | 11·8 | | 7·0 | 25·6 | 45·2 |
| Australia | 1971 | 10·1 | 6·5 | 15·6 | 7·9 | 7·6 | 52·3 |
| German F.R. | 1970 | 9·8 | 2·2 | 17·5 | 8·9 | 7·6 | 54·0 |
| Argentina | 1970 | 7·5 | 1·5 | 11·4 | 11·9 | 14·4 | 53·3 |
| Japan | 1970 | 6·6 | 3·9 | 13·8 | 11·8 | 18·9 | 45·0 |
| Brazil | 1970 | 4·8 | 1·7 | 5·3 | 7·4 | 44·0 | 36·8 |
| Egypt | 1966 | 4·4 | 1·6 | 5·0 | 5·8 | 45·6 | 37·6 |
| India | 1971 | 2·7 | 0·7 | 3·0 | 4·2 | 72·0 | 17·4 |

(*Sources*: USSR, Narodnoe Khozyaistvo 1975, pp. 440, 530, 532, 533, 538.
Other countries, ILO, *Yearbook of Labour Statistics 1977*, Table 2B, pp. 168 et seq.)

suspects, is generally true of their way of doing business. Far fewer letters, far smaller offices . . . Much more seems to be decided by more senior staff, and by word of mouth, by personal dealings or at meetings.'[9]

Some of the forms that national differences may take are shown in the more detailed comparison of Great Britain and the United States in Table 1.3. For this purpose, we have reallocated the British data to accord with the 'socio-economic groups' used by Alba M. Edwards in his official study for the United States.[10] American and British usages have some marked contrasts: the American 'clerical and kindred' group includes not only office workers but also radio operators, laboratory assistants, caretakers, messengers, baggagemen, postmen, telegraphists and telephonists; the 'skilled workers' are restricted much more closely to the traditional crafts, but include bus conductors who are graded as semi-skilled in the British scheme. 'Conductors (railroad)' are given a still more elevated status and classified with 'other proprietors and managers'.[11]

TABLE 1.3 Percentage of occupied population in occupational groups, United States (1910–70) and Great Britain (1911–71)

| | US<br>GB | 1910<br>1911 | 1930<br>1931 | 1950<br>1951 | 1970<br>1971 |
|---|---|---|---|---|---|
| 1. Professional and semi-profes-<br>sional | US<br>GB | 4·4<br>4·1 | 6·1<br>4·4 | 7·5<br>6·1 | 14·2<br>10·6 |
| 2. Proprietors, managers,<br>officials | US<br>GB | 23·0<br>10·4 | 19·9<br>10·6 | 16·3<br>10·6 | 12·7<br>12·3 |
| *of whom* farmers | US<br>GB | 16·5<br>1·6 | 12·4<br>1·6 | 7·5<br>0·9 | 2·2<br>0·9 |
| 3. Clerical and kindred | US<br>GB | 5·2<br>7·3 | 10·0<br>9·2 | 13·3<br>12·7 | 17·4<br>15·7 |
| 4. Sales | US<br>GB | 5·0<br>5·7 | 6·3<br>6·1 | 6·9<br>5·4 | 6·2<br>9·0 |
| 5. Skilled workers and foremen | US<br>GB | 11·7<br>13·9 | 12·9<br>15·0 | 13·8<br>16·8 | 12·9<br>15·5 |
| 6. Service | US<br>GB | 6·8<br>10·4 | 6·9<br>9·4 | 7·4<br>6·1 | 12·4<br>11·8 |
| 7. Farm labourers | US<br>GB | 14·5<br>6·5 | 8·6<br>4·4 | 4·6<br>3·2 | 1·7<br>1·1 |
| 8. Semi-skilled and unskilled,<br>not elsewhere classified | US<br>GB | 29·4<br>41·7 | 29·3<br>40·9 | 30·2<br>39·1 | 22·4<br>24·0 |

*Source*: See text.

Of course, there are many factors at work occasioning the curious similarities and differences shown in Table 1.3. One is the difference in size of the two countries, with its effects on agriculture and transport. In 1910, farm employment absorbed 31 per cent of the labour force in the United States, and only 8·1 per cent in Britain. In 1950, the percentages had become 12·1 and 4·1, but by 1970–1, the difference in proportions had almost disappeared: 3·1 per cent in the United States and 2·8 per cent in Britain.[12] In general, the similarities are more striking than the differences, and it seems surprising that the superior wealth and industrial advancement of the United States has not resulted in a much greater difference in the proportion of white-collar workers.

In the case of non-administrative office workers (or *clerks* in the British sense) the proportions are remarkably similar until 1950:[13]

| United States %| | Great Britain %| |
|---|---|---|---|
| 1910 | 4·0 | 1911 | 4·8 |
| 1920 | 6·6 | 1921 | 6·7 |
| 1930 | 7·3 | 1931 | 7·0 |
| 1950 | 10·4 | 1951 | 10·7 |
| 1970 | 16·5 | 1971 | 13·9 |

This suggests a certain inevitability about certain aspects of occupational distribution, dependent on technique and social advance, that overrides national boundaries. However, the relative size of the occupational classes is the result of many influences. Of immediate interest in assessing the significance of their growth or decline is a consideration of variations in the numbers in the occupations of which each class is composed, and it is to this that we shall now turn.

## 4. CHANGES WITHIN THE OCCUPATIONAL CLASSES

### (A) CLASS 1A (HIGHER PROFESSIONS)

In 1911, the dominant group amongst the higher professions consisted of the 53,000 ministers of religion; after that, came the 36,000 doctors and dentists, and then the 26,000 lawyers. The 10,000 professional engineers were a smaller group than the naval and army officers, writers or chartered accountants. There were fewer than 5,000 scientists. In the years that followed, those in the technological professions increased with extraordinary rapidity: Table 1.4 shows their size and growth alongside that of the other major groups in class 1A. The group, comprising engineers, architects, surveyors and ship-designers, increased at a compound annual rate of 4·75 per cent between 1911 and 1921; 4·0 per cent between 1921 and 1931 and 5·0 per cent between 1931 and 1951. This rate was fractionally increased to 5·1 per cent for the twenty years from 1951 to 1971. The major increase for mechanical and electrical engineers was in the decade to 1931, when their numbers rose from 2000 to 12,000. This was an era, of course, in which material life was being transformed by the application of electricity and the proliferation of the motor car.

TABLE 1.4 Higher professions (constituents of class 1A), 1911–71
(thousands)

|  | 1911 | 1921 | 1931 | 1951 | 1971 | % of 1911 |
|---|---|---|---|---|---|---|
| Church | 53 | 45 | 48 | 49 | 41 | 77 |
| Medicine | 36 | 38 | 46 | 62 | 80 | 222 |
| Law | 26 | 22 | 23 | 27 | 39 | 150 |
| Engineering[a] | 25 | 35 | 51 | 138 | 425 | 1700 |
| Writing[b] | 15 | 14 | 21 | 26 | 51 | 340 |
| Armed forces[c] | 14 | 19 | 16 | 46 | 34 | 243 |
| Accounting | 11 | 9 | 16 | 37 | 77 | 700 |
| Science[d] | 5 | 13 | 20 | 49 | 77 | 1540 |
| Total | 185 | 195 | 241 | 434 | 824 | 448 |
| All occupational classes | 18,347 | 19,333 | 21,029 | 22,514 | 25,021 | 136 |

[a] Includes surveyors, architects and ship-designers.
[b] Includes editors and journalists.
[c] Commissioned officers. 1971: census 'Armed forces' divided in same proportions to numbers for officers and others provided by Ministry of Defence.
[d] Includes statisticians and economists.

Compared with 1911, the constitution of the higher professional class has changed markedly. A representative gathering in 1911 would have included one scientist, two accountants, three officers, three writers, five engineers, five lawyers, seven doctors and dentists and ten churchmen. In 1971, there would have been eight scientists, eight accountants, five officers, five writers, four lawyers, eight doctors and dentists, four churchmen and forty-four engineers.

*Industrial Status*

In 1931, 34 per cent of the class were employers or self-employed; by 1971, the proportion had fallen to 16 per cent. Indeed, the percentage of non-employees is reduced to 12 for 1971 if the 34,020 doctors and dentists returned as employers or self-employed are regarded instead as employees of the National Health Service.[14] Lawyers, architects, accountants and writers presented the largest proportion of employers or self-employed outside medicine, but it was only in the legal profession in 1951 that employees remained in the minority:

|  | Percentages | | |
|---|---|---|---|
|  | *1931* | *1951* | *1971* |
| Lawyers | | | |
|   Employers | 59 | 39 | 47 |
|   Self-employed | 18 | 18 | 6 |
|   Employees | 22 | 42 | 46 |
| Architects | | | |
|   Employers | 27 | 13 | 14 |
|   Self-employed | 26 | 12 | 7 |
|   Employees | 47 | 75 | 78 |
| Accountants | | | |
|   Employers | 39 | 21 | 17 |
|   Self-employed | 12 | 10 | 4 |
|   Employees | 49 | 69 | 78 |
| Authors, editors, journalists | | | |
|   Employers | 4 | 1 | 2 |
|   Self-employed | 26 | 21 | 16 |
|   Employees | 70 | 78 | 82 |

It is the self-employed who have been most reduced; the numbers of employers have remained fairly stable since 1951 or, in the case of the lawyers, have risen substantially. Is this another sign of the demise of the independent worker which, along with shoemakers, tinkers and tailors, has perhaps affected the learned professions? Certainly, the numbers of those practising on their own show a strong downward trend. More are absorbed into other businesses as firms grow and find it advantageous to establish their own law, architectural and public relations departments. But here too there might be a trend towards incorporation which would *ipso facto* convert practitioners from employers or self-employed to employees. We can check on this by examining the numbers of each profession employed in that industry whose product is their specific service—that is, the number of professional accountants (occupational code 209) engaged in accountancy services (industry code 871) and so on.

The proportions of these professions employed in their own industries in 1961 and 1971 were as follows:[15]

|  | *1961* | *1971* |
|---|---|---|
| Lawyers | 83·5 | 82·6 |
| Architects and surveyors | 40·0 | 37·8 |
| Accountants[16] | 54·0 | 54·0 |
| Authors, editors, journalists | 21·0 | 17·2 |

The proportions working on their own or in firms providing their professional services have fallen—except in the case of accountants where there has been no change. So the fall in the number of employers and self-employed is not due to a process of incorporation, but to more firms in other industries employing their own lawyers, architects, and so on, instead of calling them in for consultation. All the same, the numbers in professional practice have risen over the ten years: by 14 per cent for lawyers, 29 per cent for architects and surveyors, 11 per cent for accountants and 4·5 per cent for authors, editors, journalists.

*Distribution by Sex*

Women have formed only a small proportion of the higher professions: 6 per cent in 1911 and 8 per cent in 1951, while in 1971 the proportion was very nearly back to 6 per cent. Their numbers and proportions in the higher professional groups were as follows:

|  | 1951 | | 1971 | |
| --- | --- | --- | --- | --- |
|  | *Nos.* | % | *Nos.* | % |
| Church | 13,001 | 26 | 5410 | 13 |
| Medicine | 7613 | 15½ | 15,040 | 19 |
| Law | 838 | 3 | 2470 | 6 |
| Engineering[a] | 1361 | 1 | 4050 | 1 |
| Writing[b] | 4988 | 24 | 12,680 | 25 |
| Accounting | 705 | 2 | 2650 | 3 |
| Science | 4938 | 10 | 6380 | 8 |
| Total | 33,444 | 9 | 48,680 | 6 |

[a] Inc. surveyors, architects and ship-designers.

[b] inc. editors and journalists. The inclusion of officers in the armed forces reduces the female proportion to a little over 8 per cent in 1951.

The number of professional women has increased healthily enough— by nearly 50 per cent—but not fast enough to keep up with the men, so that the overall proportion has fallen. One reason is that the engineering group has increased so substantially, and it is the group with the lowest proportion of women. If both it and the armed services are excluded from the calculation, the percentage of women becomes 13 in 1951 and 12 in 1971. There are some slight signs of hope for sex equality: the proportion of women doctors and dentists is now quite substantial; the number of lawyers has tripled and the number of accountants nearly quadrupled. But the process is very slow and has a long way to go.

(B) CLASS 1B (LOWER PROFESSIONS)

Nurses and teachers constituted 57 per cent of this class in 1951 and 58 per cent in 1971. The rise in their numbers has been proceeding steadily since the latter half of the nineteenth century, making a considerable contribution towards the transformation of society. The number of nurses doubled between 1881 and 1911, and more than doubled (a factor of 2·5) between 1911 and 1951. The number of teachers (including university teachers) increased by a factor of 1·5 between 1881 and 1911 and of 1·25 between 1911 and 1951, and between 1951 and 1971, doubled.

But there are other occupations in this class whose rise has been of such recent origin that they were of insufficient importance for separate listing in 1911: draughtsmen were included with clerks; laboratory assistants with physicists, metallurgists and others as 'persons engaged in scientific pursuits'. Nor were librarians or social welfare workers separately distinguished, and aviators (or pilots, aeroplane) were classified with acrobats and professors of legerdemain under the subhead 'Performer, showman: exhibition, games-service'. Most of the occupations included rose in numbers between 1911 and 1921; in the few cases where a decline occurred (engineering officers on board ship, painters and sculptors, musicians and music teachers) it was small. As far as can be estimated, the class total rose from about 560,000 to 680,000.

Table 1.5 shows the major changes between 1921 and 1971.

Between 1921 and 1971, the lower professions increased by a multiple of 2·86, very rapidly in comparison with that of the average for all occupational classes, but much slower than the 4·23 for the higher professions. On the other hand, their rate of growth was almost equal, and impressively high, for the twenty years from 1951 to 1971.

The growth in the number of nurses has been high and consistent over the years: at the rate of 2·9 per cent per year between 1921 and 1931, 3·0 per cent per year between 1931 and 1951 and 2·5 per cent per year between 1951 and 1971. At 2·5 per cent growth per year, a number doubles every twenty-eight years. By contrast, other medical auxiliaries (those professionally qualified other than doctors, dentists and nurses), who had increased at 4·9 per cent a year between 1931 and 1951, decelerated in the next twenty years: the number of males remained unchanged while the females increased by an average of 1·7 per cent per year.

After a slow increase between 1931 and 1951 (0·8 per cent per year), there was an explosion of teachers (5·4 per cent a year) between 1951 and 1971. Both lab technicians and draughtsmen increased substantially between 1931 and 1951 (9·5 and 4·2 per cent a year, respectively) and more moderately between 1951 and 1971 (2·9 and 0·8 per cent per year).

Overall, these estimable people increased at 1·9 per cent per year between 1931 and 1951, and 3·0 per cent per year between 1951 and 1971.

TABLE 1.5  Lower professions (constituents of class IB), 1921–71 (thousands)

|  |  | 1921 | 1931 | 1951 | 1971 | % of 1921 |
|---|---|---|---|---|---|---|
| Nurses | M | 2 | 4 | 29 | 38 | 1900 |
|  | F | 113 | 141 | 237 | 401 | 355 |
| Others in medicine[a] | M | 17 | 19 | 41 | 41 | 241 |
|  | F | 4 | 8 | 29 | 41 | 1025 |
| Teachers[b] | M | 77 | 89 | 133 | 307 | 400 |
|  | F | 210 | 206 | 207 | 381 | 181 |
| Draughtsmen[c] | M | 34 | 53 | 120 | 142 | 418 |
|  | F | 4 | 6 | 14 | 17 | 425 |
| Laboratory technicians | M | 4 | 9 | 51 | 76 | 1900 |
|  | F | 1 | 2 | 18 | 48 | 4800 |
| Librarians | M | 1 | 3 | 5 | ·· | ·· |
|  | F | 1 | 4 | 11 | ·· | ·· |
| Social welfare workers | M | 1 | 5 | 10 | 22 | 2200 |
|  | F | 2 | 4 | 14 | 40 | 2000 |
| Navigating and engineer- ing officers, aircrew | M | 37 | 36 | 30 | 27 | 73 |
|  | F | — | — | — | — | — |
| Arts[d] | M | 42 | 49 | 39 | 53 | 126 |
|  | F | 40 | 42 | 27 | 28 | 70 |
| Others[e] | M | 59 | 30 | 35 | 241 | 408 |
|  | F | 25 | 9 | 8 | 44 | 176 |
| All in class IB | M | 276 | 300 | 492 | 946 | 343 |
|  | F | 404 | 427 | 567 | 1000 | 248 |
| Total |  | 680 | 728 | 1059 | 1946 | 286 |
| All occupational classes |  | 19,333 | 21,029 | 22,514 | 25,021 | 129 |

[a] Includes veterinary surgeons, pharmacists and opticians.
[b] Excludes music teachers, 1921–51.
[c] Includes industrial designers.
[d] Includes painters, producers, actors, musicians and, until 1951, music teachers.
[e] Includes articled students in 1921 and 1931. 1971: categories 169, 216, 217, 220.

*Distribution by Sex*

Numbers of males and females in the main occupational groups have been shown in Table 1.5. Not only are women now established in what were almost exclusively male professions, but the reverse has taken place too: nowadays, about one nurse in ten is a man, while men accounted for the entire increase in teachers between 1911 and 1951, but matched the women one for one in the rise between 1951 and 1971. It is only amongst the navigating and engineering officers in the mercantile marine, and aircrew, that segregation seems to have been preserved.

(c) CLASS 2A(EMPLOYERS AND PROPRIETORS)

All employers are included in this class, except those in occupational class 1, but only those self-employed proprietors for whose occupation the control of property is decisive.[17] Thus farmers, shopkeepers and boarding-house proprietors are included, while window-cleaners, building craftsmen and tailors working on their own account are not.

The industrial distribution of those in class 2A is summarised in Table 1.6. Until 1931, the class grew at about the same pace as the occupied population; after that, as we have noticed, its 21 per cent decline to 1951 is balanced by an increase in the number of managers. After that, managers increased at a faster rate than employers and proprietors declined.

In 1951, nearly three-quarters of class 2A were in farming or the distributive trades; in 1971, 57 per cent. But outside these two spheres and that of own-account catering, the trend, since 1951, has been strongly upward. The net result, all the same, is a slight fall since 1951, compounded of a rise of 36 per cent in the number of employers and a fall of 34 per cent in those on their own account.

*Distribution by Sex*

It is only as boarding-house keepers that women have been in the majority; within this occupation there was a male resurgence between 1931 and 1951, when the number of men boarding-house proprietors almost doubled to 8000, while the number of women so engaged was reduced by half to 29,000. In 1971, boarding-houses were not distinguished from hotels, but for the two combined in the twenty years to 1971, the number of men rose while that of women declined. In these and the other catering trades, numbers moved as follows:

TABLE 1.6 Employers and proprietors (constituents of class 2A), 1911–71 (thousands)

| | 1911 | 1921 | 1931 | 1951 | 1971 | % of 1911 |
|---|---|---|---|---|---|---|
| **Farmers** | | | | | | |
| Employers | 172 | 167 | 163 | 123 | 102 | 59 |
| Own account | 73 | 135 | 114 | 179 | 131 | 179 |
| Total | 245 | 302 | 277 | 302 | 233 | 95 |
| **Mining and manufacturing** | | | | | | |
| Employers | 173 | 178 | 167 | 55 | 97 | 56 |
| **Building and decorating** | | | | | | |
| Employers | 70 | 42 | 58 | 38 | 54 | 77 |
| **Road transport**[a] | | | | | | |
| Employers | 13 | 15 | 19 | 9 | 31 | 238 |
| Own account | 21 | 37 | 40 | 38 | 55 | 262 |
| Total | 34 | 52 | 59 | 47 | 85 | 250 |
| **Distributive trade** | | | | | | |
| Employers | 220 | 182 | 217 | 128 | 197 | 90 |
| Own account | 275 | 286 | 362 | 312 | 194 | 71 |
| Total | 495 | 468 | 579 | 440 | 391 | 79 |
| **Catering**[b] | | | | | | |
| Own account | 70 | 132 | 125 | 111 | 56 | 80 |
| **Personal service**[c] | | | | | | |
| Employers | 79 | 58 | 58 | 54 | 139 | 121 |
| **Others in class 2A** | | | | | | |
| Employers[d] | 36 | 50 | 45 | 50 | | |
| Own account | 30 | 36 | 41 | 21 | . . | . . |
| **All class 2A** | | | | | | |
| Employers | 763 | 692 | 727 | 457 | 621 | 81 |
| Own account | 469 | 626 | 682 | 661 | 435 | 93 |
| Total | 1232 | 1318 | 1409 | 1118 | 1056 | 86 |

[a] Includes garages.
[b] Includes restaurants, boarding houses, hotels and public houses.
[c] In 1971, personal service and sport and recreation were combined.
[d] Includes commercial travellers, finance and insurance brokers, auctioneers. Own account and employees are included in class 2B.

|                                      |   | *Thousands* 1951 | 1971 |
|--------------------------------------|---|------|------|
| Boarding-house and hotel keepers     | M | 11·9 | 16·1 |
|                                      | F | 31·6 | 19·2 |
| Publicans and innkeepers             | M | 27·6 | 32·5 |
|                                      | F | 7·9  | 14·7 |
| Restaurateurs                        | M | 17·6 | 27·4 |
|                                      | F | 12·3 | 16·3 |
| Totals                               | M | 57·1 | 76·0 |
|                                      | F | 51·8 | 50·2 |

Women form a high proportion of the employers in the distributive trades, one that rose from 28 per cent in 1951 to 34 per cent in 1971. It is surprising to find 26,000 women amongst the employers and proprietors in farming in 1911: just over 10 per cent of the total. By 1951, their numbers had fallen to 20,000, a little under 7 per cent of the total. But between 1951 and 1971, their numbers rose to 25,000, while the number of men continued to decline, so that women were back to the proportion of 1911. As employers in manufacturing, it is only in the clothing industry that they are found in any significant number (1,870 in 1971), and there they represent nearly a quarter of the total.

(D) CLASS 2B (MANAGERS AND ADMINISTRATORS)

In census terminology, a manager is an employee (not describing himself as a foreman, supervisor or inspector) managing any number of people.[18] The range of authority is clearly very wide. The 1971 census returned 723,730 employers and 1,671,350 managers, but they are spread over a large number of establishments, varying greatly in size. The Department of Employment's census of employment for 1976 recorded 162,352 units with one employee each, and 588,588 with between two and ten employees and, at the other end of the range, 1903 establishments with a thousand or more employees.[19] Employers, being peculiar to unincorporated businesses, would be concentrated in the smaller units, while the bigger outfits would be limited companies with a hierarchy of managers.

Table 1.7 shows class 2B classified by industrial sector. In part, the figures merely express the relative rise or decline of the various sectors or

TABLE 1.7 Managers and administrators (constituents of class 2B), 1911–71 (thousands)

| | 1911 | 1921 | 1931 | 1951 | 1971 | % of 1911 |
|---|---|---|---|---|---|---|
| Land and agriculture[a] | (7) | 16 | 18 | 18 | 28 | (400) |
| Public service[b] | (34) | (62) | 52 | 124 | 150 | (441) |
| Office managers | n.d. | 18 | 35 | 61 | 76 | .. |
| Mining and manufacturing | 63 | 93 | 80 | 214 | 321 | 510 |
| Building and contracting | n.d. | 5 | 7 | 33 | 79 | .. |
| Brokers, agents[c] | | | | | | |
| Own account | 21 | 26 | 27 | 22 | 28 | |
| Employees | 137 | 132 | 190 | 209 | 447 | |
| Total | 158 | 158 | 217 | 231 | 475 | (301) |
| Retail and wholesale trade | (115) | 121 | 132 | 258 | 372 | (323) |
| Catering[d] | 146 | 90 | 64 | 84 | 94 | 64 |
| Transport[e] | (29) | 46 | 48 | 67 | (4) ⎤ | |
| Finance | (27) | 38 | 57 | 58 | n.d. ⎬ | (432) |
| Others in class 2B | 50 | 115 | 140 | 98 | 454 ⎦ | |
| All in class 2B | 629 | 704 | 770 | 1246 | 2054 | 327 |
| All occupational classes | 18,347 | 19,333 | 21,029 | 22,514 | 25,021 | 136 |

[a] In 1911, farm managers only.
[b] 1951 codes 610, 611 and 612, higher clerical officers and above. 1911 and 1921: estimated from the *Report of the Committee on Pay, etc., of State Servants* (Anderson Committee) (London: HMSO, 1923), and Royal Commission on the Civil Service (1929–31), *Appendix to Part I of Minutes of Evidence: Introductory Memoranda Relating to the Civil Service; Submitted by the Treasury* (London: HMSO, 1929).
[c] Including buyers, sales managers, advertising agents, estate agents, auctioneers and commercial travellers. Does not include stockbrokers. 1971: see note a to Table 1.10.
[d] Restaurants, boarding houses, hotels, public houses.
[e] Including garage managers and shipbrokers, except in 1971, when they were included in code 180, managers n.e.c. In Table 1.7, they are included in 'others in class 2B' in 1971.

*Note*: Numbers in brackets include estimates for, or exclude, some categories not distinguished in the year concerned.

the propensity of firms towards incorporation. We must go further if we are to measure organic changes. It would be interesting if we could classify the managers by numbers of subordinates, but the data are not available. We can, however, compare the number of employed persons per employer or manager in various industrial groups for the various years, and this is done in Table 1.8.[20]

TABLE 1.8 Staff per employer and manager in various industrial groups, 1911–71

|  | *1911* | *1921* | *1931* | *1951* | *1971* |
|---|---|---|---|---|---|
| Mining and non-metallic mining products | 96 | 100 | 102 | 82 | 49 |
| Chemical and allied | 18 | 32 | 31 | 33 | 14 |
| Metals, engineering and allied | 28 | 34 | 36 | 35 | 17 |
| Textiles, leather, textile and leather goods | 29 | 27 | 33 | 33 | 18 |
| All the above (weighted average) | 33 | 36 | 40 | 38 | 20 |

Table 1.8 shows a curious constancy in the number of staff per employer or manager between 1921 and 1951, followed by a marked reduction in the next twenty years. One can see this change reflected in Table 1.1, where the aggregate number of managers and administrators rose by 65 per cent between 1951 and 1971, while the absolute number of skilled and semi-skilled manual workers fell, and unskilled workers increased by less than 8 per cent. Of course managers have to manage machines and output, purchases and sales, as well as other employees.

*Status of Managers*
The census tables for 1951 for the first and last time classified managers into three status groups which are of analytic interest:

|  | *All* | | *General managers, directors, etc.* | | *Branch or primary dept. managers* | | *Office or subsidiary dept. managers* | |
|---|---|---|---|---|---|---|---|---|
|  | *000s* | *%* | *000s* | *%* | *000s* | *%* | *000s* | *%* |
| Men | 665 | 82·4 | 167 | 89·7 | 413 | 78·5 | 85 | 89·4 |
| Women | 142 | 17·6 | 19 | 10·3 | 113 | 21·5 | 10 | 10·6 |
| All | 807 | 100·0 | 186 | 100·0 | 526 | 100·0 | 95 | 100·0 |

We may get further information on distribution by status, however, by referring to the Department of Employment's New Earnings Survey.[21] For April 1977, their sample gives the following distribution for men:

| | Men | |
|---|---|---|
| | *Nos.* | % |
| General management | 1666 | 27·0 |
| Production and works managers, works foremen | 865 | 14·0 |
| Engineering maintenance managers | 366 | 5·9 |
| Transport, warehouse, office managers | 1892 | 30·7 |
| Department store, supermarket managers | 301 | 4·9 |
| Others in distributive trades | 747 | 12·1 |
| Hotel, catering, club or public house managers | 322 | 5·2 |
| All | 6159 | 100·0 |

Again, we find about a quarter of the total constituted by general managers. 'Office or subsidiary department managers' formed 13 per cent of the men in 1951, while in 1977 the percentage would be about 35, but the comparison is not sufficiently close to have much meaning.

*Distribution by Sex*
Women formed 20 per cent of all managers in 1911, 17 per cent in 1921, 13 per cent in 1931, 15 per cent in 1951 and 16 per cent in 1971. The New Earnings Survey of 1977 picked up too few women in general management to warrant their separate listing,[22] and of all those listed as managers women constituted only 9 per cent.

The extent to which women operate as managers is nowhere very high except in restaurants, though here, as with hotels and public houses, it actually fell between 1951 and 1971. But in most cases it has been creeping up over the years. If it continues at the pace achieved between 1931 and 1971, women should have reached equality of numbers by the time of the census of the year 3091. They have constituted the following percentages of managers in the groups shown:

| | 1931 | 1951 | 1971 |
|---|---|---|---|
| Public service[a] | 5·8 | 15·4 | 21·3 |
| Textiles, textile goods, leather and leather goods | 9·7 | 11·2 | 12·2 |
| Retail and wholesale businesses | 16·1 | 20·7 | 29·2 |
| Banking | 0·3 | 0·7 | 3·1 |
| Restaurants | 57·9 | 67·5 | 59·4 |
| Hotels and public houses | 29·2 | 46·0 | 39·2 |

[a] Administrative and executive officers and 'other officials (not clerks)' and Civil Service higher clerical officers. In 1971, Civil Service executive officers, ministers of the Crown; MPs (n.e.c.); senior government officials; local authority senior officers and Civil Service higher clerical officers. See *Civil Service Statistics*, 1971, p. 5.

(E) CLASS 3 (CLERICAL WORKERS)

In 1911, the census recognised only one category of clerk. Indeed, while 'commercial or business clerks' were distinguished, those in the public service, finance and railways were lumped together with 'officials'.[23] Those were the days when 'female typewriters' were still a novelty, and correspondence was done in the (male) copyist's beautiful hand.

In 1921, costing and estimating clerks were distinguished and in 1931, typists. In 1951 there was a further subdivision into shorthand typists, typists, other office machine operators and book-keepers. In 1961 there was a partial reversion to 1931 and in 1971 we have

clerks, cashiers;
office machine operators;
typists, shorthand writers, secretaries.

Professionally qualified accountants have throughout been classified separately.

Table 1.9 includes insurance agents and canvassers on the grounds that this is the least inappropriate class in which to put them. They are in

TABLE 1.9  Clerical workers (constituents of class 3), 1911–71 (thousands)

|  | 1911 | 1921 | 1931 | 1951 | 1971 | % of 1911 |
|---|---|---|---|---|---|---|
| Insurance agents and canvassers[a] |  |  |  |  |  |  |
| Male | 54 | 40 | 59 | 58 | 54 | 100 |
| Female | 1 | 4 | 2 | 5 | 13 | 1300 |
| Others |  |  |  |  |  |  |
| Male | 654 | 697 | 758 | 932 | 959 | 147 |
| Female | 179 | 560 | 646. | 1409 | 2453 | 1370 |
| Total | 888 | 1301 | 1465 | 2404 | 3479 | 392 |
| All occupational classes | 18,347 | 19,333 | 21,029 | 22,514 | 25,021 | 136 |

[a] Since 1961, insurance agents and canvassers have been included with 'Salesmen, services; valuers, auctioneers.' The census statisticians did distinguish them, however, in (unpublished) tables reconciling the 1951 tables with those for 1961 for England and Wales, and they have been separated on the same proportions for 1971, 35·24 per cent for men and 56·31 per cent for women.

fact a sort of peripatetic clerk. Compared with the rest of the class, their numbers have not increased much over the years.

The twenty years to 1951 were the era of the typist, their numbers rising from 244,000 to 559,000. Between 1951 and 1971, numbers moved thus:[24]

|  | 1951 | | 1971 | |
|---|---|---|---|---|
|  | *000s* | *%* | *000s* | *%* |
| Shorthand typists, typists | 559 | 23·8 | 780 | 22·8 |
| Office machine operators | 79 | 3·4 | 170 | 5·0 |
| Book-keepers | 484 | 20·7 ⎫ | 2471 | 72·2 |
| Others | 1219 | 52·1 ⎭ |  |  |
| Total | 2341 | 100·0 | 3421 | 100·0 |

Typists increased much more than the rest of the class between 1931 and 1951. In the next twenty years they just about kept pace with it, while the office machine operators forged ahead. One would have thought that photo-copiers, tape-recorders and telecopiers would have made much greater inroads into the typists' preserve, but their numbers have increased almost as fast as those of the group as a whole. But perhaps the big change came only after 1971? This we may check by reference to the proportions shown in the New Earnings Survey. In the 1971 survey, typists, shorthand typists and secretaries constituted 19·8 per cent of all clerical workers; in April 1977, 17·6 per cent. Their rate of decline does seem to be accelerating. Whether the proportion of men typists is rising or falling is not possible to say, for there are too few of them to merit separate listing in the NES.

*Distribution by Sex*

The substitution of women for men first took place on a large scale in the First World War. Between 1911 and 1921, the increase in the number of male clerks was a little less than that in the occupied population, while female clerks were multiplied by three. In 1951, women constituted nearly 60 per cent of the class. Curiously, before the invention of the typewriter, copying by hand had been regarded as a job for men, but, in due time, the typewriter was accepted as an instrument peculiarly suitable for women. In 1951, only 3·5 per cent of the 429,000 shorthand typists were men, but 54 per cent of the 483,000 book-keepers, estimating and costing clerks. In 1971, the proportions were 3·4 per cent and just under 38 per cent. The tiny minority of male secretaries is just about maintained, but their proportion of the rest greatly depleted.

One may get a measure of the change by looking at the proportion of men to women in insurance, banking and finance. This is an industrial division, but only 13 per cent of its work force were manual workers in 1951.[25] Women formed 38·3 per cent of the work force in 1951, 43·2 per cent in 1960 and, by March 1978 had just reached a majority, with 50·9 per cent.[26]

### (F) CLASS 4 (FOREMEN, SUPERVISORS, INSPECTORS)

Foremen were distinguished from other workers in 1921, 1931 and 1951 and were posted to orders or sub-orders according to the occupations of the workers whom they supervised. Thus, in 1951, foremen supervising chemical workers were classified under order V, sub-order 2, 'Workers in chemical and allied traders'. Of the 9512 foremen so enumerated in England and Wales in 1951, 7476 worked in the chemical industry itself, while the rest supervised chemical workers in other industries.[27]

The relevant coding instruction says, 'Persons returned as foremen, overlooker, or any synonymous term should be assigned to the "foremen, overlooker" or other similarly entitled group within the appropriate Order, as indicated by the statement of the employer's business, or the kind of work or activity.'[28] The census schedule called for the foreman's department to be stated as well as the employer's name and business, but of course there is no guarantee (nor much likelihood) that a foreman will be in charge exclusively of those in the occupations with which he is bracketed. For example, the foreman of 1951 code 100 (Chemicals) might be in charge of maintenance fitters, storemen, time clerks and cleaners as well as chemical process workers.

In 1911, foremen were not distinguished in the census and reference was made to the 1906 earnings census to determine the proportion of foremen to other operatives in various industries. This has the advantage of reliance on a return from employers instead of heads of households, but the disadvantage of failing to distinguish between, for example, foremen of engineering workers in the engineering industry and foremen of non-engineering workers in the engineering industry. It is probable that, with a lower degree of vertical integration, the overlap was less extensive in 1911 than in later years, but these qualifications should be borne in mind when Table 1.10 is considered.

TABLE 1.10 Foremen and number of manual employees per foreman in various occupational groups, 1911–71

| | 1911 | | 1921 | | 1931 | | 1951 | | 1971 | |
|---|---|---|---|---|---|---|---|---|---|---|
| | 000s | Em-ployees | 000s | Em-ployees | 000s | Em-ployees | 000s | Em-ployees | 000s | Em-ployees |
| Farm bailiffs, foremen | 29 | 32 | 28 | 29 | 22 | 31 | 19 | 29 | 10 | 28 |
| Coalmining overmen etc. | 34 | 29 | 46 | 24 | 40 | 24 | 42 | 14 | 29 | 7 |
| Non-metallic mining products | 3 | 55 | 3 | 57 | 4 | 55 | 7 | 32 | 6 | 13 |
| Chemical and allied | 4 | 24 | 5 | 15 | 5 | 18 | 12 | 15 | 20 | 6 |
| Metal-making and Metal-working | 31 | 54 | 49 | 42 | 63 | 34 | 263 | 12 | 432 | 7 |
| Textiles | 45 | 30 | 40 | 26 | 38 | 38 | 26 | 27 | 21 | 13 |
| Building and contracting | 32 | 13 | 24 | 25 | 37 | 19 | 64 | 16 | 65 | 5 |
| All above | 178 | 32 | 195 | 30 | 209 | 28 | 433 | 15 | 582 | 11 |
| All in class 4 | 236 | | 279 | | 323 | | 590 | | 968 | |

From 1961, foremen and supervisors were distinguished as a status category, and almost every occupation has some of its members so allocated. In addition, occupation code 031 in 1971 distinguished foremen *per se* in the engineering and allied trades.

Table 1.10 shows the number of foremen in various occupational groups and the average number of manual process workers per foreman in each group. This is calculated by dividing the number of workers listed for the group in the occupational tables by the number of foremen shown for that occupational group.

There is clearly a tendency towards closer supervision since 1931, though a foreman is in charge of goods and machines as well as men. The effect of mechanisation, standardisation and mass production is seen in the emergence of a class of 'inspectors, viewers, testers', which was distinguished first in 1951 (except for electrical work, for which it was recognised in 1921). There were 126,000 in this category in 1951 and 184,000 in 1971.

The proportion of forewomen in the class total has increased greatly. In 1911, it was possible to distinguish only 9,700: 4·1 per cent of the class total. Then the proportions moved thus:

|      | %    |
|------|------|
| 1921 | 6·6  |
| 1931 | 8·6  |
| 1951 | 13·3 |
| 1971 | 17·3 |

(G)  CLASS 5 (SKILLED MANUAL WORKERS)

Skilled workers are specialists and, *ipso facto*, can be classified into a multitude of occupations. From the 1951 classification, 224 occupations were allocated to class 5, and a number of these were themselves composed of groups of occupations. These included sixty-seven skilled occupations in metal-making and metal-working.

Table 1.11 shows this class subdivided according to the material worked in, the product made or the service given.[29] The sexes are distinguished only where women form a significant part of the work force.

There have been very wide variations in the fortunes of the various groups, and the stability of the class total is the outcome of conflicting tendencies in the parts. Mechanisation has led to increasing employ-

TABLE 1.11 Skilled manual workers (major constituents of class 5: employees and self-employed, 1911–71 (thousands)

| | | 1911 | 1921 | 1931 | 1951 | 1971 | % of 1911 |
|---|---|---|---|---|---|---|---|
| Agricultural machine drivers and attendants | | 6 | 10 | 7 | 74 | 23 | 383 |
| Coal hewers and getters | | 586 | 615 | 495 | 226 | 96 | 16 |
| Non-metallic mining products | M | 57 | 48 | 50 | 53 | 50 | 88 |
| | F | 15 | 28 | 29 | 36 | 23 | 153 |
| | Total | 72 | 76 | 79 | 89 | 74 | 103 |
| Metal-makers and metal-workers | | 1289 | 1663 | 1581 | 2096 | 2356 | 183 |
| Textiles | M | 351 | 194 | 184 | 123 | 57 | 16 |
| | F | 654 | 526 | 533 | 322 | 111 | 17 |
| | Total | 1005 | 720 | 717 | 445 | 168 | 17 |
| Leather and textile goods[a] | M | 290 | 229 | 249 | 181 | (84) | (29) |
| | F | 483 | 328 | 293 | 198 | (103) | (21) |
| | Total | 773 | 557 | 542 | 379 | (187) | (24) |
| Wood, cane and cork | | 472 | 445 | 483 | 461 | 390 | 83 |
| Paper and printing | M | 168 | 139 | 165 | 199 | 200 | 118 |
| | F | 66 | 82 | 95 | 80 | 92 | 139 |
| | Total | 234 | 221 | 260 | 279 | 292 | 125 |
| Other manufactures | | 226 | 245 | 259 | 274 | 349 | 154 |
| Building, contract-ing, decorating[b] | | 436 | 388 | 485 | 582 | 520 | 119 |
| Railway transport | | 103 | 140 | 129 | 145 | 75 | 73 |
| Sea transport | | (59) | 79 | 75 | 52 | 33 | (56) |
| Police (other ranks) | | 55 | 64 | 68 | 80 | 91 | 165 |
| Hairdressers and manicurists | M | 39 | 34 | 46 | 35 | 24 | 62 |
| | F | 5 | 6 | 34 | 48 | 105 | 2100 |
| | Total | 44 | 40 | 80 | 83 | 129 | 293 |
| Warehousemen[c] | | n.d. | 110 | 119 | 110 | 125 | |
| Stationary engine drivers etc.[d] | | 111 | 107 | 103 | 138 | 272 | 245 |
| Others | | 137 | 93 | 137 | 103 | 214 | 156 |
| All class 5 | M | 4264 | 4405 | 4423 | 4732 | 4619 | 108 |
| | F | 1344 | 1168 | 1196 | 884 | 775 | 58 |
| Total | | 5608 | 5573 | 5619 | 5616 | 5394 | 96 |

TABLE 1.11 (*Contd.*)

| | 1911 | 1921 | 1931 | 1951 | 1971 | % of 1911 |
|---|---|---|---|---|---|---|
| All occupational classes | 18,347 | 19,333 | 21,029 | 22,514 | 25,021 | 136 |

[a] The 1971 classification does not permit a satisfactory allocation between skilled and semi-skilled clothing workers.

[b] From 1961, a substantial group of construction workers were lumped together in 'Construction workers n.e.c.'. These have been divided into skilled, semi-skilled and unskilled workers in the same proportions for 1971 as those shown in the Census Department's reconciliation of the 1951 and 1961 occupational tables, when they recoded a 5 per cent sub-sample of the 1961 returns in accordance with the classification of 1951. The results were not published but are obtainable on request.

[c] The 1971 codes 136 and 137 have been subdivided in the same proportions as prevailed in 1951 to separate warehousemen (skilled) from storekeepers and packers (semi-skilled) and warehouse and storekeepers' assistants (unskilled).

[d] Including crane drivers, drivers of civil engineering plant, switchboard attendants and battery chargers.

ment in the engineering trades and falling employment in other industries. The increase in skilled metal-makers and metal-workers between 1911 and 1971 has almost balanced the fall in the number of skilled workers in textiles, leather, and textile and leather goods.

The changes in employment have been due to a combination of changes in output per industry, output per worker and the skill mix, as well as the extent to which particular skills are used outside their 'home' industry. Engineering workers are widely used to maintain machines in other industries, but not many textile workers are employed outside the textile industry. So, in 1971, skilled textile workers were 17 per cent of their numbers of 1911, the industry employed 43 per cent of its work force of 1911 and produced 138 per cent of its product of 1911.

The ratio of skilled workers to all manual workers in various occupational groups has been as follows:[30]

| | 1911 | 1921 | 1931 | 1951 | 1971 |
|---|---|---|---|---|---|
| Coalminers | 59·4 | 56·7 | 51·2 | 38·5 | 37·5 |
| Workers in: | | | | | |
| Metal-making and metal-using | 77·9 | 77·7 | 71·7 | 66·3 | 73·2 |
| Textiles | 74·8 | 67·7 | 67·4 | 62·0 | 48·2 |
| Building, contracting, decorating | 66·7 | 57·8 | 62·8 | 50·4 | 56·4 |

*Industrial Status*

Self-employed craftsmen might have been expected to fade away in this age of growing concentration. Their numbers did decline, from 329,000 in 1911 to 251,000 in 1951, but then rebounded to 349,000 in 1971 (table 1.1). As a percentage of their class they fell from 5·9 in 1911 to 4·5 in 1951, then rose to 6·5. The major groups in 1951 and 1971 were as follows:

|  | Number | | % of total in occupation | |
|---|---|---|---|---|
|  | *1951* | *1971* | *1951* | *1971* |
| Blacksmiths | 4777 | 1560 | 9 | 6 |
| Motor mechanics | 9292 | 16,720 | 6 | 9 |
| Plumbers | 9772 | 19,450 | 10 | 14 |
| Watchmakers | 5603 | 3230 | 4 | 39 |
| Electricians | 6631 | 13,170 | 3 | 4 |
| Shoemakers | 19,039 | 3870 | 48 | 41 |
| Bakers | 10,964 | 770 | 11 | 1 |
| Carpenters and cabinet-makers | 14,437 | 45,460 | 5 | 14 |
| Building workers[a] | 44,175 | 121,530 | 14 | 38 |
| Painters and decorators[b] | 25,218 | 50,600 | 9 | 18 |
| Hairdressers | 26,690 | 24,310 | 32 | 15 |
| Photographers | 4108 | n.d. | 18 | .. |
| Total | 180,706 | 292,340 |  |  |

[a] Excluding painters and decorators.

[b] Including signwriters.

Independent blacksmiths, watchmakers, shoemakers and bakers are indeed fading from the scene, but their decline has been more than compensated by the upsurge in craftsmen connected with the building industry, components of 'the lump'.[31]

Few of the women were self-employed. In 1911, 136,000 (86 per cent) of the women in class 5 working on their own account were dressmakers. By 1921, the number of dressmakers had fallen to 66,000; by 1931, to 44,000; by 1951, to 13,000. In 1971, they were not listed separately.

*Distribution by Sex*

While the number of skilled men rose by 8 per cent between 1911 and 1971, the number of skilled women fell by 42 per cent, for as Table 1.11

shows, the women have been concentrated in the textile and clothing industries whose labour force has been much reduced.

In the case of the men, the outstanding feature has been the shift to the metal-using trades. The central grade, variously known as fitter, mechanic (not motor-mechanic) or millwright, had in it about 325,000 men in 1911. By 1921, the number was up by nearly a third to 429,000. Then followed a fall to 400,000 in 1931, then increases to 511,000 in 1951 and 595,000 in 1971. Machine-tool setters, setter-operators have grown with even greater rapidity. There were 12,000 when they were distinguished for the first time in 1931. In 1951, there were 112,000 and in 1971, 177,000.

The weight of the major groups of skilled men has varied as follows:

|  | *Percentage of all men in class 5* | | | | |
|---|---|---|---|---|---|
|  | *1911* | *1921* | *1931* | *1951* | *1971* |
| Metal-makers and metal-workers | 23 | 30 | 28 | 36·0 | 49 |
| Textile workers | 18 | 13 | 13 | 8·0 | 1 |
| Leather, and leather and textile goods | 14 | 10 | 10 | 6·5 | 2 |
| Coalface workers | 10 | 11 | 9 | 4·0 | 2 |
| Woodworkers | 8 | 8 | 10 | 8·0 | 8 |
| Building craftsmen | 8 | 7 | 9 | 10·0 | 6 |
| Others | 19 | 21 | 21 | 27·5 | 32 |
| Total | 100 | 100 | 100 | 100·0 | 100 |

The distribution of women in class 5 is shown in Table 1.12. Nothing has happened to compensate for the decline of the skilled spinners, weavers and dressmakers, who made up 72 per cent of the skilled women manual workers in 1911. Even in engineering and printing, where substantial numbers are employed, the 1971 figures were below those of 1931. Milliners have almost vanished from the scene, their flights of fancy that used to enliven the world of fashion now performed by the hairdressers who constitute the one bouyant feature of the class.

( H )   CLASS 6 ( SEMI-SKILLED MANUAL WORKERS )

Table 1.13 gives a preliminary survey of class 6, by dividing it into seven sections.

TABLE 1.12 Distribution of women within class 5 (skilled workers), chief occupational groups including self-employed, 1911–71 (thousands)

| | 1911 | 1921 | 1931 | 1951 | 1971 | % of 1911 |
|---|---|---|---|---|---|---|
| Pottery | 14 | 24 | 24 | 28 | 23 | 164 |
| Metals and engineering | 47 | 83 | 94 | 76 | 88 | 187 |
| Textiles | 654 | 526 | 533 | 322 | 111 | 17 |
| Boots and shoes | 45 | 38 | 47 | 47 | | |
| Clothing cutters | 13 | 6 | 12 | 15 | | |
| Dresses and other light clothing | 317 | 162 | 126 | 59 | 103 | 23 |
| Millinery | 56 | 48 | 34 | 6 | | |
| Other hats and caps | 5 | 16 | 14 | 6 | | |
| Upholstery | 10 | 8 | 12 | 14 | | |
| Bakers and pastry-cooks | n.d. | 22 | 29 | 26 | 30 | .. |
| Sugar confectionery | 7 | 18 | 16 | 6 | n.d. | |
| Paper and printing, photography | 66 | 82 | 95 | 80 | 92 | 139 |
| French polishers | 7 | 7 | 10 | 4 | n.d. | .. |
| Hairdressers, manicurists | 5 | 6 | 34 | 48 | 105 | 2100 |
| Others | 98 | 122 | 116 | 147 | 232 | 237 |
| All women in class 5 | 1344 | 1168 | 1196 | 884 | 744 | 58 |
| All occupational classes | 18,347 | 19,333 | 21,029 | 22,514 | 25,021 | 136 |

Except for packers and storekeepers, none of the groups has kept pace with the occupied population over the sixty years to 1971. Here included are the two great reservoirs upon which other industries have been able to draw: agriculture and domestic service. Between 1921 and 1931, with a consistently high level of unemployment, the decline in the number of agricultural labourers was reduced (though not for women thus engaged), and in catering, domestic and personal service, it was strongly reversed. By 1951, the trend of 1911–21 had again asserted itself. In the ensuing twenty years, it was much accelerated in agriculture but reduced in catering etc., where for men numbers actually rose to a bit above the level of 1931.

In a period in which the volume of goods sold has multiplied by nearly five, the number of shop assistants has increased remarkably little—by 6 per cent. Like offices, shops were staffed mainly by men in 1911, and while the number of male shop assistants fell by 371,000 between 1911

TABLE 1.13 Semi-skilled workers (major divisions of class 6), 1911–71 (thousands)

| | | 1911 | 1921 | 1931 | 1951 | 1971 | % of 1911 |
|---|---|---|---|---|---|---|---|
| Agricultural laborourers, | M | 1188 | 1013 | 962 | 707 | 344 | 29 |
| foresters, fishermen | F | 100 | 81 | 49 | 88 | 66 | 66 |
| | Total | 1288 | 1094 | 1011 | 795 | 411 | 32 |
| Mining and manufactur-ing | | 1606 | 1513 | 1599 | 1828 | 1655 | 103 |
| Transport and communi-cation | | 965 | 861 | 990 | 1094 | 1010 | 105 |
| Distributive trades | M | 588 | 414 | 660 | 459 | 217 | 37 |
| | F | 342 | 425 | 503 | 652 | 767 | 224 |
| | Total | 930 | 839 | 1163 | 1111 | 984 | 106 |
| Armed services, other ranks[a] | | 196 | 221 | 173 | 531 | 218 | 111 |
| Catering, domestic and | M | 225 | 203 | 296 | 283 | 299 | 133 |
| personal service | F | 1778 | 1539 | 1813 | 1185 | 1033 | 58 |
| | Total | 2003 | 1742 | 2109 | 1468 | 1331 | 66 |
| Packers and store-keepers[b] | | (170) | 202 | 143 | 386 | (494) | (291) |
| Others in class 6 | | 86 | 71 | 71 | 126 | 210 | 244 |
| All class 6 | M | 4346 | 3859 | 4259 | 4352 | 3307 | 76 |
| | F | 2898 | 2684 | 3101 | 2978 | 3005 | 104 |
| Total | | 7244 | 6543 | 7359 | 7339 | 6312 | 87 |
| All occupational classes | | 18,347 | 19,333 | 21,029 | 22,514 | 25,021 | 136 |

[a] The 1971 census does not distinguish officers from other ranks. The 1971 figure is the total shown for census categories 221 and 222 divided proportionately to the figures provided by the Ministry of Defence.
[b] For 1971, packers and storekeepers have been separated from occupational order XX (warehousemen, storekeepers, packers, bottlers) according to the proportions obtaining in 1951.

and 1971, the number of female shop assistants rose by 425,000. What could have happenned to the disappearing men? Their loss is almost exactly matched by the increase of male nurses, teachers and draughts-men, and perhaps it is possible that professions such as these would now attract the bright young men who, sixty years ago, might have become shop assistants.

One of the most dramatic changes has been the decline in the number of indoor domestic servants in private households:

Indoor private domestic servants (thousands)

|  | 1911 | 1921 | 1931 | 1951 | 1971 |
|---|---|---|---|---|---|
| Males | 45 | 31 | 37 | 9 | 4 |
| Females | 1403 | 1072 | 1262 | 343 | 194 |
| Total | 1448 | 1103 | 1299 | 352 | 198 |

But the loss of 1·25 million has been partially made up by the gain of 588,000 in the numbers employed in hotels, catering and personal service.

In Tables 1.14 and 1.15 details are given for mining and manufacturing, transport and communication. Until 1931, occupations in manufacturing barely retained their proportion in the semi-skilled class; after 1931, their numbers increased so that in 1951 they constituted 17·9 per cent of the class compared with 14·6 per cent in 1911. Between 1951 and 1971, they achieved a modest increase of 6·6 per cent, but since the class as a whole decreased by 13 per cent, they rose to 24 per cent of the class total.

TABLE 1.14 Semi-skilled workers in mining and quarrying and in various manufacturing occupations (excluding self-employed), 1911–71 (thousands)

|  | 1911 | 1921 | 1931 | 1951 | 1971 | % of 1911 |
|---|---|---|---|---|---|---|
| Non-metallic mining products and chemicals | 109 | 62 | 66 | 123 | 131 | 120 |
| Metal-making and metal-using | 237 | 224 | 257 | 510 | 634 | 268 |
| Textiles | 198 | 201 | 233 | 161 | 120 | 61 |
| Clothing and other textile goods | 371 | 335 | 365 | 375 | 306 | 82 |
| Food, drink, tobacco | 115 | 93 | 78 | 96 | 143 | 124 |
| All the above | 1030 | 915 | 999 | 1265 | 1334 | 129 |
| Mining and quarrying | 501 | 525 | 539 | 399 | 132 | 26 |
| Total | 1531 | 1440 | 1538 | 1664 | 1466 | 96 |
| Percentage of class 6 | 21 | 22 | 21 | 23 | 23 |  |

The movements in the industrial groups have been contrasting. Ceramics and chemicals expanded employment between 1931 and 1951, almost doubling their use of semi-skilled labour, and so did the metals group, while textiles declined and clothing hardly changed.

The transport group, too, has increased its share of the class: from 12 per cent in 1911 to over 18 per cent in 1951. Table 1.15 tells the economic history of this age: horse and railway, tram and barge disappear before the inexorable internal combustion engine. There has been a minor revolution, too, in the telecommunications group: telegraphists were reduced from 25,000 in 1921 to 15,000 in 1951, while telephonists increased from 26,000 to 87,000; and 1971 showed 111,000 telephonists. Telegraphists were included with radio operators in that year, to show an increase in the combined total of 2,000 over 1951. Tram and trolley-bus drivers have, of course, been largely replaced by motor bus drivers and railway firemen are no longer required, but numbers for 1971 have also been reduced. Platelayers, paviours, tunnel-miners, railway ticket collectors and the miscellany of water transport workers are no longer

TABLE 1.15 Semi-skilled workers in various occupations in transport and communication, 1911–71 (thousands)

|  | 1911 | 1921 | 1931 | 1951 | 1971 | % of 1911 |
|---|---|---|---|---|---|---|
| Platelayers, paviours, tunnel-miners | 111 | 62 | 62 | 59 | n.d. | · · |
| Railway firemen, ticket collectors, etc.[a] | 98 | 99 | 78 | 80 | n.d. | · · |
| Vehicle drivers | | | | | | |
|    Horse-drawn | 404 | 220 | 139 | 15 | n.d. | · · |
|    Trams and trolley-buses | 17 | 23 | 23 | 13 | n.d. | · · |
|    Motor | 50 | 169 | 380 | 547 | 710 | 1420 |
| Bus and tram conductors | 21 | 31 | 67 | 97 | 58 | 276 |
| Water transport[b] | 69 | 61 | 58 | 36 | n.d. | · · |
| PO manipulative etc.[c] | 118 | 124 | 139 | 210 | 242 | 205 |
| All the above | 888 | 789 | 946 | 1057 | 1010 | 114 |
| Percentage of class 6 | 12 | 12 | 13 | 14 | (16) | |

[a] Includes running-shed workers and a miscellany of workers in 1951 code 649, 'Other workers in transport and communications'.
[b] Firemen, trimmers, bargemen, boatmen, tugmen, lock-keepers, etc.
[c] Postmen, sorters, telephonists, telegraphists and 1951 code 709, 'Other workers in transport and communications'. In 1971, telegraphists were combined with radio operators and have been included in class 5.

distinguished. I would guess that these might have added another seventy or eighty thousand to the group, putting it some percentage points above its level in 1951.

### Distribution by Sex

The proportion of women in class 6 remained remarkably constant between 1911 and 1951. It was 40 per cent in 1911, 41 per cent in 1921, 42 per cent in 1931 and 41 per cent in 1951. But in 1971, they had increased to 48 per cent of the class, the major influences being the drastic decline in the numbers of men agricultural labourers and shop assistants between 1951 and 1971, while women shop assistants increased by more than 100,000. The former constancy was in part caused by the fact that the two largest men's and women's groups of 1911, agricultural labourers and domestic servants, were both drastically reduced between 1911 and 1951, the one by 500,000, the other by 700,000.

In catering, domestic and laundry services, the working force has always been largely female, but the male constituent has remained fairly steady, with an upward trend, while, since 1931, the female has been reduced. Thus men formed 11 per cent of the group in 1911 and 22 per cent in 1971.

The change in shop-assistants has already been mentioned: in 1911, there were sixty-two male shop-assistants to every thirty-eight female; in 1971, there were seventy-eight female to every nineteen male.

### (I) CLASS 7 (UNSKILLED MANUAL WORKERS)

There was a big increase in the number of unskilled workers from 1911 to 1921, from 10 to 14 per cent of the occupied population (Table 1.1). Most of this was in engineering and the other manufacturing industries that had expanded during the war. This continued, at a lower rate, up to 1931, after which the numbers and proportions of unskilled workers fell, despite a further substantial increase in their numbers in metals and engineering. Between 1951 and 1971, numbers increased, and their proportion of the occupied population remained almost constant.

Unskilled work cannot be classified occupationally in the accepted sense, though there are a few unskilled occupations that are distinguished. The numbers in these and in certain industrial divisions are shown in Table 1.16.

TABLE 1.16  Unskilled workers (major constituents of class 7: employees only, unless otherwise stated), 1911–71 (thousands)

|  | 1911 | 1921 | 1931 | 1951 | 1971 | % of 1911 |
|---|---|---|---|---|---|---|
| Building and civil engineering[a] | 197 | 252 | 352 | 493 | 388 | 197 |
| Transport[b] | 455 | 500 | 552 | 318 | 156 | 34 |
| Charwomen, office cleaners | 137 | 132 | 163 | 252 | 468 | 342 |
| Street sellers[c] |  |  |  |  |  |  |
|   Employees | 31 | 15 | 37 | 10 | 43 | 139 |
|   Own account | 46 | 52 | 73 | 29 | 23 | 50 |
|     Total | 77 | 67 | 110 | 39 | 66 | 86 |
| Warehouse and storekeepers' assistants[d] | n.d. | 58 | 66 | 82 | 104 | ·· |
| Boiler firemen and stokers | n.d. | 63 | 56 | 80 | 36 | ·· |
| Non-metallic mining products and chemicals | n.d. | 110 | 161 | 183 | 62 | ·· |
| Metals and engineering | n.d. | 238 | 349 | 529 | 354 | ·· |
| Textiles (not textile goods) | n.d. | 140 | 112 | 110 | 56 | ·· |
| All other commercial and industrial undertakings[e] | n.d. | 1127 | 1121 | 559 | 519 | ·· |
| Total, 4 preceding groups | 844 | 1615 | 1743 | 1381 | 991 | 117 |
| Others in class 7 | 57 | 53 | 73 | 64 | 144 | 253 |
| All class 7, inc. own account | 1767 | 2740 | 3115 | 2709 | 2987 | 169 |
| All occupational classes | 18,347 | 19,333 | 21,029 | 22,514 | 25,021 | 136 |

[a] See note (b) to Table 1.11.
[b] Porters (railway and hotel, etc.), lorry drivers' mates, dock labourers, messengers, lift-attendants.
[c] Costermongers, hawkers, newspaper sellers.
[d] See note (c) to Table 1.11.
[e] 1951 census code 950.

The most important changes resulting in the net loss between 1931 and 1951 are shown on p. 39.

Technical changes are again in evidence: the fall in the number of dock labourers; a stable level in the chemical and allied industry despite a great rise in output; the replacement of messengers by the telephone. But what could account for the continuing increase in the number of charwomen (charmen) and office cleaners? The reduction, no doubt, in the number of domestic servants, and the increase in the

| | | Nos. in thousands | | |
|---|---|---|---|---|
| | | *1931* | *1951* | *1951 as %<br>of 1931* |
| Dock labourers | | 120 | 81 | 67.5 |
| Messengers | M | 186 | 47 | 25 |
| | F | 21 | 3 | 14 |
| | Total | 207 | 50 | 24 |
| Porters | | 69 | 45 | 65 |
| Charwomen | M | 5 | 14 | 280 |
| | F | 158 | 238 | 151 |
| | Total | 163 | 252 | 155 |
| Chemical and allied | M | 57 | 61 | 107 |
| | F | 9 | 13 | 144 |
| | Total | 66 | 74 | 112 |
| Metal-working, engineering, electrical<br>and allied | M | 316 | 467 | 148 |
| | F | 33 | 61 | 185 |
| | Total | 349 | 528 | 151 |
| Miscellaneous | M | 989 | 432 | 44 |
| | F | 132 | 126 | 95 |
| | Total | 1121 | 558 | 50 |

number of offices. The increase in the number of cleaning contractors has been a feature of the last twenty years.

### Distribution by Sex

Labouring jobs, depending on strength without skill, are mainly performed by men; charing and office cleaning is mainly done by women and, in 1971, occupied 40 per cent of the women in class 7. But women have been used to replace men in some class 7 occupations in time of war and, owing to the scarcity of male labour, tended to remain there after 1945. There were 1,000 women working as building labourers in 1951, and over 2,000 as railway porters; but their numbers had fallen by 1971 to 900 building labourers or 'construction workers n.e.c.' and 1,250 'Porters, ticket collectors, railway'.

## 5. THE EFFECTS OF INDUSTRIAL CHANGE

There are two proximate causes for changes in occupational distribution: technical changes within industries leading to changes in skill
coefficients, and differences in the relative rate of growth of industries.

Table 1.17 shows the percentages in which, in 1951, the occupational
classes were combined in the twenty-four industrial orders of the
industrial classification.[32]

It is apparent that the proportions vary widely from industry to
industry and that differential rates of growth between industries will, of
themselves, affect the class structure of the labour force. Table 1.18
shows the industrial distribution of those occupied in five census years.
We may now combine Tables 1.17 and 1.18 in order to show the effect
on occupational patterns of the changing fortunes of the different
industrial orders. If the distribution of occupations within each
industrial order had been throughout the same as in 1951, occupational
distribution would have been as follows:

| | IA | IB | 2 | 3 | *Percentages*<br>4 | 5 | 6 | 7 | All |
|---|---|---|---|---|---|---|---|---|---|
| 1911 | 1·29 | 3·39 | 10·88 | 8·62 | 2·45 | 24·95 | 38·36 | 10·04 | 100 |
| 1921 | 1·46 | 3·61 | 10·52 | 9·52 | 2·61 | 25·11 | 36·72 | 10·46 | 100 |
| 1931 | 1·52 | 3·81 | 10·72 | 9·74 | 2·47 | 24·68 | 36·30 | 10·76 | 100 |
| 1951 | 1·96 | 4·67 | 9·95 | 10·85 | 2·69 | 25·37 | 32·84 | 11·67 | 100 |
| 1971 | 2·63 | 7·13 | 9·95 | 12·56 | 2·45 | 23·19 | 30·46 | 11·63 | 100 |

If there had been no other change but that in the relative size of
industrial orders, this is what would have happened to the relative size
of occupational classes. Changes in the size of different industries have
worked strongly in favour of the use of more professional workers and
clerks, have been almost neutral as far as skilled manual workers are
concerned, have tended to reduce substantially the proportion of the
semi-skilled and to increase slightly the proportion of the unskilled.
These changes, however, were small between 1921 and 1931, but
considerable between 1931, 1951 and 1971.

Our findings may now be summarised by comparing an index of
changes in the proportions of the occupational classes (as shown in
Table 1.1) with an index calculated from proportions shown above.
Table 1.19 gives the results. Line A shows the extent to which the
proportion of each class would have changed from one census year to

TABLE 1.17 Occupational class distribution by industry, England and Wales, 1951

| Order | Industry | Occupational class | | | | | | | | |
|---|---|---|---|---|---|---|---|---|---|---|
| | | 1A | 1B | 2 | 3 | 4 | 5 | 6 | 7 | All |
| I | Agriculture etc. | 0·03 | 0·09 | 28·61 | 0·72 | 1·83 | 7·67 | 60·81 | 0·24 | 100 |
| II | Mining | 0·65 | 0·39 | 0·91 | 3·13 | 5·65 | 39·52 | 47·64 | 2·11 | 100 |
| III | Ceramics, etc. | 0·51 | 1·35 | 4·05 | 6·76 | 2·97 | 37·93 | 19·39 | 27·04 | 100 |
| IV | Chemicals | 3·83 | 4·96 | 7·03 | 16·02 | 3·58 | 15·33 | 27·00 | 22·24 | 100 |
| V | Metal manufacture | 1·23 | 1·86 | 2·74 | 8·86 | 5·37 | 38·48 | 18·56 | 22·89 | 100 |
| VI | Engineering and shipbuilding | 1·63 | 4·01 | 4·13 | 11·37 | 6·49 | 41·17 | 18·98 | 12·20 | 100 |
| VII | Vehicles | 0·88 | 2·50 | 4·77 | 9·88 | 6·18 | 47·74 | 16·85 | 11·19 | 100 |
| VIII | Metal goods | 0·40 | 0·48 | 4·86 | 8·67 | 5·26 | 37·17 | 28·71 | 14·45 | 100 |
| IX | Precision instruments | 0·92 | 2·34 | 5·96 | 10·96 | 4·80 | 52·52 | 15·18 | 7·32 | 100 |
| X | Textiles | 0·33 | 0·77 | 3·22 | 5·14 | 3·07 | 50·49 | 23·19 | 13·79 | 100 |
| XI | Leather, etc. | 0·38 | 0·49 | 6·86 | 6·05 | 2·86 | 66·21 | 4·48 | 12·67 | 100 |
| XII | Clothing | 0·04 | 0·17 | 4·34 | 4·79 | 2·03 | 36·63 | 48·10 | 3·90 | 100 |
| XIII | Food, drink and tobacco | 0·56 | 0·72 | 6·94 | 10·77 | 3·33 | 25·97 | 30·80 | 20·90 | 100 |
| XIV | Manufactures of wood and cork | 0·13 | 0·69 | 4·98 | 5·63 | 3·02 | 63·48 | 8·77 | 13·31 | 100 |
| XV | Paper and printing | 3·52 | 1·30 | 6·87 | 12·43 | 2·78 | 44·85 | 13·91 | 14·33 | 100 |
| XVI | Other manufactured goods | 0·86 | 2·70 | 6·42 | 11·10 | 3·47 | 42·08 | 15·02 | 18·35 | 100 |
| XVII | Building and contracting | 1·22 | 0·40 | 3·88 | 3·91 | 3·78 | 57·64 | 4·36 | 24·80 | 100 |
| XVIII | Gas, electricity and water | 3·66 | 1·63 | 4·88 | 15·57 | 2·33 | 27·61 | 18·24 | 26·08 | 100 |
| XIX | Transport and communication | 0·33 | 1·75 | 4·53 | 13·05 | 3·49 | 19·63 | 41·81 | 15·41 | 100 |
| XX | Distributive trades | 0·15 | 1·04 | 30·13 | 12·35 | 0·50 | 5·55 | 43·43 | 6·85 | 100 |
| XXI | Finance | 1·31 | 0·16 | 18·97 | 66·83 | 0·22 | 2·28 | 3·88 | 6·34 | 100 |
| XXII | Public administration | 5·00 | 2·97 | 7·90 | 18·25 | 1·18 | 10·25 | 39·63 | 14·83 | 100 |
| XXIII | Professional services | 12·73 | 44·95 | 2·88 | 13·92 | 0·14 | 2·66 | 17·95 | 4·77 | 100 |
| XXIV | Miscellaneous services | 0·36 | 3·00 | 13·06 | 4·66 | 0·12 | 8·45 | 65·06 | 5·29 | 100 |
| | All | 1·96 | 4·67 | 9·95 | 10·85 | 2·69 | 25·37 | 32·84 | 11·67 | 100 |

TABLE 1.18 Distribution of occupied population (including employers, self-employed and unemployed) by industry, 1911–71 (thousands)

| Order | Industry | 1911 | % | 1921 | % | 1931 | % | 1951 | % | 1971 | % |
|---|---|---|---|---|---|---|---|---|---|---|---|
| I | Agriculture etc. | 1499 | 8.4 | 1372 | 7.3 | 1257 | 6.1 | 1142 | 5.0 | 635 | 2.7 |
| II | Mining etc. | 1128 | 6.3 | 1305 | 6.9 | 1166 | 5.7 | 861 | 3.8 | 391 | 1.6 |
| III | Ceramics, glass, etc. | 201 | 1.1 | 214 | 1.1 | 265 | 1.3 | 318 | 1.4 | 306 | 1.3 |
| IV | Chemicals | 147 | 0.8 | 215 | 1.1 | 239 | 1.2 | 442 | 2.0 | 518 | 2.1 |
| V | Metal manufacture | 509 | 2.8 | 562 | 3.0 | 524 | 2.6 | 579 | 2.6 | 551 | 2.3 |
| VI | Engineering and shipbuilding | 878 | 4.9 | 1203 | 6.4 | 1090 | 5.3 | 1801 | 8.0 | 2149 | 9.0 |
| VII | Vehicles | 291 | 1.6 | 375 | 2.0 | 402 | 2.0 | 1009 | 4.5 | 789 | 3.3 |
| VIII } IX } | Metal goods n.e.s.  Instruments, jewellery, etc. | 321 | 1.8 | 424 | 2.2 | 450 | 2.2 | 636 | 2.8 | 731 | 3.1 |
| X | Textiles | 1359 | 7.6 | 1305 | 6.9 | 1338 | 6.5 | 997 | 4.4 | 591 | 2.5 |
| XI | Leather etc. | 93 | 0.5 | 87 | 0.5 | 92 | 0.4 | 79 | 0.4 | 53 | 0.2 |
| XII | Clothing | 1159 | 6.5 | 873 | 4.6 | 880 | 4.3 | 729 | 3.2 | 470 | 2.0 |
| XIII | Food, drink and tobacco | 554 | 3.1 | 623 | 3.3 | 709 | 3.5 | 756 | 3.4 | 738 | 3.1 |
| XIV | Wood | 276 | 1.5 | 304 | 1.6 | 321 | 1.6 | 333 | 1.5 | 302 | 1.3 |
| XV | Paper and printing | 334 | 1.9 | 403 | 2.1 | 497 | 2.4 | 520 | 2.3 | 612 | 2.6 |
| XVI | Other manufactures | 96 | 0.5 | 205 | 1.1 | 235 | 1.1 | 267 | 1.2 | 325 | 1.4 |
| XVII | Building | 950 | 5.3 | 795 | 4.2 | 1122 | 5.5 | 1431 | 6.4 | 1669 | 7.0 |
| XVIII | Gas, electricity and water | 116 | 0.6 | 179 | 0.9 | 246 | 1.2 | 361 | 1.6 | 362 | 1.5 |
| XIX | Transport and communication | 1416 | 7.9 | 1570 | 8.3 | 1671 | 8.2 | 1734 | 7.7 | 1564 | 6.6 |
| XX | Distributive trades | 2133 | 11.9 | 2239 | 11.9 | 2697 | 13.2 | 2712 | 12.1 | 3016 | 12.7 |
| XXI | Finance | 199 | 1.1 | 311 | 1.6 | 366 | 1.8 | 439 | 2.0 | 952 | 4.0 |
| XXII | Public administration and defence | 701 | 3.9 | 1007 | 5.3 | 999[a] | 4.9 | 1726 | 7.7 | 1572 | 6.6 |
| XXIII | Professional services | 798 | 4.4 | 886 | 4.7 | 1067 | 5.2 | 1543 | 6.9 | 2901 | 12.2 |
| XXIV | Miscellaneous services | 2783 | 15.5 | 2398 | 12.7 | 2865 | 14.0 | 2086 | 9.3 | 2357 | 9.9 |
|  | Inadequately described |  |  |  |  |  |  |  |  | 170 | 0.7 |
|  | Total | 17,941 | 100 | 18,855 | 100 | 20,498 | 100 | 22,501 | 100 | 23,733[b] | 100 |

[a] Local authority 'institutions' distinguished in 1931, and posted to 'Professional services'. In 1921, only nurses, attendants and medical occupations extracted from XXII and posted to XXIII.

[b] Includes 7000 whose workplace was outside the UK.

the next, or from 1951 to 1971 if the skill-mix *within* each industry order had been frozen and the only changes had been in the relative size of the twenty-four orders.

Line B shows the extent to which the proportion of each class *did* change as a result of all changes—both the relative size of the industry orders and the proportions in which the classes were blended within these orders.

Line C, which shows line B as a percentage of line A, isolates the effect of changes *within* each industry order—that is, of the proportions in which each order combines the occupational classes.

To illustrate, the proportion of the occupied population in class 1B increased by 15 per cent between 1911 and 1921 (note that we are talking about the percentage increase of a percentage). If no other factor had been operating but the change in the relative size of the industry orders,

TABLE 1.19 Indexes of changes in the proportions of each occupational class due to changes in the relative size of industry orders (A), all changes (B) and changes within industry orders (C), 1911–71 (percentages)

|  |  | *1911/21* | *1921/31* | *1931/51* | *1951/71* | *1911/71* |
|---|---|---|---|---|---|---|
| IA. Higher professional | A | 113 | 104 | 129 | 134 | 204 |
|  | B | 101 | 113 | 169 | 170 | 329 |
|  | C | 89 | 109 | 131 | 127 | 161 |
| IB. Lower professional | A | 106 | 106 | 123 | 153 | 210 |
|  | B | 115 | 98 | 136 | 166 | 255 |
|  | C | 108 | 92 | 111 | 108 | 121 |
| 2. Employers, proprietors, | A | 97 | 102 | 93 | 100 | 103 |
| administrators, managers | B | 103 | 99 | 101 | 118 | 123 |
|  | C | 106 | 97 | 108 | 118 | 119 |
| 3. Clerical workers | A | 110 | 102 | 111 | 116 | 146 |
|  | B | 139 | 104 | 153 | 130 | 287 |
|  | C | 126 | 102 | 138 | 112 | 197 |
| 4. Foremen, inspectors | A | 107 | 95 | 109 | 91 | 100 |
|  | B | 112 | 107 | 170 | 148 | 300 |
|  | C | 105 | 113 | 156 | 163 | 300 |
| 5. Skilled manual workers | A | 101 | 99 | 103 | 91 | 93 |
|  | B | 94 | 93 | 93 | 86 | 71 |
|  | C | 93 | 94 | 90 | 95 | 76 |
| 6. Semi-skilled manual | A | 96 | 99 | 90 | 93 | 79 |
| workers | B | 86 | 103 | 93 | 77 | 64 |
|  | C | 90 | 104 | 103 | 83 | 81 |
| 7. Unskilled manual workers | A | 104 | 103 | 108 | 100 | 116 |
|  | B | 147 | 105 | 81 | 99 | 124 |
|  | C | 141 | 102 | 75 | 99 | 107 |

its proportion would have increased by 6 per cent. We then deduce that changes in the use of this class *within* industries was also working strongly in its favour and, by itself, would have raised the proportion by 8 per cent. In the next decade, these factors were working in opposite directions: changes *between* orders would have raised the proportion by 6 per cent, while changes *within* orders would have reduced it by 8 per cent, the combined result being a fall of 2 per cent.

For both lower and higher professionals, the growth of industries has been more potent than their proportions within each industry; for foremen, the reverse has been true—more of them have been employed, regardless of industry. The same applied to clerical workers until 1951, after which the industrial tide became a bit stronger than the occupational tide, though both were rising strongly. For skilled workers, changes in the relative size of industries were almost neutral, while changes within industries have exercised a consistent downward pressure. Between 1951 and 1971, both combined to reduce the overall proportion by 14 per cent. For the semi-skilled the effect of both influences was almost equal in their cumulative downward effect. For the unskilled, pressures contrasted for 1911–21 and 1931–51, whilst being almost equal in the other two periods.

Over the whole span, movements between industries have dominated with respect to professionals, skilled and unskilled manual workers, and movements within industries with respect to employers and managers, clerical workers and foremen. For semi-skilled workers, the two movements have been almost equal.


## 6. CURRENT TRENDS

The population census comes but once in a decade, since the fit of curiosity that led to a quinquennial inquiry in 1966 was not permitted to reassert itself in 1976. However, we can get a glimpse of what is going on by reference to the New Earnings Survey (NES). This was held in October 1968, and then in April each year from 1970. It seeks to obtain information about 1 per cent of the employee population by requiring employers to complete a questionnaire concerning employees, whose National Insurance number ends in two specified digits. In 1978 and 1979, the number was 14, thus embracing one employee in a hundred.

As the name implies, the information sought is mainly concerned with earnings, but employers are also required to pick a job title from CODOT (*Classification of Occupations and Directory of Occupational*

*Titles*) and to give a brief description of the work performed. Thus, when classified by occupation, the results give a random sample of the numbers engaged in each occupation. Details are not given for occupations with less than 100 employees, but the report for 1979 identifies about 175 occupations for men and 50 for women. Not all of these can be posted to the occupational groups used in this book, for many of the categories cover jobs in two or more classes, and there is a residue in each of the CODOT major groups that the NES does not ascribe to a particular occupation, so in Table 1.20 we have to content ourselves with combining classes IA and IB, and to harbouring a residue of manual workers who cannot be posted to classes 5, 6 or 7, and a few women in the distributive trade whose occupational class is indeterminate.

The NES in 1979 obtained 163,000 usable returns, just over 0·7 per cent of the employee population, or 1 in 136. The sampling error, given by the square root of the number shown for any occupation, becomes rather large for occupations with small numbers. For an occupation of 1000, it would be plus or minus 3 per cent; for 100, it would be 10 per cent. If the standard errors are larger than possible year-by-year changes, then short-term comparisons cannot be made. Accordingly, in Table 1.20, we assess changes over a span of six years, from 1973, when

TABLE 1.20 Percentages of full-time employees in occupational classes, NES, 1973 and 1979

|  | 1973 | | | 1979 | | |
|---|---|---|---|---|---|---|
|  | M | F | T | M | F | T |
| 1. Professions | 13·4 | 17·2 | 14·5 | 15·7 | 20·2 | 17·1 |
| 2B. Managers and administrators | 13·4 | 3·1 | 10·4 | 16·4 | 4·5 | 12·7 |
| Sales, unclassified |  | 0·5 | 0·1 |  | 0·6 | 0·2 |
| 3. Clerks | 6·7 | 37·7 | 15·8 | 5·9 | 38·7 | 16·0 |
| 4. Foremen | 7·0 | 3·4 | 6·0 | 6·9 | 3·8 | 5·9 |
| *Manual workers* |  |  |  |  |  |  |
| 5. Skilled | 19·3 | 4·9 | 15·1 | 19·2 | 4·2 | 14·7 |
| 6. Semi-skilled | 19·8 | 18·3 | 19·3 | 19·1 | 16·3 | 18·2 |
| 7. Unskilled | 5·8 | 2·7 | 4·9 | 4·7 | 1·8 | 3·8 |
| Manual, unclassified | 14·6 | 12·2 | 13·9 | 12·1 | 9·9 | 11·4 |
|  | 100 | 100 | 100 | 100 | 100 | 100 |

(Men: 21 and over; women: 18 and over)

CODOT was first applied, to 1979, and combine the occupations into the much larger occupational classes, so that any trends that are in operation will outweigh the sampling errors.

Table 1.20 shows managers and administrators to be the fastest growing group: their proportions were up 22·4 per cent for men, 45 per cent for women, 22·1 per cent overall. Next came the professionals, with 17·2 per cent for men, 17·4 for women and 17·9 overall.

Forewomen, still a small group, show a rise of 11·8 per cent, and women clerks of 2·6 per cent, but all the other groups are in decline, both relatively and in absolute numbers. Overall, class 4 (Foremen and – women) have just about held their own, and clerks have registered a rise of a bit over 1 per cent. This is much below their rate of increase for the decade to 1971, which was 1·5 per cent per year.

For the whole group of manual workers, there was a fall of 9·6 per cent. They formed 53·2 per cent of the employee population in 1973 and 48·1 per cent in 1979: we have entered an age numerically dominated by white collar workers. The unskilled have fallen most, then the group we have been unable to classify, then the semi-skilled. The skilled have been reduced by only 2·65 per cent.

Note that the data refer to adult full-time workers. Of men employees, 2·4 per cent were part-timers in April 1973, and 3·2 per cent in April 1979. In the case of women, the percentages were 34·0 in 1973 and 36·3 in 1979.

# 2 Occupational Pay

## 1. EMPLOYEE INCOME DISTRIBUTION, 1911–12 and 1975–6

### ( A )   INCOME BEFORE TAX

In Chapter 1, we enumerated people by their jobs; in this chapter we investigate what they get paid for doing them. Employers do not buy labour as such: they buy the services of fitters, bricklayers, dress machinists, nurses, typists, physicists, and it is by occupation that rates of pay are fixed. Unfortunately (from the viewpoint of orderly presentation) there is no fixed rate for a worker engaged in a specified occupation: terms and conditions vary from employer to employer, and an individual employer may even pay diverse rates to different workers doing the same sort of job.

Average pay shown by the New Earnings Survey for 1978 was £4519 for full-time men aged 21 and over, and £2881 for full-time women aged 18 and over.[1] This chapter is aimed at discovering the dispersions about these averages, formulating them in occupational terms, and measuring the extent to which they have changed over the years.

Note that we are dealing with the earnings of individual employees, not the 'income units' in terms of which dispersion is often presented. The latter are analysed in great detail in the reports of the Royal Commission on the Distribution of Income and Wealth.[2] Income units, for tax purposes, may consist of single persons or married couples, while personal income includes income, from whatever source, accruing to an income unit. For some purposes, this is the appropriate way to measure dispersion and its changes. But here, where we are concerned with *occupational* pay, we are dealing with the price-tag put on someone for doing a particular type of work. Thus we omit unearned income, which is a return on ownership, and income from self-employment, which consists of a combination of a return on work, on ownership and, possibly, on other people's work.

The only exception is that we include Schedule D earnings with the income of occupational class 1A: the higher professions.[3] This is

47

TABLE 2.1 Distribution of annual income before tax, Great Britain (1911–12) and United Kingdom[a] (1975–6), employees numbers in thousands
1. Cumulative frequency distribution

| *1911–12* | | | | *1975–6* | | | |
|---|---|---|---|---|---|---|---|
| *Getting more than £* | *Male* | *Female* | *Total* | *Getting more than £* | *Male* | *Female* | *Total* |
| 0 | 11,665 | 4993 | 16,658 | 0 | 15,648 | 9547 | 25,195 |
| 10 | 11,621 | 4884 | 16,505 | 674 | 14,553 | 7315 | 21,868 |
| 20 | 10,984 | 4553 | 15,537 | 749 | 14,426 | 6951 | 21,377 |
| 40 | 9807 | 3097 | 12,904 | 999 | 14,048 | 5858 | 19,906 |
| 60 | 6879 | 667 | 7546 | 1249 | 13,594 | 4768 | 18,362 |
| 80 | 4355 | 175 | 4530 | 1499 | 13,077 | 3788 | 16,865 |
| 100 | 2602 | 65 | 2667 | 1749 | 12,407 | 2889 | 15,296 |
| 120 | 1185 | 9 | 1194 | 1999 | 11,526 | 2076 | 13,602 |
| 140 | 641 | 2 | 643 | 2499 | 9126 | 1007 | 10,133 |
| 160 | 451 | | 451 | 2999 | 6386 | 523 | 6909 |
| 200 | 277 | | 277 | 3999 | 2523 | 159 | 2682 |
| 300 | 125 | | 125 | 4999 | 1059 | 51 | 1110 |
| 400 | 72 | | 72 | 5999 | 528 | 20 | 548 |
| 500 | 44 | | 44 | 7999 | 197 | 6 | 203 |
| 600 | 30 | | 30 | 9999 | 96 | 3 | 99 |
| 700 | 22 | | 22 | 11,999 | 51 | 0·9 | 51·9 |
| 800 | 17 | | 17 | 14,999 | 22 | 0·4 | 22·4 |
| 900 | 14 | | 14 | 19,999 | 8 | 0·17 | 8·17 |
| 1000 | 9 | | 9 | 49,999 | 0·4 | 0·035 | 0·435 |
| 2000 | 1·8 | | 1·8 | 99,999 | 0·046 | 0·001 | 0·047 |
| 3000 | 0·75 | | 0·75 | | | | |
| 4000 | 0·4 | | 0·4 | | | | |
| 5000 | 0·2 | | 0·2 | | | | |

[a] The inclusion of Northern Ireland in 1975–6 lowers the mean by 0·14 per cent.

because, as noted in Chapter 1, a high proportion of the higher professionals are self-employed and it would give a false impression of the status of the class if they were omitted.

It would be of great interest to include the earnings of all those pursuing trades and occupations as self-employed workers, including those who inhabit the 'black economy' discovered by social scientists

2. Deciles and highest centiles and milliles (pounds)

|  | *1911–12* | | | *Deciles* | *1975–6* | | |
|---|---|---|---|---|---|---|---|
|  | *Male* | *Female* | *Both* |  | *Male* | *Female* | *Both* |
| 1 | 28 | 22 | 25 | 1 | 999 | 225 | 410 |
| 2 | 43 | 35 | 38 | 2 | 1700 | 500 | 940 |
| 3 | 51 | 37 | 43 | 3 | 2100 | 800 | 1350 |
| 4 | 59 | 41 | 49 | 4 | 2430 | 1025 | 1770 |
| 5 *Median* | 67 | 43 | 56 | 5 *Median* | 2740 | 1240 | 2125 |
| 6 | 76 | 45 | 65 | 6 | 3020 | 1490 | 2520 |
| 7 | 88 | 49 | 76 | 7 | 3350 | 1760 | 2900 |
| 8 | 103 | 55 | 92 | 8 | 3760 | 2060 | 3400 |
| 9 | 121 | 64 | 112 | 9 | 4600 | 2520 | 4100 |
|  |  |  |  | Highest centile |  |  |  |
| 99 | 310 | 103 | 265 | 99 | 9000 | 4550 | 7680 |
|  |  |  |  | Highest millile |  |  |  |
| 999 | 945 | 128 | 810 | 999 | 16,250 | 7400 | 14,600 |

3. Percentages of medians

|  | *1911–12* | | | *Deciles* | *1975–6* | | |
|---|---|---|---|---|---|---|---|
|  | *Male* | *Female* | *Both* |  | *Male* | *Female* | *Both* |
| 1 | 42 | 51 | 45 | 1 | 36 | 18 | 19 |
| 2 | 64 | 81 | 68 | 2 | 62 | 40 | 44 |
| 3 | 76 | 86 | 77 | 3 | 77 | 65 | 64 |
| 4 | 88 | 95 | 88 | 4 | 89 | 83 | 83 |
| 5 | 100 | 100 | 100 | 5 | 100 | 100 | 100 |
| 6 | 113 | 105 | 116 | 6 | 110 | 120 | 119 |
| 7 | 131 | 114 | 136 | 7 | 122 | 142 | 136 |
| 8 | 154 | 128 | 164 | 8 | 137 | 166 | 160 |
| 9 | 181 | 149 | 200 | 9 | 168 | 203 | 193 |
|  |  |  |  | Highest centile |  |  |  |
| 99 | 463 | 240 | 473 | 99 | 328 | 367 | 361 |
|  |  |  |  | Highest millile |  |  |  |
| 999 | 1410 | 298 | 1446 | 999 | 593 | 597 | 687 |

and financial journalists in recent times, but the necessary data is not available.[4]

Table 2.1 confines itself to the income of employees, and shows their distribution in income ranges near the beginning and near the end of our period of study. The 1975–6 data come from tax returns; for 1911–12, tax data embrace only the top 3 per cent of the employee population and other sources have been used for the remainder. Methods and sources are described in Appendix C.

Parts 2 and 3 of Table 2.1 process the data in part 1 so that we may more easily interpret it. Curiously, for males the dispersion of pay above the median has narrowed, while for women, both above and below, it has widened. We saw in Chapter 1 how women had invaded the higher occupations as sex barriers were reduced; later, in this chapter, we shall see that their average pay was the same percentage of the male average (54 per cent) in 1913–14 as in 1960, that by 1970 it had actually declined somewhat, but that after 1970 it began creeping up.

More equality for men; less equality for women. But *less* equality between men and women in the lower reaches—all the way up to the seventh decile (Q70)—and less inequality between them after that. In 1911–12, women got a third of men's pay at the highest centile (Q99), by 1975–6 they were getting half. At the highest millile (Q999) it was 13·5 per cent in the earlier year, 45·5 per cent in the later.

( B )   QUANTILES AT CONSTANT PRICES

We can do something to achieve a more constant measure by inflating 1911–12 incomes in accordance with the rise between then and 1975–6 of the retail price index.[5] With the former year's prices = 100, the latter's are 1262, that is, 12·6 times as high.

We see that it is about the sixth and seventh deciles that the increase has been greatest, levels heavily representative of men manual workers–the modern yeomen of England. They are three times as affluent as their grandfathers, if one permits affluence to be measured apart from the quality of life, about whose changes opinions differ.

On the other hand, at the lowest decile, real income has not risen very much—less even than at the highest millile. Who are these poor people who have enjoyed so small a share of the rise of affluence? Ten per cent of employees in the year 1975–6 got an average of £7·88 per week or less. But according to the New Earnings Survey for April 1975,[6] only 0·5 per cent of women aged 18 and over in full-time employment got less than £15 per week, while at the lowest decile, they averaged £23·00 per

TABLE 2.2 Quantiles at 1975–6 prices

| 1911–12 | | Deciles | 1975–6 | |
|---|---|---|---|---|
| | | | % of 1911–12 | |
| 1 | 315 | | 410 | 130 |
| 2 | 479 | | 940 | 196 |
| 3 | 542 | | 1350 | 249 |
| 4 | 617 | | 1770 | 287 |
| 5 Median | 706 | | 2125 | 301 |
| 6 | 819 | | 2520 | 308 |
| 7 | 958 | | 2900 | 303 |
| 8 | 1159 | | 3400 | 293 |
| 9 | 1411 | | 4100 | 291 |
| | | Highest centile | | |
| 99 | 3339 | | 7680 | 230 |
| | | Highest millile | | |
| 999 | 10,206 | | 14,600 | 143 |

week (£1196 per year).[7] Part-time women workers, on the other hand, worked on average 21·4 hours per week and, at the lowest decile, received 55·3 pence per hour: £11·83 per week, £615 per year.[8] So, up to the second decile, those concerned must have been part-time women workers plus workers who worked only part of the year.[9] We may say, then, that the bulk of full-time workers were getting incomes with three times the purchasing power of their peers on the eve of the First World War.

### (C) INCOME AFTER TAXES AND BENEFITS

If one wants to compare purchasing power now and in some previous year, should one not take disposable income you may ask, that is, income after the deduction of income tax and, perhaps, national insurance deductions? In so far as the sum total of income-earners are concerned, the answer must be no, for what is taxed is also consumed, the only difference being that we consume it whether we like it or not: by way of schooling for our children, health services, security and the other things that governments provide for the benefit of the populace. Of course, we may forego some of these services by not sending our children to government schools or not using the National Health Service. Then, if we want to determine whether people are 'better off' now than they were sixty or seventy years ago we have to do a complicated cost-benefit analysis with many value judgements: television *v.* music-halls, cars *v.* carriages, old and new fashions in crime and warfare, as well as the arduousness and interest of work.

But when it is a matter of comparing incomes at different levels, then of course the redistribution that is effected by taxes and social benefits is of relevance. We may neglect social payments for 1911–12, for health and unemployment insurance was just on the eve of being introduced.[10] Income tax stood at 1*s.* 2*d.* in the pound for incomes of over £160, with a maximum average of 9*d.* per pound of income up to £2000 of income, and 1*s.* per £ for incomes over £2,000 and up to £3,000. Supertax was charged when income exceeded £5000 at 6*d.* in the pound on the amount by which income exceeded £3000. Less than 4 per cent of employees would have paid income tax in 1911–12. A married man at the highest centile (£310) would have paid £8 15*s.*, an overall average of 6·77*d.* per £. At the highest millile, a married man would have paid £35 8*s.* 9*d.*

In 1975–6, a married man's tax-free allowance was £955, plus an additional personal allowance of £280. After the deduction of these allowances, he would pay 35 per cent on the first £4500, 40 per cent on the next £500, 45 per cent on the next £1000, and so on until 83 per cent was taken on income of over £20,000 in excess of allowances.

After tax comparisons at 1975–6 prices would then be as follows:

|  | *1911–12*<br>£ | *1975–6*<br>£ | *% of*<br>*1911–12* |
|---|---|---|---|
| Median | 706 | 1813·50 | 257·0 |
| Highest decile | 1411 | 3097·25 | 219·5 |
| Highest centitle | 3802 | 6126·75 | 161·0 |
| Highest millile | 11,479 | 7869·50 | 68·8 |

So the man at the highest centile is not 2·3 times better off than his peer of sixty-four years ago, but only 1·61 times, while the man at the highest millile is considerably poorer.

Of course, there are other allowances that may apply at the present time: deductions of up to £1500 for retirement annuity payments, or up to a sixth of total income for life insurance premiums, and the interest paid on loans from building societies. The man at the highest millile might well save £5000 in tax in these ways, in which case his 31 per cent fall might be converted into a 12 per cent rise.

But these are of necessity hypothetical cases, for taxes and allowances have regard not to individuals, but to 'income units' which consist of families (individuals living on their own, or man-and-wife plus dependants). It is on this basis that Inland Revenue data may be used.[11] We are no longer dealing with income derived from specific occupations, but with personal income from all sources.

To complete the calculus of redistribution, we must include benefits received as well as taxes and national insurance contributions paid. This the Central Statistical Office does for us on the basis of the Family Expenditure Survey.[12] Their calculations are based on household income – the income of tax-units and the effects on them of taxation and social payments. These, again, vary according to the constitution of the households, which range from one adult to two adults and various numbers of children. If the quartiles listed above are taken as representing household income and the constitution of the households is taken to conform with those of the Family Expenditure Survey of 1975, the net effect on quartile income of direct cash benefits, employees' National Insurance contributions, housing and food subsidies, indirect taxes and the benefits of education, National Health Services and welfare foods would be as follows:

|                   | £      |
| ----------------- | ------ |
| Median            | + 374  |
| Highest decile    | − 85   |
| Highest centile   | −413   |
| Highest millile   | −874   |

The reduction in differentials by taxation and social payments and benefits in kind is quite considerable, as you will readily observe. At the highest millile, about two-thirds of the reduction is occasioned by direct taxation; at the highest decile, about two-fifths. But the person at the highest millile in 1975–6, after marriage and additional personal allowances, would have had a marginal tax rate of 70 per cent. So each child not over eleven would have reduced his tax by £168 (70 per cent of the child allowance of £240), each child over eleven but not over sixteen by £192·50, and each child over sixteen but undergoing full-time education £213·50. And so on with other allowances. In the ranges given by the Central Statistical Office in their calculations, an average income of £2185 is increased to £2270, while an average income of £4561 is reduced to £3619. Before taxes and benefits, the higher income is 208 per cent of the lower; after taxes and benefits this is reduced to 159. The second percentage is itself 76 per cent of the first. In my calculation for the median and highest decile, a percentage of 193 is reduced to 138, the second being 71 per cent of the first. At the next level the proportionate reduction caused by taxation and benefits is about the same, but in the CSO's highest range (£8038 and above, with an average of £10,569) the differential is reduced by only 36 per cent, compared with 53 per cent in my calculation for the highest millile. The reduction in differential has been mitigated by allowances not included in my calculation.

(D) INCOME AND WEALTH

In Table 2.1 we observed a strong narrowing above the median in the spread of male incomes in 1975–6 as compared with 1911–12, and a strong widening of differentials in female incomes. This resulted in an overall narrowing, because of the dominance of male incomes. After tax, income at the highest centile was still 61 per cent greater in real terms in 1975 than in 1911 (compared with 157 per cent at the median), but at the highest millile it was 31 per cent lower. Social benefits, National Insurance payments and indirect taxes in 1975 would raise the median by about 20 per cent and reduce the highest centiles and milliles, respectively, by about 8 and 11 per cent. The CSO calculations suggest that the effect of taxes and social receipts and payments would not be so severe at the highest millile as I have suggested, but even so the narrowing has been pretty drastic.

This chapter is concerned with the earned income of employees, except in the case of the higher professions for whom self-employed income is included. At this point, though, it might be of interest to introduce a digression on income from property and the ownership of wealth, and to try to identify the occupations of the very rich—subjects on which a great deal of information has become available since the first edition of this book.

We may note immediately that most of the very rich achieve that salubrious state by combining earned with unearned income. We may find data about the very rich in the surtax tables of *Inland Revenue Statistics*.[13] For the year 1972–3, 12,032 of those assessed for surtax had incomes of £20,000 or more. In aggregate, their income consisted of £200,600,000 from employment and £183,100,000 from property.

Only 772 of them had no earned income, while another 734 had some earned income, but less than £1,000. These were mostly, I suppose, men who had retired or the widows of wealthy men. To approach from the other side, 767 had no investment income, while 822 had some investment income but less than £1,000. The bulk had considerable investment income supported by considerable earned income: three-quarters had £5,000 or more earned income, and two-thirds had £5,000 or more investment income. Overall, these 12,032 averaged £16,672 of earned plus £15,218 of unearned income. We may generalise by saying that most of the rich are by no means idle, but rather more than double their property income by income from work.

Of the total of 20,261,000 incomes covered in the Inland Revenue survey of 1972–3, only 6,243,000 had some investment income. Accumulating from the poorest to the richest, we find that half the investment income ( £1094·9 million out of a total of £2124·5 million) was divided amongst 5,563,000 income units, while the other half was divided amongst 680,000 income units. More than 10 per cent of the income went to the richest 28,000.

The receipt of unearned income depends on the ownership of wealth, but not all wealth produces income. This makes it difficult to measure wealth in any significant way and leads us off on flights of philosophy or fancy. The jewels that some people keep in a deposit box in the vaults of a bank produce no income, whereas company shares or government securities do. But the jewels may have trebled their selling price since 1965, in a period when average share prices rose only 50 per cent. Take, for example, Duccio di Buoninsegna's painting, 'The Crucifixion', that was sold at Christie's in July 1976 for £1·1 million, after having been bought by the Lindsay family in 1863 for 250 guineas.[14] The initial investment had yielded a return of 7·6 per cent per annum. In real terms, allowing for the fact that the pound of 1976 could buy only about one-twelfth of that of 1863, the picture had appreciated in value by a factor of about 350.

Our understanding of this difficult subject is helped by the reports of the Royal Commission on the Distribution of Income and Wealth, established in August 1974. In their first report, they present a 'personal sector balance sheet' that estimates the value of assets held by residents of the United Kingdom.[15] Physical and financial personal assets at the end of 1973 were estimated to total £250,442 million. Some of the evaluations require heroic assumptions—for example, that consumer durables (at £17,837 million) have a life of eight years.[16] Apart from their accumulation of errors, such estimates will vary according to the assumptions on which they are based.

Personal assets then amounted to about £4600 per head of population, man, woman and child. But the question at issue is how they were divided, to which the Inland Revenue statisticians have made a gallant attempt to find an answer by assuming that the wealth of the living accords with that of the newly dead. It is generally not until someone dies that his or her possessions are evaluated so that they may be taxed and the residue divided among the heirs. Since people die at a variety of ages, one may take wealth at death in a particular age group as representative of wealth for the whole age group, thereby constructing a distribution for the whole population. One of the many limitations of this method relates to the precautions taken by wealthy people to transfer some of their wealth before they die. We may suppose that the wealthier they are, the more such precautions they will take, so that the Inland Revenue estimates would represent the lower limits of skewness.[17] These show, for 1973, that, of the adult population of the UK,

the richest 1 per cent owned 28·6 per cent of the personal wealth;
the richest 2 per cent owned 36·9 per cent of the personal wealth;
the richest 5 per cent owned 52·5 per cent of the personal wealth.

It is impossible to say what proportion of their possessions had escaped the attentions of taxmen. If it had been a quarter, their percentage shares would have risen to 35, 46 and 66.

A small section of the population enjoy, or at least possess, most of the private assets. Of these, the income-producing assets are of particular interest in the present context: that part of wealth that produces still more wealth for those who possess it. We noted that, in 1972–3, the Inland Revenue had identified a total of £2,124·5 million of investment income, of which those with total incomes of £10,000 or more got £1,189·8 million. The 82,928 incomes with not less than £10,000 a year constituted 0·4 per cent of all incomes and received 56 per cent of the investment income.

In most cases, the receiver of investment income plays a passive role: your deposit with the Post Office or a building society does not entitle you to a share in the management. More important are those who own and who, by virtue of their ownership, participate to some extent in the decision-making process. These are the owners of ordinary shares in business companies, who have a vote, in accordance with the number of their shares, at the company's general meeting. Quite a small portion of all wealth is so constituted, but is of decisive importance for the behaviour of the economy.[18]

The Royal Commission estimated the market value of quoted ordinary shares in UK companies to have been £40,520 million at the end of 1973, of which 42 per cent by value were owned by persons resident in the country. Disappointingly, the Commission is unable to tell us how the ordinary shares are distributed between individuals.[19] The best we can do is to return to *Inland Revenue Statistics*, where there is a table showing 'Dividends, interest, etc., taxed at source'. This covers interest paid on Debentures, preference shares and government securities as well as dividends on ordinary shares. We know from this the proportion of taxpayers who received income of this category, and the amounts received by those in various income ranges, but we do not know the capital value of their holdings. We shall have to content ourselves with taking yield in dividends or interest as a proxy for value. The data is presented in Table 2.3.

Of the earnings from dividends and interest, 51·9 per cent went to the 292,000 incomes of £5000 or more. If this approximated to their share of quoted ordinary shares shown as belonging to persons in 1972,[20] then we could say they owned £13,499 million out of the total of £26,010 million: an average of £46,229 each. The remaining 1,609,000 from Table 2.3 would then own an average of £7776 each. Thus it would seem that ownership by persons of shares in quoted companies is concentrated in the hands of a small number of income-receivers. We cannot specify the degree of concentration with any precision, but our calculations suggest that of the income-receivers specified by the Inland Revenue in 1972–3, 292,000 (that is, 1·4 per cent) probably owned more than half the shares owned by persons.

In considering the distribution of income, with its multitude of facets, it is important to remember that one of the 'fringe benefits' of a very high income is the ability to accumulate wealth and, from the resulting income, to become richer still. It is a great help, in this respect, to have had a rich father. Evidence in this connexion has been collected by C. D. Harbury and P. C. McMahon, who analysed the fortunes left by the fathers of a sample of top wealth leavers. They concluded,

> . . . the proportion of sons leaving £100,000 and over and having fathers who had left more than £50,000 was 58 % both in 1956–57 and 1965. The fact that between a half and two-thirds of those who left £100,000 or more in the 1950s and 1960s were preceded by fathers leaving at least £25,000 illustrates the importance of having had a moderately wealthy father.[21]

Our curiosity about the occupations of the rich is in part satisfied by Report No. 3 of the Royal Commission on the Distribution of Income and Wealth.[22] This is concerned with employee incomes of £10,000 and above at 1974–5 prices, a limit they consider equivalent to about £7500 in 1972–3 and £8500 in 1973–4. Between two and three employees in a thousand had incomes at or above this level: about 65,000 employees in the tax year 1974–5.[23]

The Commission finds the major part of this group (70 per cent) to be made up of managers. The rest consisted of judges and solicitors, finance, insurance and investment specialists, aircraft flight deck officers and, to a lesser extent, medical practitioners, some university staff, actors and professional sportsmen and the most senior civil servants and local government officers.[24]

For the self-employed we must again turn to the Inland Revenue. *Inland Revenue Statistics 1976* give us ranges of trading profits and professional earnings for sole traders and partnerships (shown separately) up to 1972. By interpolation, we may estimate that there were about 25,000 sole traders at £7500 or more, while there were 17,900 partnerships at £15,000 or more: say in all about 61,000 people.

Of the 25,000 sole traders at £7500 or more, the professions constituted 4408. Who the others were, it is not possible to say for we are not given ranges by industry. We may note, however, that the trade group with the highest average earnings was insurance, banking and finance, where 40,000 sole traders or partnerships earned an average, after capital allowances, of £4700. These would include unincorporated stock-brokers, insurance brokers and merchant bankers, so it would not be surprising if they accounted for most of those other than professionals in the top ranges.

To summarise: we may guess that by 1974–5 there were between 120,000 and 130,000 people with earned incomes of £10,000 or more (equivalent to about £7500 or more in 1972–3). About 45,000 of these would have been managers. There would have been another 20,000 employees engaged in professional or specialist capacities, and 61,000 self-employed people, the majority of whom would probably have been in the professions.[25] The evidence is of necessity impressionistic, for though the partners and sole traders have to submit accounts to the Inland Revenue once a year, it is probable that many do not keep proper books, while some of the records kept are designed to obscure rather than to reveal.

## 2. PAY BY OCCUPATIONAL CLASS

### (A) PROBLEMS OF MEASUREMENT

Some occupations are normally paid by the year, some by the month, some by the week and some by the hour.[26] Some are paid for time lost owing to illness or mishap. Most, nowadays, have an annual paid holiday, though it may vary from two weeks to six months. There is also variation in the length of the working week, which may be prolonged by paid or unpaid overtime. Finally, the effort, intensity and unpleasantness of different occupations vary through an enormous range, from the depressive boredom of the art gallery attendant to the manic fervour of the pop singer.

Not only does the expenditure of effort vary between jobs; it has, in many cases, varied greatly in the same job at different times. Many manual jobs involve much less exertion now than they did thirty or forty years ago, while conditions of work that were taken for granted then would not be tolerated today.

There is no way of standardising for these variations. We cannot quantify the expenditure of effort involved in doing a job and it is not easy even to rank different jobs in this respect, for those requiring little muscular effort sometimes involve considerable nervous strain.[27] Instead, we skirt the problem by saying that what we shall set out to measure is the price of engaging a worker in a particular occupation for one year or fifty-two weeks. For the worker, it is the earnings that can be extracted (before tax and other statutory deductions) for a year's work, including payments for overtime and deductions for short-time.[28]

In Chapter 1 we plotted the occupational structure in years determined by the census of population; logically, it might seem that we should choose the same years for plotting pay structure, but here we are subject to two restraints: one concerning the limitations of the available information, the other the instability of the pay structure over much of our period of study. The years 1921 and 1951 were both periods of violent economic change, one the aftermath of the First World War, the other the middle of the Korean War; and 1931 was a year of falling prices, rising unemployment and deepening depression.

But there were periods of comparative stability from 1906 to 1914, 1923 to 1928, and 1934 to 1938, and it is at some point in each of these periods that we construct our pay structure. For more recent years, we were guided by expediency to choose 1955–6 because this was the period for which the Royal Commission on Doctors' and Dentists' Remuneration collected its information about professional incomes, and 1959–60 because that marked the end of the period covered in the first edition and was a year following major readjustments in pay. Then, in 1968, the Department of Employment inaugurated its New Earnings Survey, which it repeated in 1970 and has since continued at annual intervals.[29] The 1970 survey had a number of improvements over that of 1968: for one thing, usable returns had doubled from 84,000 to 170,000, and this is quite important for pricing occupations with small numbers. Thus I have taken 1970 and 1978 (the latest year for which full returns are available at time of writing) as reference years for the extension of the occupational class averages.

We proceed now to build up the class averages by assessing pay for the constituent occupations in each of the seven periods.

(B) OCCUPATIONAL CLASS 1A (HIGHER PROFESSIONS)

*Men*

For the years 1913/14, 1922/3 and 1955/6, professional earnings are well documented[30] and, for these years, we are able to produce measures of dispersion. These are shown in Table 2.3.

TABLE 2.3 Professional earnings, 1913/14, 1922/3 and 1955/6

|  | 1913/14 £ | 1922/3 £ | 1922/3 % of 1913/14 | 1955/6 £ | 1955/6 % of 1922/3 | 1955/6 % of 1913/14 |
|---|---|---|---|---|---|---|
| **Barristers** |  |  |  |  |  |  |
| Highest decile | 1820 | 3450 | 189 | 5003 | 145 | 275 |
| Upper quartile | 680 | 1533 | 225 | 2619 | 171 | 385 |
| Median | 210 | 580 | 276 | 1251 | 216 | 596 |
| Lower quartile | 155 | 235 | 152 | 579 | 246 | 373 |
| **Solicitors** |  |  |  |  |  |  |
| Highest decile | 1410 | 2413 | 171 | 3983 | 165 | 282 |
| Upper quartile | 790 | 1453 | 184 | 2630 | 181 | 333 |
| Median | 390 | 811 | 208 | 1688 | 208 | 434 |
| Lower quartile | 185 | 434 | 234 | 1041 | 240 | 562 |
| **Doctors** |  |  |  |  |  |  |
| Highest decile | 1200 | 1757 | 146 | 3544 | 202 | 295 |
| Upper quartile | 700 | 1142 | 163 | 2865 | 251 | 409 |
| Median | 370 | 723 | 195 | 2300 | 318 | 622 |
| Lower quartile | 195 | 439 | 225 | 1794 | 409 | 920 |
| **Dentists** |  |  |  |  |  |  |
| Highest decile | 1140 | 1681 | 147 | 3746 | 223 | 328 |
| Upper quartile | 600 | 950 | 158 | 2806 | 295 | 468 |
| Median | 310 | 514 | 166 | 2090 | 407 | 674 |
| Lower quartile | 155 | 294 | 190 | 1437 | 489 | 928 |

Over the whole span, the changes display some similarity: income at the median has multiplied six or seven times, at the lower quartile about nine times (except in the case of the solicitors), at the upper quartile about four times and at the highest decile about three times.

Within this pattern, there have been considerable fluctuations in relativities. The averages for the medians and quartiles for each profession and their relation to the averages for the four professions were as follows:

|            | 1913/14 | | 1922/3 | | 1955/6 | |
|            | £ | % of average | £ | % of average | £ | % of average |
|------------|-----|-----|-----|-----|------|-----|
| Barristers | 348 | 90  | 783 | 103 | 1483 | 77  |
| Solicitors | 455 | 118 | 899 | 118 | 1786 | 93  |
| Doctors    | 422 | 109 | 768 | 101 | 2320 | 121 |
| Dentists   | 322 | 83  | 586 | 77  | 2111 | 110 |
| Average    | 387 | 100 | 759 | 100 | 1925 | 100 |

There have been interesting fluctuations over the years: a gain by barristers in 1922 and a more than proportionate fall in 1955. To some extent, this may be explained by changes in the age structure: the First World War destroyed a high proportion of young men from the professions and, at the Bar, the earnings spread is extraordinarily wide. The road to success is long and hard but the prize (as measured by the highest decile) is considerable. At that level, barristers' earnings are much in excess of those in other professions.

Within each profession, there has been a general narrowing of differentials though, in the case of barristers, the lower quartile was no nearer the upper quartile in 1955 than in 1913.

|            | Lower quartile as per cent of upper quartile | | | Median as per cent of highest decile | | |
|            | 1913/14 | 1922/3 | 1955/6 | 1913/14 | 1922/3 | 1955/6 |
|------------|---------|--------|--------|---------|--------|--------|
| Barristers | 23      | 15     | 22     | 11      | 17     | 25     |
| Solicitors | 23      | 30     | 40     | 28      | 34     | 42     |
| Doctors    | 28      | 38     | 63     | 31      | 41     | 65     |
| Dentists   | 26      | 31     | 51     | 27      | 30     | 56     |

The career pattern of barristers was much the same in 1956 as it had been in 1914, but for the others there has been a great compression of the range of earnings, evident both in 1922 and 1955.

We are able to include data for the medical practitioners for 1935/7 by virtue of the investigation by Sir Austin Bradford Hill.[31] Their earnings in 1935/7 and 1955/6 were as follows:

|                 | 1935/7<br>£ | 1955/6<br>£ | 1955/6<br>% of 1935/7 |
|-----------------|-------------|-------------|-----------------------|
| Highest decile  | 1750        | 3148        | 180                   |
| Upper quartile  | 1380        | 2640        | 191                   |
| Median          | 1010        | 2058        | 204                   |
| Lower quartile  | 740         | 1528        | 206                   |

There has been little change in the lower quartile/median ratio but the lower quartile shows a modest rise with reference to the upper quartile: from 54 per cent in 1935/7 to 58 per cent in 1955/6. The median was 58 per cent of the highest decile in the earlier period and 65 per cent in the later.

For a comparison between 1922/3 and 1935/7, the earnings for the later year must be raised to allow for the inclusion of consultants and assistants. In 1955/6, this inclusion raises the highest decile by 12·5 per cent, the upper quartile by 8·5 per cent, the median by 11·7 per cent and the lower quartile by 17·4 per cent. The best we can do is to raise the figures for 1935/7 in like proportion. The comparison is then as follows:

|                 | 1922/3<br>£ | 1935/7<br>£ | 1935/7<br>% of 1922/3 |
|-----------------|-------------|-------------|-----------------------|
| Highest decile  | 1757        | 1969        | 112                   |
| Upper quartile  | 1142        | 1497        | 131                   |
| Median          | 723         | 1128        | 156                   |
| Lower quartile  | 439         | 869         | 198                   |

There appears to have been both a substantial rise in incomes and a substantial narrowing of differentials. The lower quartile was 38 per cent of the upper quartile in 1922/3 and 58 per cent in 1935/7. Thus, the major narrowing between 1913 and 1955 took place at some time between 1922/3 and 1935/7.

TABLE 2.4 Average male professional earnings (occupational class 1A), various years, 1913–14 to 1960 (pounds)

| | 1913–14 | 1922–4 | 1935–7 | 1955–6 | 1960 | % of 1913–14 |
|---|---|---|---|---|---|---|
| Barristers | 478 | 1124 | (1090) | 2032 | ‥ | ‥ |
| Solicitors | 568 | 1096 | (1238) | 2086 | ‥ | ‥ |
| Dentists | 368 | 601 | 676 | 2273 | 2500 | 679 |
| General practitioners | 395 | 756 | 1094 | 2102 | 2552 | 646 |
| Clergy | 206 | 332 | 370 | (582)[a] | (582)[a] | (283) |
| Army officers | 170 | 390 | 205 | 695 | 1091 | 642 |
| Engineers | 292 | 468 | — | 1497 | 1973 | 676 |
| Chemists | 314 | 556 | 512 | 1373 | 1717 | 547 |
| Averages | | | | | | |
| Unweighted | 349 | 665 | 741 | 1580 | 1736[b] | 579 |
| Current weights | 328 | 582 | 703 | 1428 | 1755[b] | 606 |
| 1913–14 average increased in step with current | | | | | | |
| weighted average | 328 | 582 | 634 | 1541 | 2034 | 620 |

[a] 1957.

[b] Averages for those shown in column above.

*Note*: For sources and methods of estimation, see Appendix D.

In Table 2.4, we estimate the averages for the four professions so far considered and, with some other professions added and doctors and dentists brought up to 1960, calculate weighted and unweighted averages for the class.[32]

Over the whole period, the increases for dentists, general practitioners, army officers, and engineers have been of similar magnitude. We do not know how barristers and solicitors fared between 1955/6 and 1960. If we grant them the 32 per cent which was the weighted average for the others, their earnings in 1960 would be 531 and 459 per cent respectively of 1913/14. The solicitors have done badly; chemists and barristers have had about four-fifths of the average increase of the others.

While dispersion within each profession was reduced between 1913/14 and 1922/4, that between the professions increased. The mean deviation was 32 per cent of the average in the pre-war year, 47 per cent in the post-war. By 1955/6, it was down to 37 per cent.

The cost of living index stood at about 425 in 1960, with 1913/14 = 100, so that, on average, higher professional real incomes before tax had increased by nearly 40 per cent; for the parochial clergy, however, real income had fallen by about 30 per cent. Their position was fairly satisfactory until 1935, but after that, they fell substantially in real and relative terms. Relatively, the bishops of the Church of England did even worse: their income, net of expenses, fell from an average of £3400 in 1913/14 to £2700 in 1924. In 1957, at £3200, it was still below the money level of 1913/14 and thus less than a quarter of the real level of that year.

High Court judges, like other high-ranking people paid out of public funds, were also left to suffer from the fall in the value of money. Their 1913 salary of £5000 was not changed until after the Second World War, and in 1960, at £8000, they were getting only 60 per cent more than their 1913 level. County court judges had had an increase of 193 per cent to £4400. In 1913/14, they had received 220 per cent of the barristers' upper quartile; in 1922/3, 111 per cent; in 1955/6, 107 per cent.[33]

Now we turn to the New Earnings Survey for 1970, with which we must try to establish the appropriate link. We are not given averages for all the occupations distinguished, though that is the figure most suitable for our purposes, and in some cases we must make do with the average for the quantiles.

Engineers are well represented: we have 2817 of various sorts, whose average earnings, including those whose pay was affected by absence,[34] were £38·50 per week, or £2002 per year.[35] From the averages of the quantiles, we can add in various other occupations to get:[36]

| Nos. | | Pay £ |
|------|------|------|
| 2817 | Engineers | 2002 |
| 425 | Natural scientists | 2325 |
| 174 | Technologists | 2034 |
| 455 | Accountants | 2146 |
| 190 | Architects/Planners | 2309 |
| 359 | Surveyors | 1893 |
| 104 | Solicitors | 2240 |
| 146 | Authors, editors, journalists | 2280 |
| 186 | Medical and dental practitioners | 3126 |
| 4856 | Weighted average | 2105 |

The immediate impression is that the figures are curiously low. The average for 1955–6, derived from the Pilkington Report was £1835.[37] Of course, the NES figures do not include the earnings of the self-employed which, as we shall see, raise the average by about 20 per cent, but even £2526 (£2105 + 20 per cent) seems implausibly low.[38] An explanation is suggested by a comparison of the numbers given for each occupation in the 1971 census of population with those in the NES multiplied by 127.[39] The NES has an excess of engineers and a deficit of everyone else, the differences being:

| | |
|---|---:|
| Engineers | + 64,169 |
| Natural scientists | − 8175 |
| Technologists | − 2722 |
| Accountants | − 335 |
| Architects/planners | − 5670 |
| Surveyors | − 8637 |
| Lawyers | − 3012 |
| Authors | − 14,238 |
| Doctors, dentists | − 11,008 |

That the NES picks up too few of a particular profession does not bring the purity of the sample into question, but that it has an excess of 64,000 engineers suggests that employers (or their wage clerks) may not have been sufficiently discriminating about those of their employees whom they described as such.[40] Enquiries in industry reveal that the term 'engineer' is often applied to 'the engineering grades' of fitter, turner and other apprenticed engineering craftsmen. The same problem does not seem to occur in respect of other professional occupations.

Fortunately, we have the *Surveys of Professional Engineers* conducted periodically by the Council of Engineering Institutions.[41] In Table 2.5, data from these surveys have been substituted for that from the NES, with the average for the quantiles plotted by interpolation between 1968 and 1971 to represent the position in April 1970. Earnings of the self-employed are already included.

For the self-employed earnings of the other major professions we may refer to the Inland Revenue Reports.[42] However, the Inland Revenue tables do not distinguish between Schedule D earnings of the full-time self-employed and those whose Schedule D earnings are supplementary to their income as employees. In the compilation of Table 2.5, the employee earnings of those other than engineers are taken to be satisfactorily represented by the NES; the averages, including that for the engineers from the *Survey of Professional Engineers*, have been multiplied by the number of employees as shown for each profession in the 1971 population census; we have added to this total the total of self-employed earnings for the relevant profession as shown by the Inland Revenue, and divided the total in each case by the number of employees plus self-employed shown in the census. This serves both to trim the earnings of the full-time self-employed and to enhance the salaries of the employees by their self-employed income. Note, though, that we do not have self-employed income for the natural scientists, technologists, surveyors or writers. It is not possible to say whether the inclusion of self-employed income would raise or lower the average for the writers; some freelance writers have high incomes and others, no doubt, live in penury. There are not enough self-employed scientists to make much difference, but the surveyors present a more serious problem, for 13·5 per cent of them were self-employed in 1971. If this made a difference to their average earnings of the same proportion as that made to the architects' average by the inclusion of the 20·8 per cent self-employed architects, then the surveyors' average would be raised from £1893 to £2059, that is, by 8·76 per cent, and this would raise the average for all those shown in Table 2.5 from £2742 to £2757, an addition of 0·5 per cent.

TABLE 2.5 Earnings in the higher professions, 1970, employees and self-employed, males, as adjusted[a]

|  | Numbers[b] | | Average earnings £ |
|---|---|---|---|
|  | Employees | Self-employed |  |
| Engineers | 293,590 | 9150 | 2712 |
| Natural scientists[c] | 62,150 | 660 | 2325 |
| Technologists[d] | 24,820 | 450 | 2034 |
| Accountants | 58,120 | 15,840 | 2582 |
| Architects/planners | 29,800 | 7830 | 2621 |
| Surveyors | 55,010 | 8590 | (1893) |
| Lawyers[e] | 16,220 | 19,810 | 3974 |
| Doctors and dentists | 34,630 | 30,350 | 4235 |
| Authors, editors, journalists | 32,780 | 6010 | 2280 |
| All | 607,120 | 98,700 | 2742[f] |

[a] As explained in text.
[b] As per 1971 census occupational tables.
[c] In census, chemists, physical and biological scientists.
[d] Numbers include metallurgists.
[e] Judges, barristers, advocates, solicitors.
[f] Weighted average of employees and self-employed.

It is interesting to note that the substitution of 1951 weights for those shown in Table 2.5 makes little difference to the average; it is reduced from £2742 to £2740. Changes in occupational structure have made almost no difference. Let us go back to 1955–6, however, and construct a link with 1970 by matching occupations.

TABLE 2.6 Earnings for higher professional men in matched occupations, 1955–6 and 1970

| | Nos. 1951 000 | 1955–6 £ | Nos. 1971 000 | 1970 £ | % of 1955–6 |
|---|---|---|---|---|---|
| Accountants | 36·1 | 1814 | 74·0 | 2582 | 142 |
| Architects | 17·0 | 1365 | 37·6 | 2621 | 192 |
| Army officers | 46·0 | 695 | 34·0 | 2770 | 399 |
| Clergy | 36·9 | 582 | 35·7 | 1456 | 250 |
| Doctors & dentists[a] | 53·2 | 2370 | 65·0 | 4235 | 179 |
| Engineers | 82·9 | 1497 | 302·7 | 2712 | 181 |
| Lawyers | 26·5 | 2054 | 36·0 | 3974 | 193 |
| Scientists | 36·8[b] | 1373[c] | 62·9 | 2325 | 169 |
| All | 335·4 | 1483 | 647·9 | 2811 | 190 |

[a] Including consultants and senior hospital medical officers.
[b] Chemists, biologists and other scientists.
[c] Chemists.
*Notes*: For sources, see Appendix D.

Table 2.6 establishes a link between 1955–6 and 1970. For a link between 1970 and 1978, we turn to the NES. We must assume away one interesting question: whether self-employed income rose faster or slower than employee income for, at time of writing, the Inland Revenue has reached only 1975 in the analysis of Schedule D professional earnings. So Table 2.7 applies only to employees.

We may now extend the current-weighted averages shown in Table 2.4 using the links suggested by Tables 2.6 and 2.7, to give the following series for higher professional men:

| | £ | % of previous year |
|---|---|---|
| 1913–14 | 328 | — |
| 1922–4 | 582 | 177 |
| 1935–7 | 634 | 109 |
| 1955–6 | 1541 | 243 |
| 1960 | 2034 | 132 |
| 1970 | 2928[a] | 144 |
| 1978 | 8286 | 283 |

[a] 190 per cent of 1955–6.

TABLE 2.7 Average professional earnings (occupational class 1A), male employees, NES 1970 and 1978

| | 1970 | | 1978 | | |
| | Nos. | £ | Nos. | £ | % of 1970 |
|---|---|---|---|---|---|
| Accountants | 455 | 2146 | 916 | 5569 | 260 |
| Architects/planners | 190 | 2309 | 165 | 6110 | 265 |
| Authors, editors, journalists | 146 | 2280 | 148 | 6072 | 266 |
| Engineers | 2817 | 2002 | 2434 | 5935 | 296 |
| Lawyers | 104 | 2240 | 166 | 6436 | 287 |
| Medical and dental practitioners | 186 | 3126 | 226 | 8570 | 274 |
| Scientists | 425 | 2325 | 442 | 6037 | 260 |
| Surveyors | 359 | 1893 | 386 | 5102 | 270 |
| Technologists | 174 | 2034 | 137 | 5565 | 274 |
| All | 4856 | 2105 | 5020 | 5948 | 283 |

*Women*

For the years before 1955–6, we have insufficient data to estimate average income for women in the higher professions. For most occupations in the Civil Service, they received three-quarters or four-fifths of the men's rate. The Bradford Hill inquiry into the income of general practitioners showed an average for 1936–8 of £1060 for men and £548 for women,[43] but until the Second World War their numbers in this occupational class were too small to make much difference to the women's average for all classes.

For 1955–6, the Pilkington Commission[44] gives us the following averages for women professionals:

| | £ | % of men's average |
|---|---|---|
| General medical practitioners | 1591 | 74 |
| Assistant general medical practitioners | 945 | 93 |
| Medical consultants | 2773 | 82 |
| Senior hospital medical officers | 1611 | 79 |
| Average | 1722 | 78 |
| General dental practitioners | 1630 | 71 |

The Institute of Chemistry had 245 women in its inquiry for 1956. In the age group 26–30, their median pay was 79 per cent of the men's median; at 36–40, it was 73 per cent; at 46–50, 67 per cent.

Though professional fees for those working on their own account are generally the same and though equal pay has been applied in the public service for some time to the professionally qualified, age-distribution, time worked and prejudice combine to lower women's earnings, so that we may guess that, for all women professionals, the average would be about 75 per cent of that for men, that is, £1156 for 1955–6 and £1525 for 1960.

The task of measuring the pay of women professionals has become only a little easier since 1960. The enquiry conducted by the Social Survey for the Pilkington Commission yielded a very small proportion of women. Between 1911 and 1971, women in the higher professions increased nearly five-fold, but in 1971 there were still only 50,000 of them out of a total of 824,000 in the class. Over the previous twenty years, their proportion had actually fallen, from 8·3 to 6·1 per cent.

The result is that insufficient women higher professionals appear in the NES to satisfy the condition for the separate listing of the occupations concerned. But in correspondence, the Department of Employment has provided data upon which estimates may be made of the relation of men's and women's earnings in 1970 and 1978.

In the survey in 1970 171 women higher professionals appeared, and 216 in 1978. The weighted average in 1970 was £1770 and in 1978 £4830, respectively 71 and 74 per cent of the men's average for the same occupations averaged according to the number of women in each occupation.

It is curious to note, however, that the overall average of women professionals compared with that for men was 84 per cent in 1970 and had fallen to 81 per cent in 1978. This is due to the fact that there are negligible numbers of women surveyors, engineers and technologists, while these occupations constitute the greater part of men professionals. Though they are amongst the lowest paid of the professions, the engineers enjoyed an exceptionally high increase in pay between 1970 and 1978, as may be seen in Table 2.6.

To continue the series for women professionals, we take 84 per cent of the men's average of £2928 for 1970 and 81 per cent of £8286 for 1978, that is, £2460 and £6712.

(C) OCCUPATIONAL CLASS 1B (LOWER PROFESSIONS)

Table 2.8 shows pay movements in the lower professions. Between 1913 and 1960, women have generally done much better then men: the 1960 average for qualified teachers was 589 per cent of 1913 for men and 778 for women, while in the public service the movement towards equal pay for men and women was completed at the beginning of 1961. But headmasters averaged 36 per cent more than certified assistants in 1913; the same in 1924; and 41 per cent more in 1960. In 1924, section leaders had a lead of 12 per cent over draughtsmen aged over thirty; in 1936, 14 per cent; in 1955, 11 per cent; but in 1960, 16 per cent.

TABLE 2.8 Pay in the lower professions (constituents of class 1B), various years, 1913–60 (pounds)

|  | 1913 | 1924 | 1936 | 1955 | 1960 | % of 1913 |
|---|---|---|---|---|---|---|
| Men |  |  |  |  |  |  |
| Qualified teachers[a] | 154 | 353 | 348 | 613 | 907 | 589 |
| Draughtsmen[b] | 126 | 250 | 253 | 679 | 905 | 718 |
| Veterinary inspectors[c] | 381 | 506 | 548 | 1016 | 1248 | 328 |
| Laboratory assitants[c] | 132 | 201 | 186 | 420 | 536 | 406 |
| Weighted average |  |  |  |  |  |  |
|   Current weights | 155 | 320 | 308 | 610 | 847 | 546 |
|   1911 weights | 155 | 334 | 332 | 634 | 929 | 599 |
| Women |  |  |  |  |  |  |
| Qualified teachers[a] | 104·5 | 272 | 265 | 524 | 813 | 778 |
| Nurses[d] | 55 | 106 | 133 | 362 | 424 | 771 |
|   Weighted average |  |  |  |  |  |  |
|   Current weights | 89 | 214 | 211 | 438 | 606 | 680 |
|   1911 weights | 89 | 222 | 223 | 473 | 689 | 774 |

[a] Annual reports of the Ministry of Education and (1913–36) *Statistical Abstract for the United Kingdom*, Board of Trade (London: HMSO, annual).
[b] 1924–60, from annual census of Draughtsmen's and Allied Technicians' Association; 1913, 1924 deflated as for Post Office Engineering Draughtsmen, 2nd Class.
[c] Civil Service.
[d] Includes value of board, lodging, uniform and other allowances. 1913: 1902 average for 13 hospitals, raised in proportion to the increase in scale averages for female clerks in the Civil Service and manipulate workers (women) in the Post Office. 1902 figures from B. Abel-Smith, *A History of the Nursing Profession* (London: Heinemann, 1960), p. 280. 1936 and after: average of minimum and maximum of ward sisters and staff nurses and rate for 2nd year probationers plus estimate for board, etc. averaged by 1937 weights.

In the nursing profession, differentials narrowed until 1955:

|  | *Percentages* | | | |
|  | *1924* | *1936* | *1955* | *1960* |
|---|---|---|---|---|
| Ward sister | 100 | 100 | 100 | 100 |
| Staff nurse | 43 | 45 | 85 | 72 |
| 2nd year probationer | 27 | 28 | 50 | 42 |

The occupations shown in Table 2.8 made up about half the men in 1911 and rather more than 60 per cent of them in 1951. The teachers and nurses constituted 83 per cent of the women in 1911 and 78 per cent in 1951.

### 1970 and 1978

The link with the NES is less difficult to make than was the case with the higher professionals. For one thing, there are two and a half times as many lower professionals, so that they come through to the NES in statistically respectable numbers; for another, in 1971 only 4·3 per cent of them were employers or self-employed, compared with 16·7 per cent of class 1A, so that Schedule D earnings (which are in any case unavailable) may be ignored. Table 2.9 shows numbers and earnings (expressed in pounds per year) from the NES.

The men's average in 1978 was 293 per cent of 1970, the shift in numbers between the groups having resulted in a small rise in the average for all the groups. If the relative size of the groups had remained unchanged, the overall rise would have been reduced by 4 percentage points. Likewise, with fixed weights the women's average in 1978 is reduced from 318 to 309 per cent of 1970. The women have done better than the men but have a long way to go before achieving equality. Their average was 67 per cent of the men's in 1970 and 72 per cent in 1978.

Now we can make a bridge between 1960 and 1970 by taking the occupations common to Tables 2.8 and 2.9 and measuring the changes between the two years. The mean from Table 2.8 can then be raised commensurately, while the change between 1970 and 1978 is given by Table 2.9.

The change in occupational distribution has added two percentage points to the 1970 averages in each case. Now we use these changes, with

TABLE 2.9 Pay in the lower professions (constituents of class 1B), 1970 and 1978

| | 1970 | | 1978 | | |
|---|---|---|---|---|---|
| | Nos.[a] | £ | Nos.[a] | £ | as % of 1970 |
| **Men** | | | | | |
| Technicians and draughtsmen | 3080 | 1612 | 2470 | 4716 | 293 |
| Teachers | 2261 | 2018 | 2761 | 5686 | 282 |
| Welfare workers | 100 | 1560 | 442 | 4332 | 278 |
| Nursing[b] | 441 | 1235 | 442 | 4074 | 330 |
| Purchasing officers and buyers | 219 | 1752 | 364 | 5299 | 302 |
| Ships officers[c] | 176 | 2618 | 262 | 7087 | 271 |
| All men | 6277 | 1764 | 6741 | 5170 | 293 |
| **Women** | | | | | |
| Technicians | 478 | 952 | 247 | 3260 | 342 |
| Teachers | 2203 | 1503 | 3129 | 4568 | 304 |
| Nursing and welfare | 3066 | 978 | 3464 | 3019 | 309 |
| All women | 5747 | 1175 | 6840 | 3736 | 318 |

[a] I.e., in the NES sample.
[b] In 1970, 148 male nurses, 188 ambulence men and hospital ward orderlies, 105 other medical, dental, nursing and welfare staff. In 1978, 137 nurse administrators and executives, 166 registered and enrolled nurses and 139 ambulance men.
[c] In 1970, includes aircrew and pilots.

| | 1960 | | 1970 | | 1970 as |
|---|---|---|---|---|---|
| | Nos.[a] | £ | Nos.[b] | £ | % of 1960 |
| **Men** | | | | | |
| Teachers | 133 | 907 | 307 | 2018 | 222 |
| Draughtsmen | 120 | 905 | 142 } | 1612 | 208 |
| Lab assistants | 51 | 536 | 76 } | | |
| | 304 | 844 | 525 | 1849 | 219 |
| **Women** | | | | | |
| Teachers | 207 | 813 | 381 | 1503 | 185 |
| Nurses | 237 | 424 | 401 | 959 | 226 |
| | 444 | 605 | 782 | 1224 | 202 |

[a] For 1951, from Chapter 1, Table 1.5, above.
[b] For 1971, loc. cit.

those shown in Table 2.9 to give a continuous series from 1913 to 1978. This is shown in Table 2.10.

TABLE 2.10 Averages for lower professional earnings (occupational class 1B) various years, 1913–78

|  | Men | | Women | |
|---|---|---|---|---|
|  | £ | % of previous year | £ | % of previous year |
| 1913 | 155 |  | 89 |  |
| 1924 | 320 | 206 | 214 | 240 |
| 1936 | 308 | 96 | 211 | 99 |
| 1955 | 610 | 198 | 438 | 208 |
| 1960 | 847 | 139 | 606 | 138 |
| 1970 | 1855 | 219 | 1224 | 202 |
| 1978 | 5435 | 293 | 3892 | 318 |

(D) OCCUPATIONAL CLASS 2B (ADMINISTRATORS AND MANAGERS)

Administrators in the public service are greatly outnumbered by business managers: in 1951, they formed 124,000 out of 1,246,000; in 1971, 150,000 out of 2,054,000. Yet they are an important sub-species, whose pay represents a public evaluation of the type of labour with which we are concerned. Table 2.11 shows pay at seven levels in the Civil Service.

TABLE 2.11 Salaries of administrators and managers in the Civil Service (men) (occupational class 2B), various years, 1913–78 (London rates) (pounds)

|  | 1913 | 1924 | 1936 | 1955 | 1960 | 1970 | 1978 | % of 1913 |
|---|---|---|---|---|---|---|---|---|
| Chancellor of the Exchequer | 5000 | 5000 | 5000 | 5000 | 5000 | 9 200 | 14,300 | 286 |
| Permanent Secretary of the Treasury[a] | 2250 | 3500 | 3500 | 5000 | 8000 | 12,700 | 22,422 | 996 |
| Deputy Secretary[b] | 1500 | 2200 | 2200 | 3250 | 5000 | 8050 | 15,629 | 1042 |
| Assistant Secretary[c] | 1150 | 1382 | 1345 | 2117 | 3115 | 5201 | 11,759 | 1022 |
| Principal[d] | 855 | 1073 | 1017 | 1794 | 2181 | 3627 | 8323 | 973 |
| Assistant Principal[e] | 380 | 563 | 509 | 743 | 1064 | — | — | — |
| Executive Officer[f] | 195 | 383 | 379 | 721 | 936 | 1515 | 3951 | 2026 |

[a] 10 point scale average.
[b] 10 point scale average. 1913, Assistant Secretary; 1955, Second Secretary.
[c] 10 Point scale average. 1913, Principal Clerks.
[d] 20 point scale average. 1913, 1st Class Clerks.
[e] 20 Point scale average. 1913, 2nd Class Clerks.
[f] 30 point scale average. 1913, Lower Division and Lower Division Higher Grade.

The Chancellor, like bishops and judges, enjoyed extraordinary wealth in the years before the First World War. In 1913 he, like the High Court judges, had an after-tax income three or four times more than the highest decile of the professional men shown in Table 2.3. At 1978 prices, it would have been worth about £80,000.

But by 1955, the public administrators were in general a rather depressed class. Principals were getting 210 per cent of the scale average of 1913, compared with 300 per cent for Chief Veterinary Officers, 333 per cent for solicitors and 409 per cent for doctors at the upper quartile, and 293 per cent for the Deputy Government Chemist, the income of all of whom was of a similar order in 1913.

Executive Officers did better, but still much worse than teachers, draughtsmen or librarians.

But another significant thing is the very high increases which were given between 1955 and 1960 after the reassessment of the position of Civil Servants *vis-à-vis* their peers in outside employment. Deputy Secretaries, for example, received an increase in pay nearly equal to the annual income of two Executive Officers. But even with these increases, only Executive Officers in 1960 had a real income higher than that of their equivalent in 1913. That of Principals had been almost halved.

*Business Managers: Pay at the Top*
The task of assessing the pay levels and movements for business managers is much more difficult. We are faced with an immense range of duties and responsibilities that defy standardisation; and, even where standards have been established, by a wide dispersion, between different firms, in the pay for similar jobs.[45] None the less, we shall try to establish two things: changes in business salaries at the very highest level and at or about the mode.

A comparison between 1913/14 and 1924/5 can be made in some detail by virtue of the Inland Revenue report mentioned above in connexion with pay in the higher professions.[46] This showed the rank order of individuals in ten industrial groups who, in 1913/14, were at annual salaries of £2000, £1000, £500 and £200 and the salaries of individuals of the same rank order in 1924/5. In addition, it showed the number getting more than £2000 in 1913/14, and their average in that year, and the average for the same number, counting from the top of the salary range, in 1924/5. These were as follows:

| 1913/14 | 1924/5 | |
| £ | £ | % of 1913/14 |
|---|---|---|
| 4321[a] | 8292[a] | 192 |
| 2000 | 4034 | 202 |
| 1000 | 1933 | 193 |
| 500 | 1045 | 209 |
| 200 | 483 | 241 |

[a] There were 212 getting more than £2000 in 1913/14 and their average salary was £4321. In 1914/5, the top 212 averaged £8292.

The increase of the £2000 man was greater than that of the £1000 man and only slightly less than that of the £500 man. The increase in the average for the top 212 was almost identical to that of the man at £1000. It is only at the £200 level that a substantially higher increase occurs. Thus the egalitarian forces, active between £200 and £500, at higher levels seem to have played themselves out, and there is an extraordinary similarity in the increases of those at £500 and above.

The highest-paid company employees maintained their relative position despite the crises of war and slump. How they fared in the inter-war years we cannot say, but after the Second World War, the Inland Revenue again published tables showing tax-payers by ranges of income, which they had ceased to do early in World War I. With these, we may take up the story again.

We know that in the Inland Revenue sample the 212 highest-paid employees averaged £4321 in 1913–14 and £8292 in 1924–5, and we are also told that the sample included roughly 5 per cent of company employees assessed to tax. If it was a representative sample, then about 212 × 20 = 4,240 at the top were getting an average of £4321 in 1913–14. The number of men in occupational class 2B increased by about 110 per cent between 1911 and 1951 and, assuming the rate of increase constant from top to bottom of the pay hierarchy, we might then conclude that the equivalent of the top 4240 in 1913 would be the top 9000 of 1957–8.

There were 17·2 thousand employees in the United Kingdom in 1957–8 with salary of £5000 or more.[47] Further, there were 26,059 surtax payers with earned incomes of £5000 or more and for these we are told the numbers in various income ranges up to £20,000 and the number with earned income over £20,000, with the total earned income for each range. Out of 26·1 thousand, 17·2 thousand were employees. On this proportion (0·66) of employees to self-employed, there would be 10,380 in the range £6000 and over. Of course not all of these would be managers, though it is probable that most of them were.[48] In any case, this is near enough to 9000 for the rough justice of the method used here. Their average pay was £9190 in 1957–8 and £9582 in 1958–9.

Between 1951 and 1971, the number of men in occupational class 2B increased by 64 per cent, so 9000 becomes 14,760. The average for the top 14,760 male employees in 1975–6 was about £22,400.[49] So we have a series for this high-paid group:

|           | £      |
|-----------|--------|
| 1913–14   | 4321   |
| 1924–5    | 8292   |
| 1957–8    | 9190   |
| 1958–9    | 9582   |
| 1975–6    | 22,400 |

Before the First World War, their income was about sixty-four times the median for all men, forty-five times that of a moulder in the metal-working industry and thirteen times the average for the higher professions. In 1975–6, these ratios had been reduced to 8, 8 and 3·5, before tax.

Of course, the £22,400 would be drastically reduced by tax: a man with wife, two children, mortgage, and life insurance might be left with about £11,000. On the other hand, he would be provided with a free car, employer's superannuation contribution and other fringe benefits costing the employer about £7000.[50]

Since the first edition of this book, a great deal more information has become available about the salaries of company directors, in terms of the Companies Act of 1967. We see a financial wonderland, deprived of guidelines, where enormous salaries are enormously reduced by tax and then reconstituted by benefits in varying degree.[51] We shall return in Chapter 4 to the problem of interpreting these phenomena, but now must proceed with the problem of calculating an average or mode that will represent class 2B in the pay hierarchy.[52]

*Pay in the Middle*

How did the average or typical manager fare in these years—the administrator between the foremen and clerk, on the one side, and the chairman of the board on the other? In Chapter 4 we shall ask whether there is operational significance in such an abstraction; for present purposes we assume that it makes sense to postulate an archetypal manager whose fortunes we assess down the years, relative to those of professionals, clerks, foremen, skilled manual workers and the rest.

We calculated that there were 574,000 such people in 1911.[53] In the Inland Revenue 5 per cent sample of 1913–14, there were 14,237 employees at more than £200 per year: multiplied by twenty to represent the universe of managers, the £200 man would then be 284,740th from the top, very near the 287,000th position that would represent the median of the range. By 1924–5, as we have seen, this had become £483.

We may get some measure of the inter-war changes by comparing the average for employees getting more than £250 in 1922–3 and 1938–9.[54] The averages, weighted by the total number of managers in the relevant industries in 1921 and 1931 respectively, were £534 in 1922–3 and £490 in 1938–9: a reduction of 8 per cent. This accords with the downward drift in the inter-war years for a number of the occupations that we have already priced. It would have reduced the £483 of 1924–5 to £444 in 1938–9.

For the generality of managers, we have no bridge to carry us over the Second World War and can produce only an impression of where the median would lie. But before we do so, it will be useful to look at the data for bankers and shop managers whom we are able to treat with greater precision.

For data as at 1 January 1956 and 1961, we are greatly obliged to the Committee of London Clearing Bankers who conducted a special inquiry in order to give us the dispersion of their (white-collar) employees by salary range.[55] We were able to produce a comparable dispersion for 1924 by combining the Inland Revenue data with that produced by Bowley from his inquiry of that year.[56] The data do not distinguish between bank managers or assistant managers and those in non-managerial positions, but the highest decile, near the threshold of managerial status, gives an indication of how salaries moved in the upper levels. The number of women in managerial positions is small enough to have little statistical significance. For the men, the highest deciles were as follows:

| 1924–5 | £ 702 | 100 | |
|---|---|---|---|
| 1 Jan. 1956 | 1360 | 194 | 100 |
| 1 Jan. 1961 [a] | 1840 | | 135 |

[a] Excluding payments for overtime, which added 0·9 per cent to remuneration in the year ended 1 January 1956 and 4·4 per cent in the year ended 1 January 1961. Overtime would not normally be paid to managers.

For 1924 and 1925, the pay of shop managers can be estimated from the trade board inquiries into the grocery, drapery, outfitting, fancy goods and meat trades.[57] The numbers of managers and assistants are given, but in the pay ranges their distribution is not distinguished, so that we must assume that managers come at the top of the respective pay distributions. For managers, then, the averages are £230 for men and £157 for women. But there are in addition a number of managers not employed in shops but working on the administrative side of the business. For them, we have no information for 1924/5, but in the 1938 data[58] their inclusion with the shop managers raises the average by 11·4 per cent for men and 2·7 per cent for women. The averages for 1924/5 similarly adjusted become:

Men    £256
Women   £161

Now the £160 average for women shop managers approximates to the average shown in Bowley's investigation in 1924 for women in the distributive trade in the pay range £125 and over. This amounted to £155 in 1924 and, in 1938 (Marley and Campion) to £162. This is an increase of about five per cent, that would raise the 1924 level to about £168 in 1938.

In 1960 minimum provincial 'A' rates for grocery branch managers for weekly sales of £2400 were £972 for the co-operative societies and £954 for the multiple grocery trade in England and Wales, 380 per cent to 372 per cent of 1924. But these minima understate the level of earnings. A large provision chain store quoted to us a range of £1025 to £2400 for branch managers, effective from the latter part of 1959. Another large chain store quoted a range for 1960 of £1150 to £2240. In this case, the firm was able to give comparable data for 1939, when the range was £260 to £520, so that 1960 levels would have been 442 to 431 per cent of 1939.

For other managers, it is not possible to produce statistics that are consistent with the pre-war material. However, a number of investigations have been made in recent years into pay levels of various sorts of managers and from these it is possible to get an idea of the managerial pay structure.

In 1960, we invited twelve large companies to rate five jobs for which detailed descriptions were supplied. Specifically, they were asked to put each job through the company's process of job evaluation so as to determine the pay and conditions that would attach to it if it were to be performed in their own company.

After the replies had been analysed, the participants met to discuss the results. In general, it was felt that the replies were comparable and gave a realistic view of salary levels and terms of employment in the organisations concerned.

Quoted levels for each job showed a wide dispersion, but this is a general characteristic of salaries for jobs at this level. For the chief accountant the deviation from the average scale minimum itself averaged £412 and from the maximum £441 (sign ignored), 18 per cent in the one case and 13 per cent in the other. Similar dispersions characterised the other jobs.

The question relating to the incumbent aged 45 was partly aimed at assessing the way in which salaries had increased in the four years to

TABLE 2.12 Salaries of five managerial occupations, July 1960, with changes between 1956 and 1960

| | Range of scale, July 1960 | Normal working hours | Annual holiday | Company pension contri- butions | Salary for incumbent aged 45 in post 5 years | |
| --- | --- | --- | --- | --- | --- | --- |
| | | | | | Year ended 1.4.56 | 1.4.60 |
| | £ | Hours | Weeks | % | £ | £ |
| Chief accountant | 2245–3276 | 37.9 | 2.6 | 7.2 | 2054 | 2663 |
| Production manager | 2170–3331 | 40.0 | 3.0 | 7.2 | 2066 | 2713 |
| Shift superintendent | 1304–1942 | 39.6 | 2.9 | 6.8 | 1296 | 1653 |
| Divisional sales manager | 2087–3129 | 37.9 | 2.8 | 7.4 | 2148 | 2673 |
| Area sales manager | 1322–2023 | 37.7 | 2.7 | 7.3 | 1314 | 1652 |

April 1960 and partly as a further move towards standardisation. But here again, dispersion was wide. For the chief accountant, with an average increase over the four years of 29·6 per cent, the average deviation was 13 per cent. This, again, typified the increases for the other occupations.

Further inquiries were held, with the Institute of Personnel Management, in 1962 and 1964, with eighty-eight companies participating in the one and forty-five in the other. On both occasions, twelve jobs were rated instead of only five. A small-scale repeat, with the aid of twelve companies, was held in 1977. These, too, were characterised by wide mean deviations in pay for each job (between 15 and 25 per cent of the mean) though the pay structure presented by a comparison of the means of the jobs remained recognisable.[59]

Another indication of pay levels and increases is given by the results of the inquiries of the Institution of Works Managers, conducted in the early parts of 1954 and 1960.[60] From those surveys, the category 'general and works managers (excluding directors)' was taken for each year and equal weight given to the distribution of those controlling 1 to 250, 251 to 500, 501 to 1000 and over 1000. Pay levels at various points were as follows:

| | 1954 £ | 1960 £ | 1960 as % of 1954 |
|---|---|---|---|
| Highest decile | 2450 | 3360 | 137 |
| Upper quartile | 1937 | 2430 | 125 |
| Median | 1515 | 1844 | 122 |
| Lower quartile | 1094 | 1375 | 126 |
| Lowest decile | 844 | 1078 | 128 |

Pay levels for the works managers in 1954 were almost identical to those for graduates aged 35–9 in the investigation conducted by the Royal Commission on Doctors' and Dentists' Remuneration.[61]

In a survey by George Copeman relating to 700 managers in 1959[62] 38 per cent were getting less than £1500; 40 per cent between £1500 and £2499; 18 per cent between £2500 and £4999 and 4 per cent £5000 and over. This suggests a median somewhere in the range £1800 to £1900. Copeman's averages for production managers and personnel managers accord closely with those subsequently published by the Institution of Works Managers (1960) and the Institute of Personnel Management (February/March 1961).[63]

For production management, with the age-range averages weighted together according to the age distribution shown in the Instituion of Works Managers *Remuneration Survey*, Copeman's average is £2014, while the average of the highest and lowest deciles, quartiles and median from the Institution of Works Managers survey is £2043. For personnel managers, the two sets of averages compare as follows:

| Age | Copeman[a] £ | IPM £ |
| --- | --- | --- |
| 25–34 | 1315 | 1239 |
| 35–44 | 1715 | 1711 |
| 45 and over | 1984 | 2016 |

[a] Simple average of age ranges 25–9 and 30–4, etc.

The evidence shows a wide range of pay and function, but what evidence we have suggests that median pay for men in 1960 was about £1800 to £1900, with average pay in the neighbourhood of £2000, and an increase between 1955/6 and 1960 averaging between 20 and 30 per cent.

For women, the average shown by the inquiry on graduates in industry quoted above, was about 50 per cent of that for men. In the Institute of Personnel Management inquiry, 1961, the women's average was 70 per cent of the men's in the case of personnel officers and personnel assistants. But because there were proportionately fewer women in the higher categories, the women's average was only 60 per cent of the men's. The Institute of Personnel Management report for 1956 gives only medians and quartiles, whose sum was 58 per cent of the men's. As a genralisation, it seems safe to say that, for managers, women's pay averaged between 50 and 60 per cent of men's between 1955 and 1960. Thus, in Table 2.15 we show women's pay at 55 per cent of men's for 1955/6 and 1960. But in 1924/5, there were comparatively few women managers except in retail trade and catering, so that their average would not have varied much from the £161 shown above for the retail trade. This was 63 per cent of the men's average for managers in distribution but only 34 per cent of the estimated median for all men managers.

*1970 and 1978*
When, at the end of the fifties, we began seeking data on managerial

salaries, we were confronted by uncharted wastes; by the 1970s, the wastes had been abundantly charted, but by charts that disagreed. One might have hoped that the NES would solve the problem: in 1970, they collected data for the earnings of 6061 men described as managers, three-quarters of whom were allocated to specified categories. The standard errors of the mean of the five categories for whom means are given are all below 1·8 per cent, while for the eleven categories for whom dispersions and quantiles but no means are given, the highest standard error of the median is 5·1 per cent.[64]

None the less, we are confronted by the same problem we encountered with the engineers, but in a more acute form: the earnings presented by the NES for some of the most important managerial categories are much below those found by enquiries directed specially at managerial pay. For example,

1970

|  | AIC/Inbucon[a] £ | NES £ |
|---|---|---|
| Managing directors | 8101 | 4348 |
| General managers | 6834 | 3546 |
| Company secretaries | 4264 | 2606 |
| Personnel managers | 3448 | 2307 |

1975

|  | Hay/MSL[b] £ | NES £ |
|---|---|---|
| Works managers | 12,030 | |
| Production managers | 9130 | } 3786 |
| General foremen | 4830 | |

[a] Royal Commission on the Distribution of Income and Wealth, *Report No. 3*, p. 57.
[b] Ibid., p. 46.

One can only speculate on the reasons for these differences.[65] Are we confronted by a dual economy like that in Japan, where great corporations (with which the management consultants are concerned) contrast with a multitude of small ones? Or is it that the wage clerks who complete the NES forms are less fastidious about whom they call a manager? Every registered company will have a manager, or managing director, however small it may be, even if the managerial functions are combined with book-keeping and answering the phone.

We shall return to those problems in Chapter 4; meanwhile a way must be found of projecting the 1960 average for managers to 1970, after which we may follow the NES for movements in, though not absolute amounts of, managers' earnings. We ask, what could a representative manager, at £1850 (or between (£1800 and £1900) in 1960, be expected to be earning in 1970?

We have reliable guide-lines from 1959 for the course of the combined average for administrative, technical (including professional) and clerical employees in manufacturing industries, mining and quarrying, construction, gas, electricity and water, national and local government, banking, insurance and publicly-owned transport,[66] with males and females shown separately.[67]

There is also a separate series from 1955 to 1970 for the earnings of non-manual workers, with clerical staff shown separately, for the public sector plus banking and insurance.[68]

Table 2.13 presents the data for 1960 and 1970. Banking and insurance have lagged, women have done better than men, and clerical workers (at least in the public sector, banking and insurance) have done worse than the rest. It is noteworthy that in this period non-manual men did just about as well as manual men, while non-manual women did slightly better than manual women.

TABLE 2.13 Earnings of non-manual workers (men and women), 1960 and 1970 (pounds per week)

|  |  | 1960 | 1970 | % of 1960 |
|---|---|---|---|---|
| Production industries | M | 19·18 | 36·25 | 189 |
|  | F | 7·97 | 15·51 | 195 |
| National and local government | M | 18·87 | 36·00 | 191 |
|  | F | 12·30 | 22·78 | 185 |
| Banking and insurance | M | 20·30 | 34·63 | 171 |
|  | F | 8·60 | 16·02 | 186 |
| Clerks in the public sector, banking and insurance | M | 13·10 | 22·58 | 172 |
|  | F | 9·85 | 17·49 | 178 |
| Others in the public sector, banking and insurance | M | 21·66 | 39·44 | 182 |
|  | F | 12·76 | 24·29 | 190 |
| All the above | M | 19·10 | 36·12 | 189 |
|  | F | 10·15 | 19·59 | 193 |

*Sources*: see text.

Of course, managers form only part of the workers represented in Table 2.13. For data relating specifically to them, we must turn to the management consultants who have conducted regular enquiries into their levels of pay. Associated Industrial Consultants (AIC) arrived at increases between 1960 and 1964 of 18 per cent for a company secretary (£2400 to £2830), 25 per cent for a sales manager (£2500 to £3125), 27·2 per cent for a chief engineer (£1650 to £2100) and 27·5 per cent for a chief accountant (£2000 to £2550).[69] These are not too far from the differences suggested by the pilot study reported in Table 2.12, above, and the full-scale enquiry of 1964. These showed increases at the minimum and maximum, respectively, of chief accountant 33 and 33·5 per cent; production manager 41 and 33 per cent; divisional sales manager 25 and 25 per cent; area sales manager 39 and 33 per cent. It was only the shift superintendent who was out of step, with increases of 48 per cent at the minimum and 45 per cent at the maximum, and this, it seems, was because his title had been changed to 'production superintendent', thus conferring on him higher status, though the job description remained unchanged.[70]

For the period 1964 to 1970, we have a Hay-MSL calculation, of 35 per cent increase for a job at £5000 in 1964, to 53 per cent for a job at £1500 in 1964.[71] If we give our representative manager an increase of 27 per cent on his £1850 for the period 1960 to 1964 he would get £2350, which would entitle him to a further increase of 45 per cent on the Hay-MSL scale to bring him to £3407 in 1970: an increase of 84 per cent from 1960 to 1970, not too far from the increase of 89 per cent shown for all white-collar workers in Table 2.13.[72] This is 15 per cent above the Hay-MSL B grade and about 82 per cent of their C grade.[73] It is also 1·2 per cent below the AIC/Inbucon Personnel Manager and 80 per cent of their company secretary. £1850 was 77 per cent of their company secretary in 1960.[74]

For the increase appropriate to the period 1970–8, let us now refer to the NES. Our trials are not yet over, for there were two breaks in this series: the first when a new classification was introduced in 1973; the second when National Insurance cards were discontinued and, from 1975, the NES tracked down the employers of its sample of employees through the Inland Revenue's PAYE cards. This last had the peculiar effect of bringing into the sample a great many managing directors who before had escaped the NES net and whose pay was substantially below the other top managers in the sample.

The survey of 1974 has 934 in group I (general management), while that of 1975 has 1375. The change of method increased the sample by 47 per cent, but also changed the nature of the population sampled. Over the year, the average for all non-manual workers rose by 24·8 per cent, but the average for group I actually fell, from £103.70 to £102.40 per week. In 1974, there were 106 at less than £50 a week; in 1975 there were 274.

How much increase could a manager at £103.70 be expected to get? The highest decile (Q90) of group II (professional and related supporting management and administration) was £103 in 1974. In 1975, it was £118.40, an increase of 14·9 per cent. There were others in management at similar levels:

|  | 1974<br>£ | 1975<br>£ | % increase |
|---|---|---|---|
| Company secretaries, Q90 | 115·10 | 140·50 | 22·1 |
| Finance, insurance, tax, etc. | | | |
|    specialists, Q75 | 101·10 | 115·10 | 13·8 |
| Personnel managers, Q90 | 104·50 | 128·30 | 22·8 |
| Marketing and sales managers, Q90 | 111·60 | 129·00 | 15·6 |

There is evidence of egalitarian influences:

Group II increases, 1974–5

|  | per cent |
|---|---|
| Median | 20·6 |
| Q75 | 17·9 |
| Q90 | 14·9 |

But it seems unlikely that the average for grade I managers would have risen by less than the increase at the highest decile for grade II managers. Thus it is reasonable to give them the 15 per cent that the figures suggest. For purposes of comparison with earlier years, from 1975 and after grade I pay should be raised by 15 per cent, while their numbers should be reduced by 32 per cent.

The principal effect, in the present context, of the change of classification introduced in 1973, was the inclusion of works foremen with works managers and production managers. The *Classification of Occupations and Directory of Occupational Titles* (CODOT) from which the *List of Key Occupations* (KOS) is drawn defines the top grade of foreman in very much the same terms as works or production manager.[75] But while they all 'plan, organise, direct and co-ordinate', the works manager is responsible to the general manager or his equivalent, and operates through other managers and executives, while the general foreman operates through trade foremen or gangers.

What difference does it make if we disentangle them? in 1972,

664 works, production managers averaged £51.50.
772 senior or higher level foremen averaged £42.60.
1436 together would have averaged £46.70.[76]

The works, production managers constituted 46 per cent of the total, and received 110 per cent of the average earnings; the senior or higher level foremen constituted 54 per cent of the total and received 91 per cent of the average earnings. These are the ratios by which pay and numbers of the two groups are separated for subsequent years.

Table 2.14 now presents the data for 1970 and 1978, with 1975 included for purposes of comparison.

Table 2.14 gives a general increase of 60·5 per cent between 1970 and 1975, and this turns out to be less than the increases found by Hay-MSL and reported to the Royal Commission. These were 74·6 per cent for a salary of £2950 in 1970; 85·5 on a salary of £6030 and 57 per cent on a salary of £14,400.[77] On the other hand, the increases between July 1970 and July 1974 reported to the Commission by the British Institute of Management (derived from AIC/Inbucon) accord satisfactorily with those for NES April 1970 to April 1974 and are certainly not in excess of them:[78] for company secretaries each showed an increase of 43 per cent; for chief engineers, AIC/Inbucon shows 44 per cent; for production and works managers (as corrected) the NES 51 per cent; for personnel managers, AIC/Inbucon 53 per cent, NES 61 per cent.

Between 1975 and 1978, Table 2.14 shows an average increase of 47·5 per cent, which accords fairly well with that shown in the relevant British Institute of Management annual surveys.

If we round the salary for our representative manager to £3400 in 1970 (to avoid illusions of exactitude), and then give him the increase suggested by Table 2.14, he would end up at £8058 in 1978.

*Women, 1970 and 1978*
We left women in 1955 and 1960 with pay between 50 and 60 per cent of that of the men in class 2B. In the NES for 1970, no mean is shown for women managers, but the mean of the quantiles is £1263, which is 52·6

per cent of that for the men. In 1978, no women are shown in group I (general management), but there are 805 in group II (professional and related supporting management and administration) and 789 in group

TABLE 2.14 Pay for managers (men) from the NES 1970, 1975 and 1978

| | 1970 Nos. | £ | 1975 Nos. | £ | 1978 Nos. | £ | % of 1970 |
|---|---|---|---|---|---|---|---|
| General management | | | 935[a] | 6122[a] | 1128[a] | 8910[a] | 219[b] |
| Company chairman, director | 667 | 4348 | | | | | |
| General, divisional manager | 360 | 3546 | | | | | |
| Company secretary | 182 | 2606 | 159 | 4457 | 175 | 6651 | 255 |
| Personnel or training | 162 | 2307 | | | | | |
| Personnel and industrial relations | | | 197 | 4503 | 256 | 6561 | 284[c] |
| Marketing, advertising, sales | 525 | 2761 | | | | | |
| Marketing, sales | | | 684 | 4365 | 926 | 6791 ⎫ | |
| Advertising and public relations | | | 103 | 4014 | 132 | 5861 ⎬ 242[d] | |
| Works, production | 684 | 2262 | 527[a] | 4158[a] | 396[a] | 6318[a] | 279 |
| Engineering maintenance | | | 253 | 3588 | 330 | 5756 | .. |
| Transport | 153 | 1723 | 265 | 3648 | 275 | 5127 | 298 |
| Office | 685 | 2236 | 855 | 4030 | 1126 | 6022 | 269 |
| Site or yard | 121 | 1803 | | | | | |
| Retail shop, department | 811 | 1414 | | | | | |
| Warehousing, etc. | | | 368 | 3203 | 484 | 4768 | .. |
| Wholesale | | | 148 | 3305 | 134 | 4821 | .. |
| Department store, super-market, etc. | | | 272 | 2944 | 263 | 4552 ⎫ | |
| Branches, other shops | | | 367 | 2730 | 386 | 4104 ⎬ 291[e] | |
| Independent shops | | | 123 | 2179 | 161 | 3460 ⎭ | |
| Hotel, catering, etc. | 168 | 1384 | 250 | 2402 | 331 | 3642 | 263 |
| General administrators, national government | | | 425 | 4648 | 101 | 7510 | .. |
| General administrators, local government | | | 167 | 4380 | 164 | 5988 | .. |
| Other managers | 1612 | 2548 | 1264 | 3680 | 1261 | 5236 | 205 |
| All | 6130 | 2532 | 7363 | 4065 | 8029 | 5996 | 237 |

[a] Corrected as described in text.
[b] 1970: company chairman, director + divisional manager.
[c] 1970: personnel or training.
[d] 1970: marketing, advertising, sales.
[e] 1970: retail shop, department.
Note: where earnings means are not given in the NES, averages of the quantiles are used.

VI (managerial excluding general management). The average for these two groups is £3768, which is 62·8 per cent of that for men shown in Table 2.14, which accords with what we know about the movement of women's pay between 1970 and 1978. In Table 2.15, the pay of women managers is given as 55 per cent of that of men from 1955 to 1970, and 63 per cent in 1978.

TABLE 2.15  Pay for representative managers (occupational class 2B), men and women, various years, 1913–14 to 1978

|  | Men | | Women | |
|  | £ | % of previous year | £ | % of previous year |
| --- | --- | --- | --- | --- |
| 1913–14 | 200 | | .. | |
| 1924–5 | 480 | 240 | 160 | .. |
| 1938 | 440 | 92 | .. | .. |
| 1955–6 | 1480 | 336 | 800 | .. |
| 1960 | 1850 | 125 | 1000 | 125 |
| 1970 | 3400 | 184 | 1870 | 187 |
| 1978 | 8050 | 237 | 5070 | 271 |

(E) OCCUPATIONAL CLASS 3 (CLERKS)

Continuing our journey down the scale, we come to occupational class 3, clerical workers. Part of their pay history may be traced from several inquiries that have been conducted during the period of our study. The Cannan Committee collected information about the pay of clerks in various industries for the years 1909 or 1910.[79]

For 1929–30, we have a dispersion of 2799 males and 1915 females living within the London area, from the house sample inquiry of the New London Survey.[80]

Since 1942, the Office Management Association (later the Institute of Office Management and now the Institute of Administrative Management) has taken a census of clerks' pay every two years, and since 1968 we have the New Earnings Surveys. The *Clerical Salaries Analysis* of the Institute of Administrative Management embraces some 30,000 males and 60,000 females and matches the NES well: for adult men in 1968, the CSA shows an average of quantiles of £19·48 to the NES 22·4. The figures for women are £12·8 and £14·2.

For the years to 1960 or 1961, we can add evidence from the Civil Service, railways and banks.[81] The data are assembled in Table 2.16.

In the first period, male clerks in business appear to have done much less well than those in the other sectors. As has been mentioned, the figures in the second column relate to 1929 and are based on the London Survey, corrected for the exclusion of clerks from middle-class families. Klingender suggests that there must have been a substantial cut in the salaries paid in this sector between 1924 and 1929, which, at the lower quartile, would have amounted about 60 per cent.[82] However, this hardly credible suggestion is based on a comparison of his figures, extracted from the London Survey records, and Bowley and Stamp's survey of 1924. Klingender seems to think that their figures for salaries relate exclusively to clerical workers,[83] but in fact they included all salaried employees so that the income shown would necessarily be above that for clerks alone.[84]

It is possible, of course, that the authors of the *New Survey of London Life and Labour* may have underestimated the depressing effect of excluding middle-class families.[85] But no fresh evidence has been found to help to decide the issue.

Up to 1955 there seems to have been a general tendency for the lower-paid to rise faster than the higher-paid; after 1955, in the case of clerks in business, this tendency is gently reversed.

For women, the movement for clerks in business between 1909–10 and 1924 is very similar to that for clerks in the Civil Service: there is some confirmation of this given by the Cadbury records.[86] Women clerks in that company averaged £57 in 1912 (£2 above the business upper quartile shown in Table 2.16) and £127 in 1924; 1924 pay was 222·7 per cent of 1912, close to the upper quartile's 218 per cent.

Between 1935 and 1955, the inverse correlation between degree of increase and salary level shows even more clearly for the women than it did for the men. This may partly be for the very reason that women's pay was in any case much below that for men. For business and banks, where we have measures of dispersion, there was a surprisingly constant relationship between the quartiles or first decile and median (as the case may be) pre- and post-World War I, followed by a substantial narrowing pre-and post-World War II. For male business clerks, $Q_{25}$ as percentage of $Q_{75}$ was as follows:

|      | Per cent |
| ---- | -------- |
| 1911 | 41 |
| 1929 | 41 |
| 1955 | 78 |
| 1960 | 76 |

TABLE 2.16 Clerks' pay (occupational class 3), various years 1911–13 to 1960 (pounds)

|  | 1911–13 | 1924 | 1935 | 1955 | 1960 | % of 1911–13 |
|---|---|---|---|---|---|---|
| *Men* | | | | | | |
| CS clerical officers | 116 | 284 | 260 | 503 | 661 | 570 |
| In business | | | | | | |
| Q75 | 148[a] | 213[b] | . . | 570[c] | 762 | 515 |
| Q50 | 96[a] | 159[b] | . . | 500[c] | 663 | 691 |
| Q25 | 60[a] | 87[b] | . . | 447[c] | 582 | 970 |
| Railway clerks | 76 | 221 | 224 | 559 | 751 | 988 |
| In banks | | | | | | |
| Q50 | 142 | 280 | 368[d] | 850 | 1040 | 732 |
| Q25 | 83 | 149 | 227[d] | 650 | 802 | 966 |
| Q10 | 46 | 92 | 103[d] | 380 | 396 | 861 |
| Weighted average | 99 | 182 | 192[f] | 523 | 682 | 689 |
| *Women* | | | | | | |
| CS clerical officers | . . | 206 | 190 | 396 | 586 | . . |
| CS clerical assistants | . . | 143 | 130 | 327 | 481 | . . |
|  | 87 | 177 | 163 | 369 | 544 | 626 |
| CS shorthand typists | 79 | 179 | 162 | 367[e] | 491[e] | 622 |
| CS typists | 65 | 147 | 125 | 315 | 432[e] | 665 |
| Civil Service | 81 | 171 | 155 | 360 | 520 | 642 |
| In business | | | | | | |
| Q75 | 55[a] | 120[b] | . . | 344[c] | 471 | 856 |
| Q50 | 40[a] | 84[b] | . . | 304[c] | 409 | 1022 |
| Q25 | . . | 58[b] | . . | 267[c] | 356 | . . |
| In banks | | | | | | |
| Q75 | . . | . . | 204[d] | 460 | 560 | . . |
| Q50 | . . | 178 | 143[d] | 360 | 412 | . . |
| Q25 | . . | 145 | 104[d] | 278 | 348 | . . |
| Weighted average | 45 | 106 | 99[f] | 317 | 427 | 949 |

[a] 1909–10.
[b] 1929.
[c] Average of March 1954 and March 1956.
[d] 1938.
[e] Grade I.
[f] Assuming business clerks as in previous columns.

*Notes*: Where quartiles, medians or deciles are shown, they are given equal weight in calculating the mean. Where only two quantiles are given, only the median is used with weight equal to the total number of clerks in the group.

For females, the median was 73 per cent of the upper quartile in 1911 and 70 per cent in 1929, while the $Q_1/Q_3$ percentage was as follows:

|      | %  |
|------|----|
| 1929 | 48 |
| 1955 | 78 |
| 1960 | 76 |

For bank clerks, the 1st deciles (or, for women, lower quartiles) as percentages of the medians (or upper quartiles) were as follows:

|         | Per cent | |
|---------|-----|-------|
|         | *Men* | *Women* |
| 1913–14 | 32 | — |
| 1922–3  | 33 | — |
| 1938    | 28 | 51 |
| 1955    | 45 | 60 |
| 1960    | 38 | 62 |

But, as in the case of men, the egalitarian principle again reverses itself between 1955 and 1960, both in the Civil Service and in business.

Between men and women, differentials have narrowed between each pair of years except 1924 and 1935. Thus, in 1909/10, the women's average was 45 per cent of the men's, and in 1960, 63 per cent. In the Civil Service, however, equal pay was achieved in January 1961.

---

For clerks in business, 1924, the data of the *New Survey of London Life and Labour* relating to 1929 have been corrected in the way suggested in the report to compensate for the exclusion from the survey of clerks in some middle-class families (vol. viii, p. 300). A further adjustment has been made to exclude clerks in the public service, transport, banking and insurance, and this lowers the male average by about £15 per year and the female by £4·6 per year. For the weighted averages, the 1929 London Survey figures have been used both for 1924 and 1935.

In banks, overtime pay for those entitled to it added 0·9 per cent to pay in 1955 and 4·4 per cent in 1960. Upper quartiles were not available for men in 1911–13 or 1935. For 1924, 1955 and 1960 they were, respectively, £507, £990 and £1325.

The NES now takes up the story. After 1972, as we noted, there was a change in classification, with the emphasis on industry rather than grade: we now have finance, insurance, etc. clerks; production and materials controlling clerks, and so on, rather than the division into senior, intermediate and junior used pre-1973 and in the *Clerical Salaries Analysis* of the Institute of Administrative Management. Thus the analysis of change between 1970 and 1978 is somewhat limited. After we have extracted supervisors, postmen, telephonists, mail sorters, messengers and receptionists, we find that the men's average of 1978 is 277 per cent of 1970, while the women's is 325. We can in addition compare the progress of women secretary shorthand typists, copy and audio typists and office machine operators:

1978 as % of 1970

|  | Nos. | Earnings |
|---|---|---|
| All women clerks | 117 | 325 |
| Secretary, shorthand-typists | 92 | 326 |
| Copy, audio typists | 108 | 342 |
| Office machine operators | 71 | 346 |

Pay for 1970 and 1978 is shown in Table 2.17, along with that for the previous years.

TABLE 2.17  Clerks' pay (occupational class 3), various years, 1911–13 to 1978

|  | Men | | Women | |
|---|---|---|---|---|
|  | £ | % of previous year | £ | % of previous year |
| 1911–13 | 99 |  | 45 |  |
| 1924 | 182 | 184 | 106 | 235 |
| 1935 | 192 | 105 | 99 | 93 |
| 1955 | 523 | 272 | 317 | 320 |
| 1960 | 682 | 130 | 427 | 135 |
| 1970 | 1337 | 196 | 839 | 196 |
| 1978 | 3701 | 277 | 2730 | 325 |

(F) OCCUPATIONAL CLASS 4 (FOREMEN, SUPERVISORS, INSPECTORS)

*Men*

The earnings reports of 1906[87] distinguish foremen from other occupational categories so that there is no difficulty in establishing their pay level for that year. There is also sufficient information available for the period post-World War II to get an approximation of their present position. Between the wars however, our knowledge is limited to a small number of cases.

Foremen are as a rule manual workers promoted from the ranks and their pay is generally fixed in relation to the pay of those they supervise. The major determinant is the level of the highest-paid occupation in the foreman's charge, in addition to which he will receive a plus-rate for supervision. Thus, if we can establish what was thought to be the appropriate plus-rate in any period we may add this to the rate for the relevant group of manual workers to give the foreman's rate. In 1906, the relation of foremen's pay to the average for men in their charge was as follows:

Foremen's average earnings

|  | £ | % of men's average |
|---|---|---|
| Textiles | 100 | 140 |
| Clothing | 105 | 146 |
| Metals and engineering | 134 | 161 |
| Paper and printing | 127 | 139 |
| Pottery, chemicals, etc. | 111 | 149 |
| Food and drink | 104 | 140 |
| Other manufacturing industries | 105 | 144 |
| Building, woodworking | 118 | 146 |
| Public utilities and railways | 86 | 132 |
| Weighted average | 113 | 145·5 |

Most of the averages lay between 140 and 150 per cent of men's earnings in the industries concerned. In metals and engineering, the differential was higher: more than 160 per cent in the major branches of the industry. It was also high in gas and electricity supply, but rather lower for local authority services and transport.

For the post-1945 period, we have the study of the National Institute

of Industrial Psychology.[88] For 446 'level B' foremen[89] averages
(converted to annual rates) were:

|  | £ | % of men's average |
|---|---|---|
| Metals, engineering, etc. | 520 | 131 |
| Chemicals | 517 | 138 |
| Textiles | 484 | 134 |
| Clothing | 476 | 131 |
| Food, drink, tobacco | 481 | 140 |
| Weighted average | 511 | 132·5 |
| Other | 476 | . . |

In food, drink and tobacco the 40 per cent differential is the same as
that for food and drink in 1906 (tobacco was not divided occupationally
in the report for that year). All the other sectors show a reduction:

|  | 1906 | 1949 | Quotient |
|---|---|---|---|
| Metals and engineering | 161 | 131 | 0·81 |
| Chemicals | 151 | 138 | 0·91 |
| Textiles | 140 | 134 | 0·95 |
| Clothing | 146 | 131 | 0·89 |

In 1958, the Institute of Personnel Management collected information
about foremen's pay.[90] For five large engineering concerns, the mid-
point of the range of pay was £908. The annual rate of earnings for men
in engineering, shipbuilding and electrical goods (mean of October 1957
and April 1958) was £692. The foremen's differential would thus have
been 31 per cent: the same as that shown for 1949.

Between July 1958 and October 1958, the Civil Service Pay Research
Unit submitted eight reports on the pay outside the Civil Service of
occupations related to the 'linked departmental classes of the technical
works, engineering and allied classes'. The Civil Service Arbitration
Tribunal finally fixed their pay in June 1960, with effect from May
1958.[91]

These classes are drawn from apprenticed craftsmen who are not less
than 26 years old, have had three years' experience as a tradesman and
have an Ordinary National Certificate or an equivalent technical

education in the appropriate subject.[92] The two lowest grades are roughly comparable to foreman and, since comparison is largely with general engineering, electronics and aircraft, the Tribunal's award may be held to reflect the pay of foremen in those industries at that time. If the scales for grades II and III are averaged over ten annual points and weighted together according to the totals in each grade, an average is obtained of £940. Average men's earnings in engineering, shipbuilding and electrical goods, vehicles and metal goods not elsewhere specified in April and October 1958 (at an annual rate), were £706. Grades II and III, on the basis of the calculation described, had a lead of 33 per cent on this.

We must now look for evidence of the situation between the wars and see how it differed from that before and after them. There are some cases in which comparisons can be made. In 1906, railway foremen earned 136 per cent of the average for railway manual workers and gangers 120 per cent of permanent way labourers (including, in 1906, lengthmen and relayers). In other years, the relationship was as follows:

|  |  | 1935 | 1960 |
|---|---|---|---|
| Foremen |  |  |  |
| Operating | £ | 263 | 938 |
|  | % of manual average | 160 | 132 |
| Maintenance and | £ | 303 | 1035 |
| construction | % of manual average | 170 | 135 |
| Gangers | £ | 146 | 815 |
|  | % of lengthmen and |  |  |
|  | relayers | 117 | 113 |

Thus, while the gangers' lead was reduced between 1906 and 1935 by three percentage points and between 1935 and 1960 by four percentage points, that of foremen increased quite substantially between 1906 and 1935 and then, between 1935 and 1960, fell to somewhat below the 1906 level.

In electricity supply, the pay and lead of shift-charge engineers moved as follows:

|  | 1924 | 1935 | 1959 |
|---|---|---|---|
| Amount (£) | 476 | 453 | 1039 |
| Per cent of manual average | 281 | 267 | 156 |

Foremen in electricity supply in 1906 had a lead of 57 per cent over the men's average, so, again, there appears to have been a reversion in more recent years to the position of 1906.

Further evidence of the rise and fall of differentials in our period of study comes from the Anderson Report of 1923.[93] In 1914, the average pay of the Civil Service inspectorate was £229, compared with an average of £81 per head for Civil Service industrial staff; in 1923, it was £443 for the inspectorate and £142·5 for the industrials. The lead had increased from 183 to 211 per cent.

In the Post Office Engineering Department in 1938, inspectors' pay was 188 per cent of that of skilled workmen class II; in 1952, it was 159 per cent.[94] The fall in the differential over the Second World War was almost identical in proportion to the rise in the inspectorate-industrial staff differential over the First World War.

In general terms, foremen seem to have had a modal lead in 1906 of between 40 and 50 per cent of the men's manual average for the industry concerned with the average at 45 per cent; between the wars, this had risen to between 60 and 65 per cent; post-1945, it returned to somewhere below the pre-1914 level, with a much-reduced inter-industry dispersion and an average lead lying between 30 and 35 per cent. Applying these estimates to the men's average from the earnings censuses,[95] we get:

|  | 1906 | 1924 | 1935 | 1955 | 1960 |
|---|---|---|---|---|---|
| Men's average (£) | 78 | 165 | 168 | 592 | 766 |
| Foremen's average (£) | 113 | 268 | 273 | 784 | 1015 |

As with the clerks, reconciliation with the NES data for 1970 and 1978 presents few problems. In 1970, supervisors and foremen had a class of their own. There were 5927 of them and their average was £1685. We have only to include 700 skilled inspectors from class 16, and this brings their average down to £1669.

For 1978, the task is more tedious, for foremen and supervisors are scattered about amongst those whom they supervise. We must again separate the works foremen from production and works managers, taking 54 per cent of the group and 91 per cent of the average earnings: 464 works foremen at £103·50 per week. For the rest, we have eighteen different groups, including supervisors of clerks, inspectors and testers, and deputies, coal mining. For ten, we are given average earnings; for the rest we must take the mean of the quantiles. The grand total is 6280 and the average pay £4685.

*Women*
There is little information available about the pay of this occupational class and, at any rate until 1939, their numbers were too small for a mode to have emerged.[96] The 1906 reports distinguish only the following:

|  | Rate £ | % of women's average |
|---|---|---|
| Hosiery | 45·5 | 126 |
| Dress, millinery, etc. (factory) | 67 | 174 |
| Shirts, blouses, underclothing | 56 | 168 |
| Tailoring (ready-made) | 49 | 151 |
| Corsets (factory) | 42 | 135 |
| Dyeing and cleaning | 58 | 161 |
| Laundries | 55 | 175 |
| Bookbinding | 48 | 145 |
| Stationery manufacture | 49 | 161 |
| Cardboard, canvas box manufacture | 46 | 151 |
| Cocoa, chocolate and sugar confectionery manufacture | 47 | 146 |
| Weighted average | 52 | 160 |

We have no evidence of what happened to the forewomen's lead between the wars, but the National Institute of Industrial Psychology study[97] shows an average in 1949 for level B forewomen of £71s. 0d. per week and for level C (supervisors responsible to a level B supervisor) of £5 14s. 0d. The B and C average was £6 6s. 0d. Women's earnings in the Ministry of Labour inquiry in October averaged £3 18s. 9d., so that forewomen's earnings, at £6 6s. 0d., would have been back at the 1906 level of 160 per cent of the women's average.

In the Post Office, there is some evidence for the rise and fall of differentials that we saw in the case of men. In 1938, telephone supervisors had a London scale averaging £280 over fifteen points; in 1953, the average was £499·5. For telephonists, the scale average (fifteen points from age eighteen) was £142 in 1938 and £309 in 1953. The supervisors' lead had fallen from 97 to 62 per cent. The fall (just over a fifth) was similar in scale to that experienced by men.

For the earlier period, the change in differentials at Cadbury's

Bournville factory gives corroboration. In 1912, forewomen's average earnings were 186 per cent of day-wage operatives and 170 per cent of piece-wage operatives. In 1924, the rank of forewoman had been divided into two: forewomen and deputy forewomen. Their earnings as a percentage of those of operatives, were as follows:

|  | Day-wage operatives | Piece-wage operatives |
|---|---|---|
| Forewomen | 360 | 251 |
| Deputy forewomen | 253 | 176 |

We cannot say what the average rise in differential was, for we do not know the numbers in the occupations concerned, but the rise ranged between 93·5 per cent for forewomen compared with day-wage operatives to 3·5 per cent for deputy forewomen compared with piece-wage operatives.

We should probably not be far wrong if we guessed that the forewomen's differential moved similarly to that of foremen, and that their 1906 lead of about 60 per cent rose to rather over 90 per cent between the wars and then returned to about 60 per cent.

In 1970, we have 1044 supervisors and forewomen in the NES, with average earnings of £1014, which gives them a lead of 51 per cent over women manual workers. In 1978, we are given six groups totalling 1606, more than half of whom are supervisors of clerks. There average earnings were £3214.

Table 2.18 gives the run of data thus accumulated.

TABLE 2.18 Earnings of foremen, forewomen, supervisors, inspectors (occupational class 4), various years, 1911–13 to 1978

|  | Men | | Women | |
|  | £ | % of previous year | £ | % of previous year |
|---|---|---|---|---|
| 1906 | 113 |  | 57 |  |
| 1924 | 268 | 237 | 154 | 270 |
| 1935 | 273 | 102 | 156 | 101 |
| 1955 | 784 | 287 | 477 | 306 |
| 1960 | 1015 | 129 | 602 | 126 |
| 1970 | 1669 | 164 | 1014 | 168 |
| 1978 | 4685 | 280 | 3214 | 317 |

(G) OCCUPATIONAL CLASS 5 (SKILLED WORKERS)

*Men*

Again, we may draw on a wide range of occupations for the calculation of the 1906 average:

| | 000s | Average earnings £ | |
|---|---|---|---|
| Coalface workers | 586 | 112 | |
| Manufacturing industry | | | |
|   Pottery turners | 14 { | 87 } | 90 |
|   Pottery throwers | | 93 } | |
|   Glass gatherers, blowers, makers | 13 | 113 | |
| Engineering and boilermaking | | | |
|   Patternmakers | 18 | 97·5 | |
|   Moulders | 99 | 95 | |
|   Smiths | 55 | 96 | |
|   Turners, fitters, erectors, millwrights | | | |
|     time | 231 { | 90 } | 95 |
|     piece | | 104 } | |
|   Platers, riveters, caulkers | | | |
|     time | 60 { | 96 } | 106 |
|     piece | | 120 } | |
| Ship- and boatbuilding and repairing | | | |
|   Platers, riveters, caulkers | | | |
|     time | 13 { | 90 } | 128 |
|     piece | | 140 } | |
|   Shipwrights | | | |
|     time | 21 { | 91 } | 92 |
|     piece | | 119 } | |
| Railway coachmakers | 4 | 93 | |
| Buffers and polishers (coal etc.) | 3 | 86 | |
| Engravers | 5 | 93 | |
| Mounters (jewellery) | 3 | 97 | |
| Cotton spinners | 114 { | 107 } | 103 |
| Wool-worsted spinners | | 74 } | |
| Cotton weavers | 115 { | 65 } | 65 |
| Wool-worsted weavers | | 65 } | |
| Textile printers | 16 | 119 | |
| Tailoring cutters (ready-made) | 19 | 81 | |
| Boot and shoe clickers | | | |
|   time | 19 { | 71 } | 71 |
|   piece | | 69 } | |
| Grain millers | 8 | 62 | |

| | 000s | Average earnings £ | |
|---|---|---|---|
| Bakers | 77 { | 76 } | 77 |
| Confectioners and pastry-cooks | | 81 } | |
| Cabinet-makers | 47 | 85 | |
| French polishers (cabinet- etc., making) | 17 | 83 | |
| Carriage-makers and body-builders | 73 | 86 | |
| Wheelwrights | 18 | 76 | |
| Compositors, general | 54 { | 90 } | 98 |
| Compositors, daily news | | 141 } | |
| Building | | | |
|   Bricklayers | 100 | 94 | |
|   Masons | 56 | 90 | |
|   Carpenters and joiners | 223 | 93 | |
|   Plumbers | 63 | 94 | |
|   Painters and decorators | 183 | 89 | |
| Electrical wiremen (electricity supply) | 8[a] | 93 | |
| Railways | | | |
|   Engine drivers | 33 | 119 | |
|   Guards | 24 | 80 | |
|   Signalmen | 30 | 71·5 | |
|   Mechanics | 27[b] | 82 | |
| Weighted averages | | | |
|   Coal | 586 | 112·0 | |
|   Manufacturing and maintenance | 1116 | 90·7 | |
|   Building and electricians | 633 | 91·8 | |
|   Railways | 114 | 89·5 | |
| All | 2449 | 96·0 | |

[a] Electricians and electrical fitters.
[b] No. shown in earnings report.

Table 2.19 gives a selection of representative occupations by which the 1906 average may be projected to the relevant years. The weights used are the numbers of skilled workers of whom the occupation cited is typical; for example, engineering fitters are taken to represent all skilled metal-workers, carpenters all skilled woodworkers, bakers all skilled food-workers.

TABLE 2.19  Earnings of skilled men (occupational class 5) various years, 1906–60 (pounds)

| | 1906[a] | 1924 | 1935 | 1955 | 1960 | % of 1906 |
|---|---|---|---|---|---|---|
| Coalface workers[b] | 112 | 180 | 149 | 834 | 922 | 831 |
| Pottery turners[c] | 90 | 153 | 166 | . . | 758 | 842 |
| Pottery throwers[c] | 110 | 198 | 203 | . . | 678 | 617 |
| Engineering fitters[d] | | | | | | |
| time | 90 | 157 | 212 | 649 | 828 | 916 |
| piece | 103 | 191 | 243 | 686 | 876 | 848 |
| Boot and shoe clickers[e] | | | | | | |
| time | 71 } | 165 | 159 | 464 } | 620 } | 731 |
| piece | 69 } | | | 555 } | 751 } | |
| Bakers[f] | 75 | 159 | 156 | 508 | 691 | 921 |
| Carpenters[g] | 98 | 191 | 176 | 507 | 674 | 688 |
| Bricklayers[g] | 94 | 191 | 176 | 507 | 674 | 717 |
| Railway engine drivers[h] | 119 | 276 | 258 | 622 | 863 | 725 |
| Railway guards[h] | 80 | 196 | 192 | 540 | 745 | 931 |
| Compositors[i] | 91 | 209 | 218 | 561 | 723 | 795 |
| Weighted average[j] | 97 | 182 | 197 | 629 | 804 | 829 |
| Unweighted average | 92 | 189 | 192·5 | 585 | 754 | 820 |

[a] Except coal, from earnings inquiry.

[b] From Finlay A. Gibson, *A Compilation of Statistics (Technological, Commercial and General) of the Coal Mining Industry of the United Kingdom* (Cardiff, *The Western Mail*, 1922). Coal earnings figures relating to June 1914 have been reduced in proportion to average earnings per shift for all coalminers and average number of shifts worked per week to approximate to earnings in 1906. *Other years:* coalface workers annual averages include payments in kind.

[c] Employers' Federation inquiries. 1960: 1959 raised by increase in earnings shown in Ministry of Labour inquiries.

[d] Employers' Federation inquiries.

[e] 1924 and 1935 average earnings for all men aged 21 and over. 1955 and 1960: Employers' Federation inquiries.

[f] 1906 earnings raised proportionately with rates for 1924 and 1935. 1955 and 1960: average quotations for 1958 from thirty-six firms notifying vacancies to employment exchanges in Edinburgh, Manchester, Birmingham and London lowered and raised respectively, proportionately to earnings in Ministry of Labour reports. Amounts include addition for overtime.

[g] 1924 and 1935, average rates thirty-nine towns. 1955 and 1960 rates Grade A districts. Amounts include addition for overtime.

[h] Total cash earnings from Ministry of Transport or British Transport Commission reports.

[i] Jobbing book and weekly newspapers. For 1924 and 1935, raised proportionately with rates in twenty-six large towns. 1955 and 1960: same methods as for bakers. Amounts include addition for overtime.

[j] Weights: number in occupation at nearest population census, except for the following: fitters—all skilled engineering workers; bakers—all skilled food-workers; carpenters—all skilled woodworkers; bricklayers—all skilled building workers except carpenters; compositors—all skilled printing workers. 1960: numbers from census 1951 adjusted in proportion to change in industrial totals for employees end-May 1951 to October 1960.

Table 2.19 gives the following indexes:

|      | Weighted | Unweighted |
|------|----------|------------|
| 1906 | 100      | 100        |
| 1924 | 188      | 205        |
| 1935 | 203      | 209        |
| 1955 | 648      | 659        |
| 1960 | 829      | 863        |

The major divergence between the two series comes between 1906 and 1924, when the weighted index is pulled down by the relatively small rise in the pay of coalface workers who, in 1924, constituted 605,000 out of the total 2,892,000 employees of whose pay the index is representative. Engineering fitters, too, were a large class whose rise in pay was below the mode. Between 1924 and 1960, by contrast, there is less divergence and it is then the weighted index that shows the greater rise: from 100 to 441 as compared with 421 in the unweighted index.

Applying the indexes to the average of £96 for 1906 we get:

|      | Weighted | Unweighted |
|------|----------|------------|
| 1906 | 96       | 96         |
| 1924 | 180      | 197        |
| 1935 | 195      | 201        |
| 1955 | 622      | 633        |
| 1960 | 796      | 828        |

We can identify thirty-two groups of skilled workers in the NES for 1970 and 1978. There are 21,480 in the sample for 1970; in 1978, less effort was exerted to separate the skilled from the semi-skilled and unskilled, and numbers are reduced to 16,114. Average earnings for 1970 are £1440 and for 1978 £4354.

*Women*
Averages for the skilled occupations about which information was available were as follows for 1906:

| | Nos. 000s | £ |
|---|---|---|
| Pottery transferers | 14 | 32 |
| Wire weavers | 1 | 21 |
| Polishers ( jewellery) | 1 | 36 |
| Chain makers (goldsmiths) | 1 | 36 |
| Ring spinners (cotton) | 15 | 39 |
| Reelers, winders, beamers, warpers (cotton) | 69 | 39 |
| Weavers (cotton) | 163 | 50 |
| Winders, reelers, warpers (wool) | 10 | 37 |
| Weavers (wool and worsted) | 49 | 39 |
| Hosiery frame tenters and knitters | 47 | 36 |
| Boot and shoe closers | | |
| time | 34 | 36 } 36 |
| piece | 10 | 38 } |
| Women's clothing cutters (factory) | 13 | 49 } 41 |
| Shirt cutters | | 38 } |
| Dress, corset and light clothing makers | 183 | 37 |
| Milliners, hat and cap makers | 53 | 37 |
| Upholsterers | 9 | 32 |
| Food and tobacco workers | 24 | 34 |
| Paper makers | 43 | 30 |
| Case makers, sewers and stitchers | | |
| (bookbinding) | 22 | 32 |
| French polishers, signwriters[a] | 7 | 26 |
| Total | 768 | 39 (average) |

[a] E. Cadbury, M. C. Matheson and G. Shann, *Women's Work and Wages* (London: Fisher Unwin, 1906).

The average of £39 compares with the range of £30 to £34 for the semi-skilled women in the clothing, engineering and laundry trades, but is well below the £50 of cotton frame tenters, shop-assistants and domestic servants (including an estimate of the value of board and lodging).

In Table 2.20 we attempt to gauge the movement of skilled women's earnings between 1906 and 1960. For pottery transferers and boot and shoe closers the information is based on returns collected by employers' associations and is satisfactory; for clothing cutters and upholsterers the figures relate directly to those occupations and probably give a fair reflection of the reality. For cotton weavers, we rely on average

TABLE 2.20　Earnings of skilled women manual workers (occupational class 5), various years, 1906–60 (pounds)

| | *1906*[a] | *1924* | *1935* | *1955* | *1960* | *% of 1906* |
|---|---|---|---|---|---|---|
| Pottery transferers[b] | 32 | 65 | 76 | 305 | 366 | 1144 |
| Cotton weaving[c] | 48 | 93 | 80 | 327 | 404 | 842 |
| Wool and worsted[c] | 35 | 94 | 80 | 303 | 378 | 1080 |
| Hosiery[c] | 36 | 75 | 93 | 329 | 394 | 1094 |
| Boot and shoe closers[d] | | | | | | |
| 　time | 32 | 94 | 86 | 260 | 344 | 1075 |
| 　piece | 37 | .. | .. | 330 | 441 | 1192 |
| Clothing cutters[e] | 41 | 100 | 103 | 322 | 410 | 1000 |
| Dressmakers[c] | 37 | 76 | 93 | 294 | 367 | 992 |
| Upholsterers[e] | 32 | 102 | 114 | 405 | 518 | 1619 |
| Average | | | | | | |
| 　weighted[f] | 40 | 87 | 86 | 317 | 395 | 987 |
| 　unweighted | 37 | 87 | 91 | 319 | 402 | 1086 |

[a] Earnings and hours inquiry.
[b] Employers' federation census; 1960 and 1955, Oct. 1959 figures adjusted proportionately with Ministry of Labour earnings averages.
[c] For sources, see text.
[d] 1924 and 1935, standard rates; 1955 and 1960, employers' federation census.
[e] 1929 (*New Survey of London Life and Labour*, vol. ii (1)) adjusted by change in women's earnings in the clothing and furniture industries 1924 and 1925.
[f] Weights: from Table 1.12, with cotton weaving, wool and worsted and hosiery combined in proportion to all females in those industries in 1911, 1921, 1931, 1955 and 1960.

women's earnings for the weaving section of the cotton textile industry: since about two-thirds of the female manual working force of this section consisted of weavers, the approximation is not too wide. But to be comparable with later years, the 1906 average for weavers (£50) must be diluted to allow for admixture of winders, warpers, sizers and drawers in, whose average was £38·5 in 1906. There were 9.4 thousand of these last in 1951, to 51.1 thousand weavers in the cotton weaving industry, and the use of these proportions brings the average for 1906 down to £48. For wool and worsted, hosiery and dressmakers, again dominated by workers of class 5, the best we can do is to follow average earnings for all women in those industries, with the assumption that they approximate to the relative movements of the earnings of skilled women.

Table 2.20 gives indexes based on 1906 as follows:

|      | Weighted | Unweighted |
|------|----------|------------|
| 1906 | 100      | 100        |
| 1924 | 217·5    | 235        |
| 1935 | 215      | 247        |
| 1955 | 795      | 873        |
| 1960 | 993      | 1101       |

Applying these indexes to the skilled women's average of £ 39 for 1906, we get:

|      | Weighted £ | Unweighted £ |
|------|------------|--------------|
| 1906 | 39         | 39           |
| 1924 | 85         | 92           |
| 1935 | 84         | 96           |
| 1955 | 310        | 340          |
| 1960 | 387        | 429          |

The weighted average is dominated by skilled textile workers who accounted for nearly half the total of skilled women workers in 1911 and 35 per cent 1951. Dressmakers formed 24 per cent of the total in 1911 and 6·7 per cent in 1951.

Cotton weavers remained above the average in 1960, but never fully recovered from their relative decline of 1906–24 and 1924–35 despite their rally between 1935 and 1955. It is this in particular that has depressed the weighted in relation to the unweighted average.

We can identify 2539 skilled full-time women workers in the NES for 1970, including 493 chefs, cooks, 450 skilled textile workers, 811 skilled sewing machinists and 191 hairdressers. In 1978, the sample is reduced to 1728, no textile workers, skilled or otherwise, are identified, though we gain 101 bookbinders. It is, perhaps, time that the Department of Employment extended its June surveys of earnings in engineering and chemicals to women: at present it is confined to adult men, though the annual enquiry into occupations in engineering for May 1977 shows that there were 15,670 female full-time craftsmen at work, and more than 300,000 semi-skilled and unskilled female employees.[98]

Average earnings shown in the NES were £677 in 1970 and £2246 in 1978.

(H) OCCUPATIONAL CLASS 6 (SEMI-SKILLED WORKERS)

*Men*

The following average earnings for 1906 are taken from the earnings reports[99] with the addition of some manipulative grades of Post Office workers,[100] shop-assistants and army privates.

|  | £ |
| --- | --- |
| Agricultural labourers | 48 |
| Manufacturing industry | |
| Cotton textiles, mixers, scutchers, grinders and card-room jobbers | 70 |
| Wool teazers, fettlers, scribblers, combers, dressers and finishers | 58 |
| Textile bleachers, crofters and dyers | 59 |
| Ready-made tailoring machinists and pressers | 72 |
| Wooden box makers | 75 |
| Shipbuilding platers' helpers | 60 |
| Shipbuilding drillers and hole cutters | 88 |
| Engineering machinemen | |
| time | 73 |
| piece | 84 |
| Letterpress assistants | 74 |
| Packers, The Potteries | 88 |
| Transport | |
| Carters and carmen (sawmilling) | 58 |
| Carters and carmen (borough and urban district councils) | 65 |
| Tram drivers | 80 |
| Bus drivers | 93 |
| Bus conductors | 70 |
| Railway platelayers | 55 |
| Railway engine firemen | 71 |
| Railway ticket collectors | 64 |
| Railway carmen and draymen | 65 |
| Post Office | |
| Postmen (London) | 81 |
| Sorters (London) | 109 |
| Telephonists (London) | 77 |
| Electricity and gas supply | |
| Boiler attendants (gas) | 85 |
| Firemen (electricity) | 81 |
| Jointers' mates (electricity) | 71 |
| Shop-assistants | 83 |
| Army privates[a] | 40 |
| Unweighted average | 72 |

|  | £ |
|---|---|
| Sectional averages | |
| Weights | £ |
| 1118  Agriculture | 48 |
| 550  Manufacturing industry | 72 |
| 665  Transport | 65 |
| 97  Post Office | 94 |
| 30  Electricity and gas | 81 |
| 546  Shop-assistants | 83 |
| 196  Army[a] | 40 |
| Weighted average | 63 |

[a]Includes pay and living-out allowance for married men.

*Note:* Manufacturing industry, transport, and electricity and gas sectional averages obtained using weights in accordance with numbers shown in the Board of Trade earnings reports. For overall average, weights according to 1911 Population Census.

TABLE 2.21  Earnings or rates for semi-skilled men (occupational class 6), various years 1906–1960 (pounds)

| | 1906 | 1924 | 1935 | 1955 | 1960 | % of 1906 |
|---|---|---|---|---|---|---|
| Packers, The Potteries[a] | 88 | 153 | 159 | .. | 653 | 742 |
| Other semi-skilled pottery workers[a] | 77 | 171 | 173 | .. | 585 | 760 |
| Engineering machinemen:[b] | | | | | | |
| time | 73 | (151) | 168 | 547 | 672 | 921 |
| piece | 84 | .. | .. | 634 | 808 | 962 |
| Railway platelayers[c] | 55 | 147 | 128 | 549 | 720 | 1309 |
| Railway engine firemen[c] | 71 | 199 | 203 | 507 | 712 | 1000 |
| Railway ticket collectors[c] | 64 | 166 | 164 | 510 | 680 | 1062 |
| Railway horse carters[c] | 65 | 151 | 147 | 458 | 634 | 975 |
| One-horse carters average rates[d] | 66 | 139 | 135 | 372 | 492 | 745 |
| Bus and tram conductors (London) rates[e] | 72 | 147 | 157 | 399 | 485 | 674 |
| Bus and tram drivers (London) rates[e] | 107 | 190 | 218 | 476 | 546 | 510 |
| Postmen (London) rates[f] | 81 | 160 | 149 | 430·5 | 527 | 651 |
| Weighted average[i] | 73 | 158 | 168 | 532 | 662 | 908 |
| Shop-assistants[g] | 83 | 120 | 113 | 390 | 487 | 587 |

Table 2.21 (*Contd.*)

|  | 1906 | 1924 | 1935 | 1955 | 1960 | % of 1906 |
|---|---|---|---|---|---|---|
| Weighted average[i] | 75 | 153 | 159 | 520 | 647 | 863 |
| Agricultural labourers[h] | 48 | 82 | 89 | 423 | 512 | 1067 |
| Weighted average[i] | 68 | 136 | 144 | 506 | 627 | 923 |
| Unweighted average | 74 | 152 | 154 | 474·5 | 607·5 | 821 |

[a] Potteries, 1924 onwards: British Pottery Manufacturers' Federation censuses.

[b] 1935 onwards: Engineering and Allied Employers' National Federation censuses. 1926: semi-skilled earnings assumed in same position relative to skilled and unskilled as in 1934.

[c] Average earnings for a week in March 1924 and 1935, *Railways (Staff) Return* (London: HMSO, annual); 1955 and 1960: *Annual Census of Staff* (London: British Transport Commission).

[d] 1914, 1924 and 1936, average of recognised rates in twelve large towns (Ministry of Labour, *Abstract of Labour Statistics*). 1955 and 1960: average of standard rate for brewing in nine districts and corn trade in four districts.

[e] Ibid.

[f] 1924, scale averaged over twenty-five years. Other years, averaged over twenty years. 1955: scale operative from 1 November 1955 to 31 March 1956. 1960: scale operative from 1 December 1958. In all cases, beginning at eighteen years of age.

[g] 1909: estimate from inquiry by National Union of Shop Assistants. See *The Case for Minimum Wages in Distributive Trades* (National Amalgamated Union of Shop Assistants, 1913). 1924–5: reports of Trade Board inquiries. 1938: Marley and Campion inquiry, 'Changes in Salaries in Great Britain, 1924–39', p. 524). 1955 and 1960: average quotations for 1958 from 155 firms notifying vacancies to employment exchanges in Edinburgh, Manchester, Birmingham and London, reduced by 17 per cent for 1955 and raised by 3·5 per cent for 1960, these being the approximate percentage changes for retail co-operative, retail multiple grocery and Retail Food Wages Council wage rates.

[h] Includes allowance for payments in kind. 1924: A. L. Bowley's estimate, *Wages and Income in the United Kingdom since 1860* (Cambridge: University Press, 1937). 1935: J. R. Bellerby's estimate for 1936–8, *Agriculture and Industry: Relative Income* (London: Macmillan, 1956).

[i] Weights: numbers in the occupation in Population Census 1911 for 1906; in immediately preceding census for subsequent years. Engineering machinemen are weighted according to the number of all semi-skilled engineers, postmen (London), *all* postmen, etc., and those other than shop-assistants and agricultural labourers are given a group weight equal to number of all semi-skilled men other than shop-assistants and agricultural labourers.

Of course, the class average is pulled down by the average for the agricultural labourer which was below that of any of the unskilled averages cited below. If agriculture is excluded, the average becomes £71, well above that of £56 for unskilled men.

We may now gauge the movement of semi-skilled earnings from Table 2.21, limited to occupations for which data are available for all or most of the five required years.

Our calculations showed a semi-skilled male average for 1906 of about £63 including agricultural labourers and £71 without them. We may now calculate average pay series for semi-skilled men by applying to these estimates the ratios of inter-year change from Table 2.21. The results are shown in Table 2.22.

TABLE 2.22 Average pay for semi-skilled men (occupational class 6), various years 1906–1960

|  | Including agriculture | | Without agriculture | |
| --- | --- | --- | --- | --- |
|  | £ | Index | £ | Index |
| 1906 | 63 | 100 | 71 | 100 |
| 1924 | 126 | 200 | 145 | 204 |
| 1935 | 134 | 212 | 151 | 212 |
| 1955 | 469 | 744 | 493 | 694 |
| 1960 | 581 | 923 | 611 | 860 |

In the event, the index including agriculture (100 : 923) is almost identical in its ratio 1906–60 with that given for semi-skilled factory and construction workers in Table 2.27 (100:923·5). But when agricultural labourers and shop-assistants are excluded the 1960 average is reduced to 908 per cent of 1906 (Table 2.21).

There have been important differences between the performance of the different groups in the various periods: between 1906 and 1924, agricultural labourers and shop-assistants were well below the average in percentage increase and bus and tram drivers did not get on much better. In the next period, bus drivers and agricultural labourers had increases much larger than the average, but shop-assistants were again near the bottom.

In the period 1935–55, agricultural workers were well in the lead and shop-assistants staged a partial recovery. In the last period, railway workers led the field, engineering machinemen and shop-assistants were very near the average and agricultural workers near the bottom.

In the beginning and end years, the occupations were ranked as follows:

| 1906 | £ | 1960 | £ |
|---|---|---|---|
| Bus and tram drivers | 107 | Engineering machinemen (piece) | 808 |
| Pottery packers | 88 | Railway platelayers | 720 |
| Engineering machinemen (piece) | 84 | Railway engine firemen | 712 |
| Shop-assistants | 83 | Ticket collectors | 680 |
| Postmen (London) | 81 | Engineering machinemen (time) | 672 |
| Semi-skilled potters | 77 | Pottery packers | 653 |
| Engineering machinemen (time) | 73 | Carters (railways) | 634 |
| Bus and tram conductors | 72 | Semi-skilled potters | 585 |
| Railway engine firemen | 71 | Bus drivers | 546 |
| One-horse carters | 66 | Postmen (London) | 527 |
| Carters (railways) | 65 | Agricultural workers | 512 |
| Ticket collectors | 64 | One-horse carters | 492 |
| Railway platelayers | 55 | Shop-assistants | 487 |
| Agricultural workers | 48 | Bus conductors | 485 |
| Unweighted average | 74 | | 607·5 |
| Average deviation | 11 | | 87·5 |

The average deviation from the unweighted average (sign ignored) amounted to 14·8 per cent of the average in 1906 and 14·4 per cent in 1960, so that the degree of dispersion was almost unchanged; but bus and tram drivers in 1960 were 90 per cent of the average compared with 145 per cent in 1906, shop-assistants had fallen to 80 from 112 per cent and agricultural labourers had risen to 84 from 65 per cent.

The NES provides twenty-three identifiable semi-skilled men's groups in 1970, including four groups of lorry driver classified by size of lorry, and embracing 20,191 workers, their average earnings £1289, which is 222 per cent of 1960. In 1978 we can identify twenty-five groups, but totalling only 13,226, mainly because the allocation of workers to skill groups has been reduced. Average pay in 1978 was £3827, that is 297 per cent of 1970.

*Women*

Table 2.23 shows movements in the average earnings of representative occupations in occupational class 6.

For the whole period, the occupations listed divide themselves into two: textile workers, shop-assistants and domestic servants whose 1960 averages as a percentage of 1906 were 734, 630 and 633, and clothing machinists, engineering machine operators and laundry workers, for

TABLE 2.23 Earnings of semi-skilled women (occupational class 6), various years, 1906–60 (pounds)

| | 1906 | 1924 | 1935 | 1955 | 1960 | % of 1906 |
|---|---|---|---|---|---|---|
| Cotton frame tenters[a] | 50 | 94 | 80 | 310 | 367 | 734 |
| Clothing machinists[b] | 34 | 78 | 73 | 294 | 434 | 1276 |
| Shop-assistants[c] | 50 | 69 | 80 | 255 | 315 | 630 |
| Waitresses[d] | .. | 113 | (113)[e] | 280 | 323 | .. |
| Domestic servants[f] | 49 | 115 | (115)[e] | 255 | 310 | 633 |
| Engineering machine operators[g] | 32 | 79 | 85 | 328 | 406 | 1269 |
| Laundries and dry cleaning[h] | 30 | 68 | 73 | 246 | 310 | 1033 |
| Weighted average | 46 | 97·6 | 99·6 | 269·2 | 339·1 | 737 |
| Index | 100 | 212 | 216 | 584 | 736 | |

[a] 1906 average earnings; 1924, 81 per cent over 1914. See *18th Abstract of Labour Statistics of the United Kingdom*, Cmd. 2740 (London: HMSO, 1926) p. 117, but excluding effect of increase in hourly rates to compensate for reduction in length of working week. Allows for 2·8 per cent increase, September 1906 to July 1914; see J. Jewkes and E. M. Gray, *Wages and Labour in the Lancashire Cotton Spinning Industry* (Manchester: University Press, 1935). 1936, 59·2 per cent over 1914. 1955 and 1960: quotations from ten firms in north-west region, May 1958, adjusted by changes in minimum rates, 1955 and 1960.

[b] Bowley gives 130 per cent increase for females making 'other clothing', 1914–24. See *Wages and Income in the United Kingdom since 1860*, p. 17. 1935: 1924 adjusted *pari passu* with women's earnings in the clothing industry. 1955 and 1960: 107 employment exchange quotations for 1958 adjusted according to changes in earnings.

[c] 1909: inquiry by National Amalgamated Union of Shop Assistants, Warehousemen and Clerks, *The Case for Minimum Wages in Distributive Trades*; 1924/5 Trade Board inquiries; 1938: Marley/Campion inquiry. 'Changes in Salary in Great Britain'; 1955 and 1960: 143 employment exchange quotations for 1958 adjusted according to per cent changes for retail co-operative societies, retail multiple grocery and wages councils for retail food and drapery, outfitting and footwear.

[d] 1929: from Trade Board reports. Average of quartiles and median by licensed hotels with more than ten bedrooms, non-licensed hotels, etc., and light refreshment and dining-rooms, without tips but including value of meals and accommodation. 1955 and 1960: average quotations for 1958 from 179 firms notifying vacancies to employment exchanges in Edinburgh, Manchester, Birmingham and London, adjusted forward and backward according to per cent changes in waitress rates, licensed residential establishments and licensed restaurants, plus £47 for value of meals.

[e] Assumes no change 1924 and 1935.

[f] W. T. Layton, 'Changes in the Wages of Domestic Servants during Fifty Years', *Journal of the Royal Statistical Society*, vol. 71, part 3 (September 1908), p. 515. 1929: housewives' returns to the *New Survey of London Life and Labour and Survey of Merseyside* (ed. D. Caradog Jones [Liverpool: University Press, 1934]). 1958/9: ninety employment exchange quotations, adjusted according to per cent changes in rates for chambermaids, licensed residential establishments, Area B.

[g] Time- and piece-workers. Federation average 1935: 1924—all women plus 12·3 per cent, to equal relationship of 1935. 1955 and 1960, Federation average.

[h] Laundries, etc.: earnings for all females.

whom the comparable figures were 1276, 1269 and 1033.[101]

The 1906 averages in the first group were all in the vicinity of £50, compared with £30 to £34 for the second. The decline, in the case of shop-assistants, comes between 1906 and 1924, after which their increases are above or near the average. In cotton, the relative fall is between both 1906 and 1924, and 1924 and 1935; then comes a recovery between 1935 and 1955, followed by a further decline. In domestic servants, by contrast, the decline was between 1935 and 1955.

By 1960, the income relationship between the service occupations and two of the three manufacturing occupations had been reversed: the averages for shop-assistants, waitresses, domestic servants, laundresses and dry cleaners were all within the band £310 to £323; engineering and clothing were in the region of £400 with cotton' midway between.

For 1970, we can find 9359 semi-skilled women workers in the NES, in eighteen groups, including 1181 semi-skilled 'not elsewhere specified'. Their average earnings were £645, which is 190 per cent of 1960.

For 1978, we can find 6638, in twelve groups, whose average is £2356, which is 365 per cent of 1970.

(I) OCCUPATIONAL CLASS 7 (UNSKILLED WORKERS)

*Men*

The earnings reports of 1906 give the following average earnings for general labourers, aged twenty and over, in the United Kingdom.[102]

|  | No. | Average earnings £ per year |
|---|---|---|
| Cotton | 1944 | 52·65 |
| Wool and worsted | 535 | 51·35 |
| Textile bleaching, printing, dyeing and finishing | 3337 | 52·4 |
| Building |  |  |
| Bricklayers' labourers | 10,814 | 60·9 |
| Masons' labourers | 4393 | 58·9 |
| Plasterers' labourers | 2185 | 62·6 |
| Painters' labourers | 1631 | 68·5 |
| Excavators | 3920 | 57·6 |
| Builders' labourers | 7706 | 62·8 |
| Civil Engineering |  |  |
| Excavators and labourers |  |  |
| time | 5952 | 54·8 |
| piece | 246 | 85·4 |

|  | No. | Average earnings £ per year |
|---|---|---|
| Sawmilling, machine joiners, etc. |  |  |
|     time | 5147 | 53·9 |
|     piece | 199 | 94·5 |
| Cabinet-making, etc. | 902 | 57·0 |
| Road, sanitary, etc. services |  |  |
| Borough and urban district councils |  |  |
|     General roadmen | 5096 | 58·3 |
|     Paviours' labourers | 2612 | 60·5 |
|     Sweepers and scavengers (able-bodied) | 20,228 | 58·9 |
|     Yardmen and general labourers | 10,361 | 59·4 |
|   County and rural district councils |  |  |
|     Road labourers | 13,208 | 41·8 |
| Gas supply | 9090 | 62·2 |
| Electric supply | 2413 | 63·5 |
| Water supply | 3211 | 59·6 |
| Tramway and omnibus services | 3428 | 65·6 |
| Pig iron manufacture | 2020 | 55·9 |
| Iron and steel | 3824 | 59·8 |
| Engineering and boilermaking |  |  |
|     time | 51,357 | 57·2 |
|     piece | 4473 | 69·1 |
| Ship- and boatbuilding and repairing | 12,534 | 54·4 |
| Railway carriage and wagon building |  |  |
|     time | 4262 | 52·2 |
|     piece | 4629 | 62·6 |
| Railways (1907): |  |  |
|     Porters (loading and traffic) | 23,906 | 50·1 |
|     Porters (goods) | 18,506 | 56·8 |
|     Engine cleaners | 9930 | 52·4 |
|     Carriage cleaners | 4478 | 52·6 |
|     Locomotive etc. labourers | 8518 | 56·5 |
|     Permanent way labourers | 27,197 | 56·3 |
| Paper manufacture | 1305 | 55·7 |
| Printing | 469 | 66·1 |
| Pottery | 459 | 56·8 |
| Bricks etc. | 1779 | 51·8 |
| Chemical manufacture | 4921 | 55·7 |
| Grain milling | 2010 | 50·3 |
| Brewery | 1033 | 59·1 |
| Cocoa, chocolate and sugar confectionery | 319 | 63·9 |
| Total | 306,487 | 56·45 (average) |

While the average for the above is £56 per year, the median for the groups (disregarding the numbers in each group) is between £57 and £58 and the unweighted average is £59. We may say that the 'representative rate' for unskilled men in 1906 lay between £55 and £60 per year, or between 94.5 and 103 per cent of the manual workers' average as shown in the Board of Trade earnings reports.

In 1924, we are much less well served with information. For many of the industries listed above we have no information about labourer's earnings. There are some for whom earnings information is available, however, and others for whom we shall have to depend on changes in standard rates. Thus we have:

TABLE 2.24  Earnings or rates for unskilled men (occupational class 7), 1906 and 1924

| | Weights | 1906 | 1924 | 1924 as % |
|---|---|---|---|---|
| | | £ per year | | of 1906 |
| Building labourers' standard rate[a] | 250 | 65 | 144 | 221·5 |
| Railway permanent way labourers[b] | 25 | 56 | 133 | 237·5 |
| Railway workshop labourers[b] | 14 | 57 | 147 | 258 |
| Railway platform porters[b] | 94 | 50 | 133 | 261 |
| Engineering labourers[c] | | | | |
| time | 170 | 57 | 116[d] | 203·5 |
| piece | 30 | 69 | 138[d] | 200 |
| Brewery labourers (London)[e] | 15 | 72 | 149 | 207 |
| Local authority labourers[f] | 30 | 58 | 138 | 238 |
| Weighted average[g] | 628 | 60 | 134 | 223 |
| Unweighted average | 8 | 60·5 | 137 | 226 |

[a] Average weekly rates in thirty-nine large towns.
[b] Average weekly earnings from *Railways ( Staff ) Return* (annual).
[c] October 1926, Employers' Federation census.
[d] 1926.
[e] 1924, Meux's Brewery.
[f] Average of rates in twenty-eight large towns.
[g] Weights: approximate numbers in 1921 in thousands.

The range of increases is from 100 per cent for engineering piece-workers to 161 per cent for platform porters. Applying the average increase of 123 per cent to the range of £55 to £60 for 1906, we get a range of £123 to £134 as likely to have included the mode in 1924.

Table 2.25 illustrates the relative positions in 1924, 1935, 1955 and 1960.

TABLE 2.25 Earnings or rates for unskilled men (occupational class 7), 1924, 1935, 1955 and 1960

| | 1924 | 1935 | | 1955 | | 1960 | |
|---|---|---|---|---|---|---|---|
| | £ | £ | % of 1924 | £ | % of 1935 | £ | % of 1955 |
| Building[a] | 144 | 131 | 91 | 419 | 320 | 496 | 118 |
| Railways[b] | | | | | | | |
| Civil eng. labourers and length-men | 133 | 135 | 101·5 | 478 | 355 | 720 | 150 |
| Shedmen | 147 | 146 | 99 | 452 | 309 | 616 | 136 |
| Signal and telegraph (1955 and 1960: handymen) | 158 | 145 | 92 | 509 | 351 | 707 | 139 |
| Marine and dock (1955 and 1960: porters) | 123 | 124 | 101 | 476 | 383 | 637 | 134 |
| Platform porters | 133 | 114 | 86 | 441 | 387 | 614 | 139 |
| London Transport stationmen/porters | 140 | 148 | 106 | ·· | ·· | 524 | ·· |
| Engineering[c] | | | | | | | |
| time | 116 | 144 | 124 | 499 | 347 | 620 | 124 |
| piece | 138 | 158 | 114 | 543 | 344 | 684 | 126 |
| Brewery labourers, London[d] | 149 | 162 | 109 | 447 | 276 | 583 | 130 |
| Local authorities[e] | 138 | 135 | 98 | 342 | 253 | 460 | 135 |
| Weighted averages | 134 | 136 | 101 | 458 | 337 | 565 | 123 |

[a] 1924 and 1935: average weekly rates in thirty-nine large towns. 1955: Grade A districts, 45¼ hours. 1960: from April, Grade A districts, forty-four hours.
[b] Earnings from *Railways (Staff) Return* or British Transport Commission *Annual Census of Staff*.
[c] From Employers' Federation censuses. 1935: 1938 average reduced by 8.1 per cent, i.e. difference in average shown in Ministry of Labour inquiries.
[d] 1924, Meux. Later years, Guinness.
[e] 1924 and 1935: average of rates in twenty-eight large towns. 1955 and 1960: Group I, weekly rates Zone A.

The calculations shown above indicate a pay level for unskilled men in 1960 9·3 times that of 1906 and we may now check this by drawing on other evidence.

Labourer's earnings in the Potteries increased 9·6 times; the basic rate for labourers in gas supply 8·0 times and in electricity supply (London) 8·6 times. Labourers other than those listed in Table 2.25 averaged £55 in 1906 and may be compared with a group of 589 employment exchange quotations for Camden Town, Birmingham and Manchester for 1957–60, which, if adjusted to take account of increases to the latter year, give an average of £469.

We may say, then, that the modal rate for unskilled men in 1960 is somewhere about nine times that for 1906.

Tables 2.25 and 2.24 give the ratios by which the unskilled average for 1906 must be raised to yield averages for the subsequent years:

| 1906 | 1924 | 1935 | 1955 | 1960 |
|------|------|------|------|------|
| £57·5 | £128 | £129 | £435 | £535 |

In the NES for 1970 we can find five groups of unskilled men, numbering 8511, with average earnings of £1154, which is 216 per cent of 1960.

In 1978, we find eight groups, but numbering only 3972, with average of £3390. This is 294 per cent of 1970.

### Women

In *Women's Work and Wages*,[103] the authors wrote: 'In the inquiry as to wages one of the outstanding facts elicited was, that whenever women had replaced men the former always received a much lower wage, and that this wage was not proportionate to the skill or intelligence required by the work but approximated to a certain fixed level—about 10s. to 12s. per week. The wage that the man previously received gave no criterion as to what the woman would get, though as a general statement approximately correct, we may say that a woman would get from one-third to one-half the wages of a man.'

The tendency to fix women's pay without particular regard to the skill or intelligence required makes it difficult to distinguish between the pay of occupational classes 5, 6 and 7 in 1906 and a greater variation appears between rates of pay of different women for the same job than between the averages for different jobs. The following are some examples of average earnings in unskilled work in 1906 (converted into annual rates):[104]

|  |  | £ |
|---|---|---|
| Rag sorters (paper manufacture): | time | 26 |
|  | piece | 28 |
| Rag cutters (paper manufacture): | time | 25 |
|  | piece | 26 |
| Folders (printing): | time | 31 |
|  | piece | 42 |
| Gummers (stationery manufacture): | time | 32 |
|  | piece | 28 |
| Soap and candle manufacture |  | 32 |
| Cleaners (borough and urban district councils) |  | 31 |

But in other industries, the 1906 reports do not distinguish unskilled occupations and sometimes give no occupational classification for women. The average for all women aged eighteen and over was £36 (annual rate) and for girls under eighteen, £20, so that the unskilled averages for the two age groups must have been somewhere below these. Cadbury et al.,[105] cite an average of 10s. per week for door-attendants aged eighteen and over; 7s. 9d. for charwomen, with a minimum of 1s. 6d. and a maximum of 2s. per day. The average earnings of firewood choppers were 9s. 10d., tin pressers 8s. 6d., mineral water bottlers 9s., laundry general workers 7s. 4d.

In August 1910, the Trade Board for the chain industry established a minimum rate of 2½d. per hour. The average normal week was 46·8 hours in 1906, for which the minimum pay in 1910 would then have been 9·7s.

In 1911, a Trade Board minimum of 2¾d. per hour was established for machine-made lace and net or 12·4s. for a 54-hour week. In 1912, 3d. per hour was laid down as a minimum for cardboard-box making. It would probably be safe to say, then, that the mode for unskilled women in 1906 would have been at an annual rate of about £26.

By the mid-twenties, the Trade Board minima had been raised to 6½d. or 7d. per hour: between 26s. and 28s. for a 48-hour week and the number of industries covered had been increased to forty-one. At an annual rate, this would represent between £67 and £73 per year. This matches the rate of £70 paid to charwomen in the Civil Service. The median remuneration of kitchen and scullery maids was shown in the Trade Board investigation of 1929 as somewhat higher: 35·5s. per week or £92 per year[106]

The earnings inquiry of 1924 did not distinguish women from girls and showed an average for females of £71. Applying the same women: females ratio as in 1935, one gets an amount of £81 as the approximate average for all grades of women's manual work. This would be higher than the average or mode for unskilled women, which would have been nearer to the Trade Board minimum of £67 and probably within the range of £70 to £75: about 2·8 times the level of 1906. From about 45 per cent of the manual average in 1906, they had risen to about 58 per cent of it in 1925.

Between the mid-1920s and the mid-1930s, there were some reductions in Trade Board minima and some increases, but in the main they were unchanged. The earnings inquiry of 1935, too, showed an average for females almost identical to that for 1924.

On 1 April 1955, the average of 105 minima laid down in wage regulation orders[107] was at an annual rate of £223. At 1 April 1956, it was £238, so that, by interpolation, the mid-1955 figure would have been £227.

The equivalent figure for mid-1960 was £283. This figure is almost identical to that yielded by the application of the occupational class proportions to the earnings distribution for manufacturing industry. Women in manufacturing industry in 1951 were divided as follows:

|  | Per cent |
|---|---|
| Occupational classes 4 and 5 | 41 |
| Occupational class 6 | 44 |
| Occupational class 7 | 15 |
| Total | 100 |

On this basis, median earnings would be at the annual rate of £510 for classes 4 and 5 combined, £373 for class 6 and £286 for class 7. The inter-period movements thus suggested are set out in Table 2.26 compared with those of the manual average and of the women's average.

TABLE 2.26 Average earnings of unskilled women workers compared with average for all women manual workers (selected industries)[a] and the manual average (selected industries)

|  | Unskilled women | Women's average[b] | Manual average |
|---|---|---|---|
| 1924 as % of 1906 | 280 | 225 | 213 |
| 1935 as % of 1924 | 100 | 101 | 101 |
| 1955 as % of 1935 | 310 | 363 | 391 |
| 1960 as % of 1955 | 125 | 126 | 127 |
| 1960 as % of 1906 | 1090 | 1044 | 1075 |

[a] Those listed in note 95.
[b] The women's constituent of the manual average.

We see here a suggestion of periods with contrasting characteristics: a first period where women's pay rises more than that of all workers and that of unskilled women more than that of all women; a third period where the reverse holds; and a second and fourth where pay at these three levels moves in step.

There are only three identifiable groups of unskilled women workers in the NES for 1970, the largest being 1006 unskilled workers not elsewhere specified. In 1978, we do not have even this degree of assurance that the sample is representative. There are only two groups, kitchen hands and other cleaners, numbering 837. Nearly 40 per cent of women manual workers are left unspecified in 1978, so that we do not know their level of skill.

For 1960, we found an average of £283. For 1970 this has increased to £610 (215 per cent of 1960), and for 1978, £2275 (373 per cent of 1970).

## 3. OCCUPATIONAL CLASS PAY STRUCTURE

Now at last we may assemble the class averages and get an overview of pay structure as it existed at the beginning and end of the sixty-five years of our study and at five periods in between. Table 2.27 presents numerous changes and failures-to-change that demand explanation[108] In the next chapter we shall track down the time and circumstances of these events and non-events as a means to identifying their causes, and in Chapter 4 we shall try to interpret them.

We are not short of phenomena to challenge our explanatory skill. Over the whole period, money incomes, according to the table, have risen by a factor of 50. Over the same period, retail prices have risen by a factor of 17 or 18, so that average pay in 1978 had about three times the purchasing power of average pay in 1913 or 1914. Is that much or little? In 1913, Great Britain was second in affluence only to the United States; in 1978, real earned income per worker employed was three times as great, so that when we look back today it is at a very different country. But the growth of wealth has been interrupted by two great wars and periods of economic decline or stagnation, so that the compound rate of growth in real income per head has been only a litte over 1·7 per cent per year. If it had not been for these disturbances and we had maintained a steady growth in output per person employed of 3 per cent a year, real income per head in 1978 would have been 6·8 times as much as in 1913.

### (A) EFFECT OF CHANGES IN CLASS PROPORTIONS

Part of the increase in average pay has been due to a shift in numbers from lower- to higher-paid classes: this is measured by the difference between the current-weighted and 1911-weighted averages. In the first period, changes in class proportions accounted for 1·6 per cent (3

TABLE 2.27 Average earnings, seven occupational classes, various years, 1913–14 to 1978

| | 1913–14 £ | 1922–4 £ | % of 1913–14 | 1935–6 £ | % of 1922–4 | 1955–6 £ | % of 1935–6 | 1960 £ | % of 1955–6 | 1970 £ | % of 1960 | 1978 £ | % of 1970 | Multiple of 1913–14 |
|---|---|---|---|---|---|---|---|---|---|---|---|---|---|---|
| **Men** | | | | | | | | | | | | | | |
| 1. Professional | | | | | | | | | | | | | | |
| A. Higher | 328 | 582 | 177 | 634 | 109 | 1541 | 243 | 2034 | 132 | 2928 | 144 | 8286 | 283 | 26 |
| B. Lower | 155 | 320 | 206 | 308 | 96 | 610 | 198 | 847 | 139 | 1885 | 223 | 5435 | 288 | 35 |
| 2B. Managers etc. | 200 | 480 | 240 | 440 | 92 | 1480 | 336 | 1850 | 125 | 3400 | 184 | 8050 | 237 | 40 |
| 3. Clerks | 99 | 182 | 184 | 192 | 105 | 523 | 272 | 682 | 130 | 1337 | 196 | 3701 | 277 | 37 |
| 4. Foremen | 123 | 268 | 218 | 273 | 102 | 784 | 287 | 1015 | 129 | 1669 | 164 | 4685 | 280 | 38 |
| Manual | | | | | | | | | | | | | | |
| 5. Skilled | 106 | 180 | 171 | 195 | 108 | 622 | 319 | 796 | 128 | 1440 | 181 | 4354 | 302 | 41 |
| 6. Semi-skilled | 69 | 126 | 183 | 134 | 106 | 469 | 350 | 581 | 124 | 1289 | 222 | 3827 | 297 | 55 |
| 7. Unskilled | 63 | 128 | 203 | 129 | 101 | 435 | 337 | 535 | 123 | 1154 | 216 | 3390 | 294 | 54 |
| Averages | | | | | | | | | | | | | | |
| Current weights[a] | 94 | 180 | 191 | 186 | 104 | 634 | 340 | 848[d] | 134 | 1707 | 201 | 4786 | 280 | 51 |
| 1911 weights | 94 | 177 | 188 | 185 | 104 | 590 | 319 | 746 | 126 | 1445 | 194 | 4241 | 293 | 45 |
| **Women** | | | | | | | | | | | | | | |
| 1. Professional | | | | | | | | | | | | | | |
| A. Higher | .. | .. | .. | .. | .. | (1156) | .. | (1525) | (132) | 2460 | 161 | 6712 | 273 | .. |
| B. Lower | 89 | 214 | 240 | 211 | 99 | 438 | 208 | 606 | 138 | 1224 | 202 | 3892 | 318 | 44 |
| 2B. Managers etc. | (80)[b] | 160 | .. | (168) | 105 | 800 | (524) | 1000 | 125 | 1870 | 187 | 5070 | 271 | 63 |
| 3. Clerks | 45 | 106 | 235 | 99 | 93 | 317 | 320 | 427 | 135 | 839 | 196 | 2730 | 325 | 61 |
| 4. Forewomen | 57 | 154 | 270 | 156 | 101 | 477 | 306 | 602 | 126 | 1014 | 168 | 3214 | 317 | 56 |

| | | | | | | | | | | | | | |
|---|---|---|---|---|---|---|---|---|---|---|---|---|---|
| **Manual** | | | | | | | | | | | | | |
| 5. Skilled | 44 | 87 | 198 | 86 | 99 | 317 | 369 | 395 | 125 | 677 | 171 | 2246 | 332 | 51 |
| 6. Semi-skilled | 50 | 98 | 196 | 100 | 102 | 269 | 270 | 339 | 126 | 645 | 190 | 2356 | 365 | 47 |
| 7. Unskilled | 28 | 73 | 261 | 73 | 100 | 227 | 280 | 283 | 125 | 610 | 215 | 2275 | 373 | 81 |
| **Averages** | | | | | | | | | | | | | |
| Current weights[a] | 50 | 103 | 204 | 104 | 101 | 319 | 307 | 417[d] | 131 | 824 | 198 | 2691 | 327 | 54 |
| 1911 weights | 50 | 103 | 205 | 104 | 101 | 307 | 295 | 402 | 131 | 731 | 182 | 2516 | 344 | 50 |
| **Men and Women** | | | | | | | | | | | | | |
| Current weighted av.[c] | 81 | 157 | 194 | 162 | 103 | 531 | 328 | 704 | 133 | 1385 | 197 | 3961 | 286 | 49 |

[a] According to number of men and women in relevant class in nearest population census year.

[b] Included in weighted average. Their exclusion lowers the average fractionally.

[c] According to proportions in occupational classes in nearest census year until 1935–6; thereafter, proportion in total labour force.

[d] Weights from G. S. Bain and R. Price, 'Union Growth and Employment Trends in the United Kingdom', *British Journal of Industrial Relations*, vol. 10, no. 3, pp. 368–9.

percentage points) of the men's rise; in the second, they had no effect; but between the mid-1920s and mid-1950s, 6.6 per cent of the rise was accounted for by the class shifts; an almost equal amount (6·3 per cent) between 1955–6 and 1960. But be it noted that the weights used for calculating the current weighted averages are those in the nearest population census year. For 1955–6, 1951 weights have been used; for 1960, weights from the census of 1961.

Between 1960 and 1970, the gap rises by another 3·6 per cent, so that the men's current-weighted average is 18 per cent higher than the 1911-weighted average. Then it appears to go into reverse, but this is because 1971 weights are used for both 1970 and 1978 at a time when the lower-paid classes did exceptionally well. In fact, the NES suggests a substantial rise in the numbers in classes 1 to 3, and a substantial fall in the numbers in classes 4 to 7:

|  | *Percentages* | | |
|  | *NES 1970* | *Census 1971* | *NES 1978* |
|---|---|---|---|
| Classes 1 to 3 (men) | 27 | 29 | 38 |
| Classes 4 to 7 (men) | 73 | 71 | 62 |

Of course, the NES does not include employers and self-employed, but their numbers are comparatively small and their spread over the two groups fairly even, so their inclusion, if we knew the numbers, would not make very much difference. We can, thus, make a calculation for 1978 to take account for the shift in proportions between the two groups. The average for classes 1 to 3 in Table 2.27 is £6565; for classes 4 to 7 it is £4043. When combined in the proportions shown in the NES for 1978, the overall average becomes £5001. This would restore the difference between the current weighted and 1911-weighted and men's average to the 18 per cent of 1970.

For women, changes of occupational class make little difference until 1955, when the advantage for the current-weighted average is 4 per cent. It remains at about that level in 1960, but by 1970 has risen to nearly 13 per cent. In 1978 (with 1971 weights) it is down to 7 per cent. But if we use the NES divisions for 1978 between classes 1 to 3 and 4 to 7, the 1978 average is raised to £2863, and the gap between the current-weighted and fix-weighted averages becomes 14 per cent, slightly higher than in 1970.[109]

(B) MEN'S AND WOMEN'S AVERAGES

Over the whole span, women have done better than men in every class except that of semi-skilled manual workers (occupational class 6), whose moderate pay increase and large numbers (accounting for nearly 33 per cent of the women in 1971) have combined to hold down the women's overall average compared to that of the men. The data is set out in Table 2.28.

The women's average moved up in the first period, the women in each class (except the managers and administrators) gaining on the men. Then inter-class movements worked against the women. Their currently-weighted average fell until, in 1955–6, it was lower than it had been in 1913, and by 1960 it had lost another percentage point. This was because of shifts between classes, that brought the current-weighted average down, while the constant-weighted average rose.

TABLE 2.28 Women's as a percentage of men's averages

|  |  | 1913–4 | 1922–4 | 1935–6 | 1955–6 | 1960 | 1970 | 1978 |
|---|---|---|---|---|---|---|---|---|
| 1A. | Higher professional | . . | . . | . . | (75) | (75) | 84 | 81 |
| 1B. | Lower professional | 57 | 67 | 69 | 72 | 72 | 65 | 72 |
| 2B. | Managers and administrators | (40) | 33 | 38 | 54 | 54 | 55 | 63 |
| 3. | Clerks | 42 | 46 | 46 | 57 | 61 | 63 | 74 |
| 4. | Foremen | 46 | 57 | 57 | 61 | 59 | 61 | 69 |
| 5. | Skilled manual | 42 | 48 | 44 | 51 | 50 | 47 | 52 |
| 6. | Semi-skilled manual | 72 | 78 | 75 | 57 | 58 | 50 | 62 |
| 7. | Unskilled manual | 44 | 57 | 57 | 52 | 53 | 53 | 67 |
| All (current weights) | | 53 | 57 | 56 | 50 | 54 | 48 | 56 |
| All (1911 weights) | | 53 | 58 | 56 | 52 | 54 | 51 | 59 |
| Unweighted average | | 49 | 55 | 55 | 58 | 58 | 60 | 67·5 |

The women clerks have shown the greatest relative improvement, though in every class women have advanced except amongst the semi-skilled. The unweighted average shows periods of advance interspersed with periods of stability; six percentage points over the First World War, three over the second. Then in 1970, the Equal Pay Act was passed, requiring the application of equal pay for men and women doing the same or broadly similar work in a series of steps to be completed by 1975 and this, it seems clear, achieved what the long-expressed sentiments of the trade unions had been unable to do.

(C) INTER-CLASS PAY STRUCTURE

In Table 2.29, class averages have been converted into percentages of the average for all classes. Thus we eliminate the confusing effect of measuring in money of inconstant value, and express the movements in the simplified form of 'pay units'. The average for each class is then shown as a percentage of the average for men and women of all classes. The all-class average becomes the unit of account, in which the earnings for each class are then expressed.

TABLE 2.29 Occupational class averages as percentages of the mean for all occupational classes, men and women (pounds)

| | | 1913–14 | 1922–4 | 1935–6 | 1955–6 | 1960 | 1970 | 1978 | Multiple of 1913–14 |
|---|---|---|---|---|---|---|---|---|---|
| **Men** | | | | | | | | | |
| 1. | Professional | | | | | | | | |
| | A. Higher | 405 | 372 | 392 | 290 | 289 | 211 | 209 | 0·5 |
| | B. Lower | 191 | 204 | 190 | 115 | 120 | 136 | 137 | 0·7 |
| 2B. | Managers etc. | 247 | 307 | 272 | 279 | 263 | 245 | 203 | 0·8 |
| 3. | Clerks | 122 | 116 | 119 | 98 | 97 | 97 | 93 | 0·8 |
| 4. | Foremen | 152 | 171 | 169 | 148 | 144 | 121 | 118 | 0·8 |
| | Manual | | | | | | | | |
| 5. | Skilled | 131 | 115 | 121 | 117 | 113 | 104 | 110 | 0·8 |
| 6. | Semi-skilled | 85 | 80 | 83 | 88 | 83 | 93 | 97 | 1·1 |
| 7. | Unskilled | 78 | 82 | 80 | 82 | 76 | 83 | 86 | 1·1 |
| Men's average (current weights) | | 116 | 114 | 115 | 119 | 120 | 123 | 121 | 1·0 |
| % mean deviation | | 68 | 73 | 70 | 48 | 47 | 35 | 30 | |
| **Women** | | | | | | | | | |
| 1. | Professional | | | | | | | | |
| | A. Higher | ·· | ·· | ·· | (218) | (217) | 178 | 169 | ·· |
| | B. Lower | 110 | 137 | 130 | 82 | 86 | 88 | 98 | 0·9 |
| 2B. | Managers etc. | 99 | 102 | 104 | 151 | 142 | 135 | 128 | 1·3 |
| 3. | Clerks | 56 | 68 | 61 | 60 | 61 | 61 | 69 | 1·2 |
| 4. | Forewomen | 70 | 98 | 96 | 90 | 86 | 73 | 81 | 1·2 |
| | Manual | | | | | | | | |
| 5. | Skilled | 54 | 56 | 53 | 60 | 56 | 49 | 57 | 1·1 |
| 6. | Semi-skilled | 62 | 63 | 62 | 51 | 48 | 47 | 59 | 1·0 |
| 7. | Unskilled | 35 | 47 | 45 | 43 | 40 | 44 | 57 | 1·6 |
| Women's average (current weights)[a] | | 62 | 66 | 64 | 60 | 59 | 59 | 68 | 1·1 |
| % mean deviation | | 31 | 37 | 38 | 67 | 67 | 59 | 43 | |

[a] The exclusion of higher professional women in 1955–6 lowers the women's average to 58 and the mean deviation to 43.

The last column of Table 2.29 gives the score for each class over the whole period. This ranks the classes as follows:

|  | Multiple of 1913–14 |
| --- | --- |
| Unskilled (W) | 1·6 |
| Managers (W) | 1·3 |
| Clerks (W) | 1·2 |
| Forewomen | 1·2 |
| Skilled (W) | 1·1 |
| Semi-skilled (M) | 1·1 |
| Unskilled (M) | 1·1 |
| Semi-skilled (W) | 1·0 |
| Lower professional (W) | 0·9 |
| Managers (M) | 0·8 |
| Clerks (M) | 0·8 |
| Foremen | 0·8 |
| Skilled (M) | 0·7 |
| Lower professional (M) | 0·7 |
| Higher professional (M) | 0·5 |

Semi-skilled women have barely retained their place in the hierarchy; unskilled women have done a lot better than the average, though they still remain at the bottom of the pile. Women managers have done so well that they have changed their rank order for level of pay from eighth to fourth. Is there a law of increases that says 'Women shall get more than men', or a law that says 'The poor shall get more than the rich'? As already noted, women have in general done better than men, but on the other hand, low-paid men have done better than higher-paid men.

But Figure 2.1 shows that these results were not achieved by a direct path. There have been many ups and downs with advantages gained and lost, but overall an edging-up by the lower-paid or less-skilled and a more marked edging down by the higher-paid and more skilled.

Of course it is not only the relative pay of each class that makes the difference: it is also the changes of numbers in each class. If there is a flow of numbers from lower to higher classes, this in itself will serve to raise the weighted average, which will cause the pay of each class, relative to the average, to fall. If, in addition, average pay is raised by the lower classes getting proportionately higher increases in pay, then the relative pay of the higher classes will fall all the more.

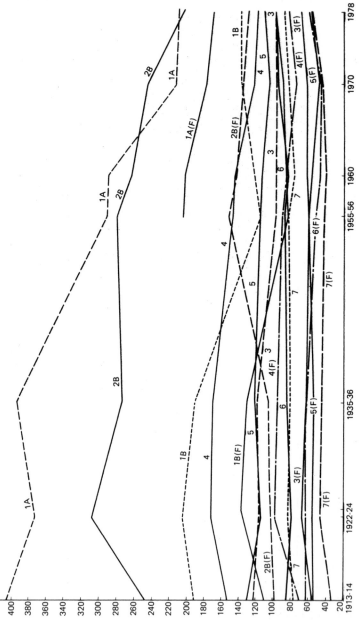

FIGURE 2.1 Occupational class averages as percentages of the mean for all occupational classes, men and women

In Table 2.30 class averages for men are expressed in terms not of the weighted average for all classes and both sexes, but as percentages of the simple average for men only. We eliminate the effects of changes in relative class numbers and focus on the changed fortunes of each class as such. The average for all men = 100 and the average for each class is expressed as a percentage of that.

TABLE 2.30 Average pay for each men's occupational class expressed as a percentage of the simple average for all men

| Class | 1913–14 | 1922–4 | 1935–6 | 1955–6 | 1960 | 1970 | 1978 |
|---|---|---|---|---|---|---|---|
| 1A | 230 | 206 | 220 | 191 | 195 | 155 | 159 |
| 1B | 109 | 113 | 107 | 75 | 81 | 100 | 104 |
| 2B | 140 | 169 | 153 | 183 | 177 | 180 | 154 |
| 3 | 69 | 64 | 67 | 65 | 65 | 71 | 71 |
| 4 | 86 | 95 | 95 | 97 | 97 | 88 | 90 |
| 5 | 74 | 64 | 68 | 77 | 76 | 76 | 83 |
| 6 | 48 | 44 | 46 | 58 | 56 | 68 | 73 |
| 7 | 44 | 45 | 45 | 54 | 51 | 61 | 65 |
| All | 100 | 100 | 100 | 100 | 100 | 100 | 100 |
| Average £ | 142·8 | 283·2 | 288·1 | 808·0 | 1042·5 | 1887·7 | 5216·0 |
| % mean deviation | 45 | 47 | 45 | 43·5 | 43·5 | 34 | 29 |

## (D) DIFFERENTIALS BETWEEN COMPLEMENTARY OCCUPATIONS

The above analysis deals with changes between great occupational classes, whose averages are themselves the results of movements in the pay of many occupations. We may get the changes into sharper focus by comparing the pay of particular occupations that are complementary to one another in the production process.

The fall in differentials between skilled and unskilled workers has been often remarked. In engineering, time-working fitters and turners in 1906 were earning 58 per cent more than time-working engineering labourers; in 1970, the difference was down to 39 per cent. Between June 1970 and June 1978, there was a further reduction from 39 to 28 per cent. The reduction in the differential itself was 43 per cent in the sixty-four years from 1906 to 1970 and 28 per cent in the eight years from 1970 to 1978.[110] The decline of differential between bricklayers and building labourers has been even more pronounced: from 50 per cent in 1906 to

13 per cent in 1978.[111] And on the railways a great fall that, after 1970, is mildly reversed:[112]

| | 1906 | | 1960 | | 1970 | | 1978 | |
|---|---|---|---|---|---|---|---|---|
| | £ | % | £ | % | £ | % | £ | % |
| Engine drivers | 119 | 238 | 863 | 141 | 32·35 | 128 | 98·49 | 135 |
| Ticket collectors | 64 | 128 | 680 | 111 | | | | |
| Senior railmen | | | | | 29·14 | 115 | 89·52 | 122 |
| Porters | 50 | 100 | 614 | 100 | | | | |
| Railmen | | | | | 25·31 | 100 | 73·08 | 100 |

As between the classes (Table 2.29 and Figure 2.2), so between these occupations, there has been no consistent movement. Between 1906 and 1924, the engineering differential fell from 72 to 35 per cent. In the next ten years it grew to 47 per cent; by 1955, it was down to 30 per cent; by 1960, up to 34; by 1970, to 39; by 1978, down to 28. For the building industry the changes are similar, though the rise in differentials between 1924 and 1935 was only 1 percentage point. But between 1955 and 1960 it was more considerable: from 21 to 36 per cent; then down to 1970, contrasting with the upward movement in engineering, so that it returned to the position of 1955, and down again to the 13 per cent of 1978.

Most of the semi-skilled men's occupations fit into the same pattern, but the large numbers in agriculture and retail distribution have followed a rhythm of their own:

| | 1924 as % of 1913 | 1935 as % of 1924 | 1955 as % of 1935 | 1960 as % of 1955 | 1970 as % of 1960 | 1978 as % of 1970 |
|---|---|---|---|---|---|---|
| Agricultural labourers | 171 | 109 | 475 | 121 | 179 | 326 |
| Shop-assistants | 145 | 94 | 345 | 125 | 232[a] | 301[a] |
| Other semi-skilled | 216 | 106 | 317 | 124 | 197 | 298 |
| Unskilled | 223 | 101 | 337 | 123 | 216 | 294 |
| Skilled | 188 | 108 | 319 | 129 | 181 | 302 |

[a] Including roundsmen.

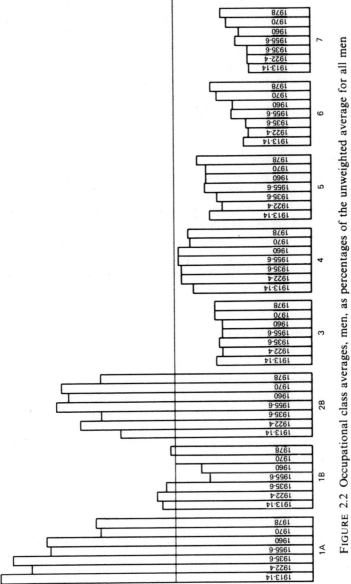

FIGURE 2.2 Occupational class averages, men, as percentages of the unweighted average for all men

Agricultural labourers were the lowest-paid male occupation in 1913; despite this, their relative position had still further deteriorated by 1924. Their atypical pattern continued to 1935, when they registered an increase even larger than that of skilled men. In the next period, too, their rise was extraordinarily high. Then, between 1955 and 1970, they lost ground, then forged ahead between 1970 and 1978. Over the whole span of our study, their earnings increased by a factor of 62·2, more than those of any group except the unskilled women and women managers.

Shop-assistants' pay sagged until 1935. Then they made a come-back, after which they held their own or gained a little ground. Over the whole period their earnings increased by a factor of 41, better than the male clerks, the same as the skilled men, but a good deal worse than the other inhabitants of class 6.

The women's groups did not conform to the patterns set by the men. In period 1 the unskilled women did much better than the others; in the second period the three manual groups moved almost in unison; in the third period, the skilled did much better than the other two and for the first time their earnings overtook and passed those of the semi-skilled; in the fourth they moved again almost in unison; in the last two periods, the skilled lagged while the semi-skilled and unskilled moved strongly ahead, both overtaking the skilled in average earnings.

## 4. END OF CHAPTER

The New Earnings Survey of April 1979 marks the end of a chapter in the development of pay structure. On 3 May, the change of government brought an end to the incomes policies that had been a feature of the seventies, so that subsequent settlements will be free of the associated constraints.

Table 2.31 summarises the changes in pay structure registered by the NES between 1978 and 1979. The method of construction is the same as that used above for measuring changes between 1970 and 1978. In such a short time-span, it is essential to match identical occupations in each group, and this has been done. Even so, the results are subject to random effects, like the date of pay settlements for large groups that may be applied after the April census, but with retrospective effect.

The money averages are not the same as those shown in Table 2.27, for reasons that have already been explained, but the percentage changes may be applied to the averages there shown to project them from 1978 to 1979.

Table 2.31 shows the continuation of the relative decline in the pay of non-manual workers. The NES shows average increases of 14 per cent for both men and women, but manual-working men have done better than this, with increases of 18 or 19 per cent extending up the hierarchy as far as foremen. Manual-working women have not done so well, which lends support to the fear that the effect on their earnings of the equal pay and equal opportunity acts may have been spent.

Amongst the non-manual workers, the increase for men and women clerks has been just about at the average, while for the higher grades women have done better then men, but all have lagged behind the manual workers. In the higher professions, women appear to have done well, but their average is based on only 205 returns in 4 occupations, with standard errors of 4.4 per cent of the average, so that the favourable trend is a suggestion rather than a conclusion.

TABLE 2.31 Occupational class averages, 1978 and 1979

|  |  |  | 1978 £ | 1979 £ | 1979 % of 1978 |
|---|---|---|---|---|---|
| 1A. | Higher professions | M | 5948 | 6658 | 112 |
|  |  | F | (4830) | (5548) | (115) |
| 1B. | Lower professions | M | 5170 | 5637 | 109 |
|  |  | F | 3736 | 4119 | 110 |
| 2B. | Managers, etc. | M | 5996 | 6796 | 113 |
|  |  | F | 3768 | 4309 | 114 |
| 3. | Clerks | M | 3701 | 4229 | 114 |
|  |  | F | 2730 | 3072 | 113 |
| 4. | Foremen/women, etc. | M | 4685 | 5526 | 118 |
|  |  | F | 3214 | 3590 | 112 |
| *Manual workers* |  |  |  |  |  |
| 5. | Skilled | M | 4354 | 5197 | 119 |
|  |  | F | 2246 | 2619 | 117 |
| 6. | Semi-skilled | M | 3827 | 4520 | 118 |
|  |  | F | 2356 | 2699 | 115 |
| 7. | Unskilled | M | 3390 | 4035 | 119 |
|  |  | F | (2275) | (2507) | 110 |
| All |  | M | 4633 | 5273 | 114 |
|  |  | F | 2881 | 3276 | 114 |

*Source*: NES occupational tables. (Employees only, April each year.)

The poor showing of the lower professions results from the rise of only 9 per cent recorded for draughtsmen and technicians (9·6 per cent for women), but more particularly from the 6 per cent rise in the teachers' average, due to the fact that their annual settlement had not yet been put into effect.

The managers have again been outstripped by those they manage, but they have at least kept pace with the clerks and done no worse than the higher professions.

What were the forces generating and restraining the changes that we have observed? The next task will be to track the course of change between the staging-posts we have so far observed in an attempt to identify the causal factors that were at work.

# 3 The Time and Circumstances of Pay Changes

We have now reconstructed the national pay and occupational structure for various years between 1906 and 1978, but this tells us nothing of the functional relation between changes in numbers and changes in pay. A rise or fall in the numbers in any occupation may go along with a rise or fall in its relative pay, perhaps because their causal factors are not connected or, in traditional economic terms, because both the demand and supply schedules may have changed, thus changing the shape or position of the curves that depict them. We have a series of snapshots for each class and its principal occupations showing pay and employment in various years; but to interpret the changes (or failures to change) we need a moving picture of the years between in which we can glimpse in action the forces whose conflicts have determined the course of events.

For the testing of the standard theory, two variables are of peculiar relevance: the levels of unemployment generally and in any occupation, and the rate and direction of price changes. The first is the best indicator we have of the strength of demand and supply, though for more recent years we can reinforce unemployment data with information about unfilled vacancies; the second is important because price changes throw on to the institutions of the labour market (firms, groups of workers, employers' associations, local or national government) the task of adjusting money contracts to give expression to the real relationships that underlie them. The varying speeds at which these institutions work may themselves cause changes in pay structure.

As a starting-point, we set out in Table 3.1 percentage unemployment and indices showing the movements in average wage rates and the cost of living between 1906 and 1978. Their changing relations are shown in Figure 3.1, a silhouette of the British economy indicating the price of labour, the price of goods and services and the demand for labour over the years.

TABLE 3.1 Indices of wage rates and the cost of living (average for 1906–10 = 100) and percentage unemployment (trade unions, 1906–23; insured workers, 1925–47; all workers, 1948–78), United Kingdom

| | 1906 | 1907 | 1908 | 1909 | 1910 | 1911 | 1912 | 1913 | 1914 | 1915 |
|---|---|---|---|---|---|---|---|---|---|---|
| Wage rates | 97 | 103 | 100 | 99 | 100 | 101 | 104 | 106 | 106 | 111–17 |
| Cost of living | 98 | 102 | 98 | 99 | 102 | 103 | 106 | 108 | 106 | 131 |
| Unemployment | 3·6 | 3·7 | 7·8 | 7·7 | 4·7 | 3·0 | 3·2 | 2·1 | 3·3 | 1·1 |

| | 1916 | 1917 | 1918 | 1919 | 1920 | 1921 | 1922 | 1923 | 1924 | 1925 |
|---|---|---|---|---|---|---|---|---|---|---|
| Wage rates | 122–7 | 143–8 | 185–191 | 223–8 | $\left\{\begin{array}{c}276\\314\end{array}\right.$ | 307 | 226 | 208 | 211 | 212 |
| Cost of living | 155 | 187 | 216 | 230 | 266 | 241 | 194 | 184 | 185 $\left\{\begin{array}{c}8·1\\10·2\end{array}\right.$ | 186 |
| Unemployment | 0·4 | 0·7 | 0·8 | 2·4 | 2·4 | 16·6 | 14·1 | 11·6 | | 11·0 |

| | 1926 | 1927 | 1928 | 1929 | 1930 | 1931 | 1932 | 1933 | 1934 | 1935 | 1936 |
|---|---|---|---|---|---|---|---|---|---|---|---|
| Wage rates | 211 | 210 | 207 | 206 | 205 | 203 | 198 | 196 | 196 | 199 | 203 |
| Cost of living | 182 | 177 | 175 | 173 | 167 | 156 | 152 | 148 | 149 | 153 | 156 |
| Unemployment | 12·3 | 9·6 | 10·7 | 10·3 | 15·8 | 21·1 | 21·9 | 19·8 | 16·6 | 15·3 | 11·9 |

| | 1937 | 1938 | 1939 | 1940 | 1941 | 1942 | 1943 | 1944 | 1945 | 1946 | 1947 |
|---|---|---|---|---|---|---|---|---|---|---|---|
| Wage rates | 210 | 218 | 218 | 245 | 264 | 288 | 300 | 313 | 327 | 353 | 365 |
| Cost of living | 164 | 166 | 170 | 198 | 216 | 231 | 237 | 242 | 245 | 249 | 266 |
| Unemployment | 10·6 | 11·1 | 8·2 | 4·4 | 1·3 | 0·6 | 0·4 | 0·4 | 0·8 | 2·5 | 1·7 |

| | 1948 | 1949 | 1950 | 1951 | 1952 | 1953 | 1954 | 1955 | 1956 | 1957 | 1958 |
|---|---|---|---|---|---|---|---|---|---|---|---|
| Wage rates | 387 | 398 | 401 | 434 | 471 | 493 | 518 | 555 | 599 | 633 | 645 |
| Cost of living | 287 | 295 | 305 | 333 | 362 | 373 | 381 | 397 | 417 | 432 | 445 |
| Unemployment | 1·4 | 1·5 | 1·5 | 1·2 | 2·0 | 1·6 | 1·3 | 1·1 | 1·2 | 1·4 | 2·1 |

| | 1959 | 1960 | 1961 | 1962 | 1963 | 1964 | 1965 | 1966 | 1967 | 1968 | 1969 |
|---|---|---|---|---|---|---|---|---|---|---|---|
| Wage rates | 666 | 684 | 712 | 739 | 765 | 801 | 836 | 875 | 908 | 968 | 1019 |
| Cost of living | 449 | 454 | 470 | 489 | 499 | 516 | 540 | 561 | 575 | 603 | 636 |
| Unemployment | 2·2 | 1·6 | 2·1 | 2·6 | 1·7 | 1·5 | 1·6 | 2·5 | 2·5 | 2·5 | 2·6 |

| | 1970 | 1971 | 1972 | 1973 | 1974 | 1975 | 1976 | 1977 | 1978 |
|---|---|---|---|---|---|---|---|---|---|
| Wage rates | 1121 | 1266 | 1441 | 1639 | 1963 | 2542 | 3033 | 3233 | 3687 |
| Cost of living | 676 | 740 | 793 | 865 | 1004 | 1247 | 1454 | 1684 | 1824 |
| Unemployment | 2·6 | 3·5 | 3·9 | 2·7 | 2·6 | 4·2 | 5·7 | 6·2 | 6·2 |

*Sources:* Unemployment: *Abstract of Labour Statistics of the United Kingdom* (London: HMSO, 1926 and 1937); *Ministry of Labour Gazette. Wages rates and cost of living, 1906–14:* A. L. Bowley, *Wages and Income in the United Kingdom since 1860,* p. 6, col. 1; 1914–20: Bowley, *Prices and Wages in the United Kingdom, 1914–1920, Economic and Social History of the World War,* British Series (Oxford: Clarendon Press, 1921), p. 106 (July each year); 1920–60: Ministry of Labour index of weekly wage rates (annual averages) and index of retail prices, *London and Cambridge Economic Bulletin.* 1961–78: *Department of Employment Gazette* or *Year Book of Labour Statistics.*

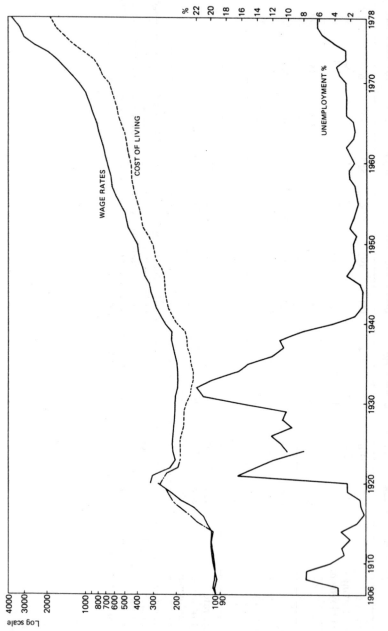

FIGURE 3.1 Indices of wage rates and cost of living (average 1906–10 = 100) and percentage unemployment, 1906–78

We have economic experiences of contrasting type against which to test the theories and to seek better ones: first, a period of fluctuating unemployment where prices and wage rates move gently together; then six years to 1920 in which wages multiply by a factor of 2·8 and prices of 2·5; then a precipitous fall in each, with high unemployment, the beginning of fifteen years of stable wage rates, high unemployment and prices that drift down until the depths of the depression in 1933. From 1939, there follows a period of about thirty years typified by full employment and a steady rise in wage rates and prices, sometimes converging so that real wage rates fall, but generally diverging so that they rise. The final movement is *allegro con brio*: ten years from 1968 in which wage rates and prices more than triple and in which unemployment begins at 2·5 and ends at 6·2 per cent.

## 1.  1906 TO 1924

A period of gently rising prices and wage rates is followed by one of mobilisation for war. A post-war boom is followed by a sharp decline with heavy unemployment and, after 1923, partial recovery. The final outcome, as we saw in Tables 2.29 and 2.30, was a radical improvement in the relative pay of the unskilled, though there was no general tendency for lower-paid classes to do better than the higher paid. Skilled and semi-skilled men on average did no better than clerks and higher professionals and considerably worse than foremen, managers and lower professionals. The pattern amongst the women was similar, except that female clerks did particularly well.

Prices rose with great rapidity on the outbreak of war and continued their rise until November 1920, so that considerable revisions in pay were required. By 8 August 1914, four days after the declaration of war, the cost of living index had risen by 15 per cent and, though there was an immediate fall from this level, by 1 January 1915 the rise was 18 per cent. Year-to-year increases were then as follows:

|  |  | *Per cent* |
|---|---|---|
| Year ended 1 January | 1916 | 23 |
|  | 1917 | 29 |
|  | 1918 | 10 |
|  | 1919 | 11 |
|  | 1920 | 3 |
| 10 months to 1 November | 1920 | 23 |

Bowley has given a detailed account of wage movements between 1914 and 1920.[1] Earlier in 1914, a wage offensive was being mounted by the trade unions; on the outbreak of war, their programmes were postponed and outstanding disputes settled. In the next six months or so, wages in many industries remained unchanged; in others, increases seldom exceeded 10 per cent. But a general move for higher rates became evident about the middle of 1915. 'The patriotic efforts of men to work their best, irrespective of wage questions and without much notice of the rise of prices . . . showed signs of diminution. The demand for labour was acute and there was no difficulty in obtaining moderate increases.'[2]

In the next phase, standard rates rose rapidly, the form of the rise varying from case to case.[3] The net effect was generally a narrowing of differentials between kindred manual occupations. Thus in 1920, the bricklayer's rate was 235 per cent of that of 1914, his labourer's 300 per cent. The engineering craftsman's rate was 231 per cent of 1914, the engineering labourer's 309 per cent.

Standard rates lagged behind prices until 1920, but earnings probably caught up sooner. Thus in July 1920, when Bowley estimated standard time- or piece-rates at 260 per cent of July 1914, returns furnished to the Ministry of Labour showed that earnings averaged 275 per cent of 1914.

How did salaries behave in this period of high demand for labour and rapidly rising prices? After 1913/14, the Commissioners of Inland Revenue no longer gave a frequency distribution for tax-paying employees in different income ranges.

Changes in total salaries liable to tax (between years with the same lower limit) are due either to an expansion of employment, a rise in pay for employees who had previously been below the limit and are now over it, or to increases in pay for those already paying tax. It is the extent of the latter that we must try to measure.

The Inland Revenue reports tell us how many Schedule E tax-payers there were in each year except 1915/16, 1916/17 and 1917/18.[4] We can fill in these years by a calculation based on total abatements.[5] Despite the downward extension of the lower limit, no increase in total salaries was registered between 1914/15 and 1915/16 for corporation and public company officials, due, no doubt, to the large number of enlistments. Between then and 1920/1, the total salary bill for this group (for employees at more than £130) rose 263 per cent. For all Schedule E income, the rise was 230 per cent.

This, of course, is much more than the increase per head, given by dividing total income by total numbers, that amounted to only 35 per cent. But the 35 per cent understates the rise for any member of the group because, when incomes are rising, there is an annual influx of those who, the year before, were below the exemption level. We may place an upper limit on the percentage increase per head by assuming that all the additional tax-payers each year were receiving only £131 and calculating what the average salary of the remainder would then be. The results of this calculation are shown in Table 3.2.

TABLE 3.2  Estimated increase in the average salary of Schedule E tax-payers with new arrivals excluded each year, 1915/16 to 1920/1

|         | Last year's average | This year's average | Per cent increase | Cumulative per cent increase |
|---------|---------------------|---------------------|-------------------|------------------------------|
| 1916/17 | 209                 | 226                 | 8·1               | 8·1                          |
| 1917/18 | 204                 | 218                 | 6·8               | 15·4                         |
| 1918/19 | 208                 | 246                 | 18·3              | 36·6                         |
| 1919/20 | 227                 | 259                 | 14·1              | 55·8                         |
| 1920/1  | 242                 | 312                 | 28·9              | 100·8                        |

Of course, the new entrants to the tax range would average more than £131 in their first tax-paying year, and the calculation in Table 3.2 overstates the increase for the remainder accordingly. None the less, we may maintain with confidence that annual increases would not be more than the percentage shown. The cumulative increase of 101 per cent between 1915/16 and 1920/1 compares with one of 154 per cent for railwaymen; 126 per cent for coalminers; 186 per cent for cotton textile workers; 113 per cent for postmen; 67 per cent for Civil Service administrators; 93 per cent for Civil Service lower division clerks.

By the end of 1920, average salaries were probably little more than double what they had been in 1914, while average weekly wage rates had risen 2·7 or 2·8 times for a working week that, in 1919, had been reduced to between 44 and 48 hours from its former range of 48 to 60 hours.[6]

The year 1919 is curious for having produced this great reduction of hours concurrently with a general rise in weekly wage rates and a sudden increase in unemployment to levels that had not been experienced since before the war. In November 1918, less than 1 per cent of insured workers were unemployed; by March 1919, their numbers had risen to nearly 9 per cent: 753,000 civilians and 306,000 ex-servicemen. From May, conditions improved and unemployment was down to 5·4 per cent by November. By March 1920, it was down to 2·8 per cent, but towards the end of the year, began rising again.

The Ministry of Labour recorded negotiated increases for 7,867,000 wage-earners in 1920, at an average of 12s. per worker per week.

By January 1919, standard wage rates had just about caught up with the cost of living, measured from July 1914; during 1919, standard rates[7] rose 9 per cent and the cost of living index just under 1 per cent, while hours of work were greatly reduced; from December 1919 to December 1920, standard ιates rose 20·4 per cent and the cost of living 19·5 per cent.

Then followed the collapse of wages that we have noted above. From December 1920 to December 1921, Bowley records a fall in standard rates of 8 per cent; for the next twelve months, of 22 per cent, and there rates rested with very little change until 1931. The average decrease recorded by the Ministry in 1921 was 17s. 6d. per week for 7·2 million workers and in 1922 a further 11s. for 7·6 million. The reductions were most severe for coalminers: an average of more than £2 per week for 1·3 million in 1921, and a further 10s. in 1922.[8] Excluding coalminers, the average reduction for 1921 was 11·7s., but for 1922 was slightly above 11s.

Wage rates, prices and unemployment moved as follows in this period:

| | | | Wholesale prices | | |
|---|---|---|---|---|---|
| | *Weekly wage rates*[a] | *Cost of living* | *All articles* | *Including iron and steel* | *Per cent unemployment of insured workers* |
| **1920** | | | | | |
| Oct. | · · | 100 | 100 | 100 | · · |
| Nov. | · · | 107 | 95 | 95 | 5·4[b] |
| Dec. | · · | 103 | 87 | 90 | 6·6[b] |
| **1921** | | | | | |
| Jan. | 100 | 101 | 81 | 85 | 11·0 |
| Feb. | 98 | 92 | 74 | 76 | 12·9 |
| March | 98 | 86 | 70 | 67 | 15·0 |
| April | 97 | 81 | 68 | 61 | 19·9 |
| May | 95 | 78 | 67 | 59 | 23·0 |
| June | 94 | 73 | 65 | 57 | 21·9 |
| July | 89 | 73 | 64 | 54 | 17·4 |
| Aug. | 87 | 74 | 63 | 52 | 15·1 |
| Sept. | 85 | 73 | 62 | 49 | 13·9 |
| Oct. | 83 | 67 | 60 | 46 | 14·3 |
| Nov. | 78 | 63 | 57 | 43 | 16·9 |
| Dec. | 77 | 60 | 56 | 41 | 17·7 |

| | Weekly wage rates[a] | Cost of living | Wholesale prices | | Per cent unemployment of insured workers |
|---|---|---|---|---|---|
| | | | All articles | Including iron and steel | |
| **1922** | | | | | |
| Jan. | 75 | 56 | 54 | 39 | 17·5 |
| Feb. | 74 | 54 | 54 | 38 | 16·9 |
| March | 72 | 52 | 53 | 37 | 15·8 |
| April | 70 | 50 | 53 | 37 | 15·6 |
| May | 68 | 49 | 53 | 37 | 14·4 |
| June | 67 | 49 | 53 | 37 | 13·5 |
| July | 66 | 51 | 53 | 37 | 12·9 |
| Aug. | 64 | 49 | 52 | 36 | 12·6 |
| Sept. | 64 | 48 | 51 | 35 | 12·5 |
| Oct. | 63 | 48 | 51 | 35 | 12·4 |
| Nov. | 62 | 49 | 52 | 35 | 12·8 |
| Dec. | 62 | 49 | 52 | 35 | 12·6 |

a Ministry of Labour index.
b United Kingdom.

The wholesale price of cotton textiles showed an even more calamitous fall: the average for 1922 was only 30 per cent of the high point reached in April 1920.

The advances in pay and conditions in 1919 had been gained with the loss in strikes of 36 million man-days; the reductions of 1921 were accompanied by the loss of 82 million man-days and those of 1922 by 20 million. But most of these man-days were lost in two great disputes: coal in 1921 (85 per cent) and engineering in 1922 (88 per cent).

Of the aggregate reductions in rates, 55 per cent in 1921 (measured in pounds per week) and 38 per cent in 1922 were under sliding scale agreements related to the cost of living, and just as these had very often benefited the lower-paid relatively more than the higher-paid, so reducing differentials, they now reduced the pay of the lower-paid relatively more, thus widening them again.

In 1921, despite the reduction in money rates, there was a rise in real rates, for, while money rates fell 23 per cent, retail prices fell just over 40 per cent. But in the next twelve months, the fall of rates was 19 per cent, almost the same as that in prices. Of course, family incomes must have suffered more than these figures suggest by the increase in unemployment, short-time working and loss of job opportunities.

Table 3.3 shows the magnitude of the changes in standard rates between 1920 and 1924.[9]

TABLE 3.3 Number of workpeople[a] reported as affected by changes in weekly full-time rates of wages and aggregate amount of such changes in the years 1920-4

| | Number of separate individuals reported as affected by | | | Amount of change in weekly rates | | |
|---|---|---|---|---|---|---|
| | *Net increase* | *Net decrease* | *Total*[b] | *Increase* | *Decrease* | *Net increase ( + ) Net decrease ( − )* |
| 1920 | 7,867,000 | 500 | 7,868,300 | 4,793,200 | 180 | + 4,793,020 |
| 1921 | 78,000 | 7,244,000 | 7,432,000 | 13,600 | 6,074,600 | − 6,061,000 |
| 1922 | 73,000 | 7,633,000 | 7,706,700 | 11,450 | 4,221,500 | − 4,210,050 |
| 1923 | 1,202,000 | 3,079,000 | 4,685,000 | 169,000 | 486,000 | − 317,000 |
| 1924 | 3,019,000 | 481,500 | 3,873,000 | 616,000 | 62,100 | + 553,900 |

[a] The statistics exclude changes affecting agricultural labourers, domestic servants, shop-assistants and clerks. In many cases the changes arranged by individual employers and affecting unorganised workers are not reported to the department.
[b] Workpeople whose wages were changed during any year and at the end of that year stood at the same level as at the beginning, are included in the above total column, though not in either of the preceding columns.

The years 1922 and 1923 were a time of almost universal reductions in wage rates; in 1923, the increase registered was largely accounted for by a modest rise in miners' rates and there was a further general reduction though on a much more moderate scale. It was not until 1924 that there was a general move in the opposite direction. So, from the level of 1920, two and a half to three times that of 1914, standard rates were reduced to about twice the 1914 level.

The Anderson Committee produced a table showing the increase in pay per head of various sections of the Civil Service between 1914 and 1923.[10] This, together with data for women civil servants,[11] was as follows:

|  | Pay per head, 1914 £ | 1923 as per cent of 1914 |
|---|---|---|
| Administrative | 662·1 | 139 |
| Professional, scientific and technical | 234·2 | 179 |
| Inspectorate | 229·0 | 193 |
| Executive and clerical | 138·0 | 170 |
| Writing assistants and typing | 65·4 | 197 |
| Manipulative | 67·4 | 220 |
| Messengers, charwomen, etc. | 49·9 | 203 |
| Industrial[a] | 80·9 | 176 |
| Women only |  |  |
|    Clerks, writing assistants, etc. | 79·5 | 186 |
|    Manipulative (mainly PO) | 61·3 | 229 |

[a] Civil Service industrial workers are skilled, semi-skilled and unskilled workers employed on repair and production in government factories, dockyards, etc. Their rates are fixed in relation to those of similar workers outside the Civil Service.

The path by which various classes reached these temporary resting points was largely the same as that noted for manual workers: a substantial rise to 1920 (1921 in the Civil Service) and a substantial fall to 1923.[12] This is shown on p. 144.

We have already noticed that salaries in general must have risen much less than wages between 1914 and 1920. But by 1923, they bore a relationship to their 1914 level similar to that of wages. Table 2.3 (professional earnings) records a narrowing of differentials within each profession, but at the median barristers' income had risen 2·76 times, solicitors' 2·08, doctors' 1·95 and dentists' 1·66.

Indexes of Civil Service Pay, 1914–24

| | 1914 | 1915 | 1916 | 1917 | 1918 | 1919 | 1920 | 1921 | 1922 | 1923 | 1924 |
|---|---|---|---|---|---|---|---|---|---|---|---|
| Administrative class | 100 | 100 | 100 | 101 | 106 | 129 | 167 | 180 | 144 | 134 | 134 |
| Executive class | 100 | 100 | 102 | 106 | 126 | 151 | 264 | 290 | 238 | 197 | 197 |
| Women clerks | 100 | 105 | 108 | 111 | 129 | 155 | 221 | 247 | 220 | 196 | 196 |
| Postmen and sorters (men) | 100 | 106 | 109 | 119 | 148 | 177 | 221 | 224 | 193 | 173 | 173 |
| PO engineers (professional) | 100 | 101 | 102 | 106 | 140 | 178 | 237 | 261 | 216 | 197 | 197 |
| PO engineers (manual) | 100 | 108 | 110 | 121 | 151 | 209 | 259 | 291 | 227 | 200 | 200 |

Certificated teachers, whose pay rose nearly two and a half times between 1914 and 1924, followed a different pattern. By 1921, the men's average had risen 2·24 times, the women's 2·47. In 1923, the ratios with 1914 had become 2·35 and 2·64 and only in 1924 did they suffer a modest decline.[13]

We have noted that salary-earners taxed in terms of Schedule E also fell behind wage-earners to 1920. Did they participate in the general reductions that followed? Table 3.4 sets out some of the data provided for the Anderson Committee by the Department of Inland Revenue.

TABLE 3.4 Salaries in public companies in various industries, 1920/1 to 1924/5 (pounds)

A. Average salaries, 1920/1 to 1922/3

|  | *1920/1* | *1921/2* | *1922/3* |
|---|---|---|---|
| Coal, metal and engineering | 364 | 368 | 359 |
| Textiles | 411 | 389 | 383 |
| Chemicals | 420 | 449 | 467 |
| Food, drink and tobacco | 378 | 398 | 408 |
| Paper | 410 | 417 | 419 |
| Shipping | 482 | 450 | 440 |
| Banking | 424 | 406 | 407 |
| Insurance | 478 | 476 | 456 |
| Wholesale and retail distribution | 355 | 327 | 320 |
| All the above | 408 | 401 | 400 |
| Railways | 302 | 282 | 275 |

B. Average of highest salaries and amount of salaries at various rank points, 1920/1 to 1924/5

| *All the above industries except railways:* | *1920/1* | *1921/2* | *1922/3* | *1924/5* |
|---|---|---|---|---|
| Average of 204 highest | 8720 | 7200 | 8100 | 8416 |
| 205th | 4350 | 4020 | 4372 | 4211 |
| 697th | 2010 | 1970 | 1955 | 1949 |
| 2462nd | 1025 | 1128 | 1114 | 1079 |
| 13,571st | 429 | 466 | 526 | 534 |
| Railways |  |  |  |  |
| Average of 8 highest | 3850 | 3600 | 4698 | 5125 |
| 9th | 3000 | 2860 | 3333 | 3750 |
| 28th | 1733 | 1615 | 1583 | 1545 |
| 122nd | 840 | 824 | 812 | 832 |
| 744th | 453 | 422 | 415 | 419 |

Salaries in the industries listed had a remarkable stability when compared with manual wage rates or earnings in the years 1920 to 1924. There are significant differences in the performance of different industries, but the average falls only 2 per cent between 1920/1 and 1922/3.

Again, for the values of salaries of different rank order or for the highest-paid, there is not much fluctuation. For all the industries listed (except railways), the top 204 fell by 17·5 per cent between 1920/1 and 1921/2, but by 1924 had returned to within 3·5 per cent of the 1920/1 level. In 1924/5, the 205th was within 3·2 per cent of the 1920/1 level; the 697th within 3 per cent, the 2462nd had actually risen 5·2 per cent and the 13,571st 24·5 per cent. Fortunes in different industries varied, some in particular suffering substantial cuts in 1922 or 1923. But, like the teachers, they neither climbed so high nor fell so far as manual workers.

A high degree of stability is manifest for the professions, too, whose averages for 1921/2 and 1922/3 are shown in Table 3.5.[14]

TABLE 3.5 Professional incomes in 1921–2 and 1922–3 (pounds)

| | Average income of those liable to tax | |
| --- | --- | --- |
| | *1921/2* | *1922/3* |
| Barristers | 1088 | 1309 |
| Solicitors | 1040 | 1173 |
| Doctors | 909 | 943 |
| Dentists | 745 | 759 |
| Scholastic professions[a] | 538 | 586 |

[a] Heads of universities and colleges, university and college teachers, headmasters and housemasters.

UNEMPLOYMENT

Unemployment data derived from National Insurance returns is classified by industry and not by occupation and until 1948 was limited, with some exceptions, to manual wage-earners. Percentages represent the number registered for employment at employment exchanges as a proportion of all insured workers in the industry in which they are normally employed or, if they are not attached to a particular industry, in the industry in which they last worked.

The series relating to those insured under the National Insurance Act of 1911 dates from September 1912, when some two million workers were included. Until 1926, the Ministry of Labour also published a series showing percentage unemployment amongst members of certain trade unions that paid unemployment benefit and made regular returns to the Ministry. Since the latter refers almost exclusively to craftsmen and the former to all workers, a comparison of the two rates gives a rough indication of the variation of unemployment at different levels of manual skill.

In engineering, shipbuilding and metal, the trade union rate was 2·2 per cent in 1913, while for all insured males in shipbuilding and engineering it was 2·6 per cent. Since skilled workers formed 78 per cent of all workers in the metal-making and -using trades, unemployment must have averaged about 4·0 per cent for the semi-skilled and unskilled. In 1921 and 1922 the related figures would have been:

|  | Percentages | |
| --- | --- | --- |
|  | 1921 | 1922 |
| Trade union | 22·1 | 27·0 |
| All | 27·1 | 28·9 |
| Semi-skilled and unskilled | 45·0 | 35·6 |

We cannot get any other near industrial comparison before 1914, but for 1921 and 1922 may compare the following:

|  | Percentages | |
| --- | --- | --- |
|  | 1921 | 1922 |
| Trade unions | | |
| Printing and bookbinding | 7·3 | 6·6 |
| Furnishing trades | 10·3 | 6·2 |
| Boots and shoes | 7·1 | 4·5 |
| Carpenters, joiners, plumbers | 4·8 | 7·6 |
| All trade unions, including above | 14·8 | 15·2 |
| National Insurance [a] | | |
| Printing, publishing and bookbinding | 7·2 | 7·2 |
| Furniture and upholstery | 12·9 | 10·0 |
| Boots and shoes | 12·3 | 10·3 |
| Building | 15·2 | 16·8 |
| All insured males | 17·0 | 16·3 |

[a] Average of rate at end of each quarter.

In November 1923 and 1924, the Ministry of Labour investigated the personal circumstances of a representative sample of claimants of unemployment benefit.[15] Here again, the high proportion of unskilled men is demonstrated, though for the women, the semi-skilled percentage was rather near their proportion of the manual work force.

| Level of skill | Males | | Females | |
|---|---|---|---|---|
| | *1923* | *1924* | *1923* | *1924* |
| Apprenticed | 2135 | 2093 | 270 | 228 |
| Trained | 2082 | 2180 | 868 | 1094 |
| Neither | 4016 | 4557 | 626 | 731 |

## 2. 1924 TO 1934

The downward rush of the early 1920s now gives way to a gentle decline. Unemployment again reaches the depths of 1921 but now the agony is prolonged over years instead of months:

| | Weekly wage rates | Cost of living | Wholesale prices | | Per cent unemployment of insured workers |
|---|---|---|---|---|---|
| | | | *All articles* | *Including iron and steel* | |
| 1924 | 100 | 100 | 100 | 100 | 10·2 |
| 5 | 102 | 101 | 96 | 88 | 11·0 |
| 6 | 101 | 98 | 89 | 86 | 12·3 |
| 7 | 101 | 96 | 85 | 84 | 9·6 |
| 8 | 99 | 95 | 84 | 79 | 10·7 |
| 9 | 99 | 94 | 82 | 80 | 10·3 |
| 1930 | 98 | 90 | 72 | 79 | 15·8 |
| 1 | 96 | 84 | 63 | 73 | 21·1 |
| 2 | 95 | 82 | 61 | 72 | 21·9 |
| 3 | 94 | 80 | 61 | 74 | 19·8 |
| 4 | 94 | 81 | 63 | 78 | 16·6 |

PAY MOVEMENTS

The dimensions of unemployment and the fall in prices are again on a grand scale, but instead of a 38 per cent fall in wage rates, there is one of

6 per cent. There is a further contrast with 1921/2, in that the fall was by no means general. Of the net fall in the weekly aggregate of £772,000 recorded by the Ministry for the years 1930 to 1933 (inclusive) nearly half was accounted for by textiles and building. Engineering rates, raised in 1927, were not reduced at all, nor were compositors' rates. Of the decreases in rates between 1924 and 1933, 59 per cent came about in terms of sliding scales tied to the cost of living index or to product prices.[16]

This stability was not merely one of appearance, for industrial earnings showed even less fluctuation than did standard rates, despite the increase in short-time working in 1931.[17]

Earnings in 1928 and 1931 as percentages of those in 1924 were as follows:

|                                                 | 1928 Oct. | 1931 Oct. |
|-------------------------------------------------|-----------|-----------|
| Pottery, bricks, glass, chemicals               | 102·5     | 96·8      |
| Metal manufacture, engineering and shipbuilding | 104·0     | 95·6      |
| Textiles                                        | 102·2     | 94·4      |
| Clothing, including laundries                   | 97·1      | 96·1      |
| Food, drink and tobacco                         | 95·8      | 94·4      |
| Wood products                                   | 102·9     | 93·4      |
| Paper and printing                              | 112·3     | 107·8     |
| Building and contracting                        | 103·0     | 100·2     |
| Gas, electricity and water                      | 103·0     | 102·3     |
| Weighted average                                | 102·4     | 96·8      |

Bowley estimated that full-time earnings in 1931 were, for males, 97.3 per cent and for females 98.5 per cent of their 1924 level.

Non-manual salaries or earnings showed even greater stability except those within the control of the government. Their course in various sectors, for the years 1924 to 1934, is shown in Table 3.6.

UNEMPLOYMENT

For the first time the unemployed were distinguished from the employed by occupation in the census of 1931. The unemployed represented 15.7 per cent of all operatives (employees, excluding managers and directors).

TABLE 3.6  Indexes of pay movements (for non-manual workers), 1924–34

| | 1924 | 1925 | 1926 | 1927 | 1928 | 1929 | 1930 | 1931 | 1932 | 1933 | 1934 |
|---|---|---|---|---|---|---|---|---|---|---|---|
| **Railway earnings** | | | | | | | | | | | |
| Station-and yard-masters and supervisory staff | 100 | 99 | 99 | 98 | 97 | 95 | 96 | 98 | 94 | 94 | 94 |
| Clerical staff | 100 | 99 | 99 | 97 | 100 | 98 | 99 | 102 | 98 | 99 | 100 |
| **Civil Servants** | | | | | | | | | | | |
| Administrative class[a] | 100 | 100 | 100 | 100 | 98 | 98 | 98 | 93 | 92 | 92 | 93 |
| **Post Office engineering** | | | | | | | | | | | |
| Professional and supervisory | 100 | 100 | 102 | 102 | 97 | 97 | 97 | 91 | 89 | 89 | 101 |
| **Certified full-time teachers[b]** | | | | | | | | | | | |
| Public elementary schools (England and Wales) average salaries: | | | | | | | | | | | |
| Men | 100 | 99 | .. | 99 | 99 | 99 | 99 | 99 | 88 | 88 | 88 |
| Women | 100 | 100 | .. | 96 | 95 | 95 | 95 | 95 | 86 | 86 | 86 |
| **Manufacturing industry (December)[c]** | 100 | 100 | 100 | 100 | 100 | 100 | 99½ | 95½ | 95 | 95 | 97 |
| Distribution (December)[c] | 100 | 100 | 100 | 100 | 100 | 100 | 100 | 99 | 99 | 99 | 99 |
| Finance (December)[c] | 100 | 100 | 100 | 100 | 100 | 100 | 98 | 95 | 95 | 95 | 95 |
| Local authorities (December)[c] | 100 | 100 | 99 | 99 | 98 | 98 | 98 | 96 | 95 | 97 | 97½ |
| Draughtsmen (all men over 30)[d] | 100 | 99 | 99 | 99 | 98 | 102 | 101 | 100 | 100 | 96 | 97 |

[a] From Guy Routh, 'Civil Service Pay, 1875 to 1950'. Economica, n.s., vol. 21, no. 83 (August 1954).
[b] Statistical Abstract for the United Kingdom, 1913 and 1924 to 1937. Cmd. 5903 (London: HMSO 1939), pp. 54 and 58.
[c] J. G. Marley and H. Campion, 'Changes in Salaries in Great Britain, 1924–39', Journal of the Royal Statistical society, vol. 103, part 4 (1940).
[d] From the Association of Engineering and Shipbuilding Draughtsmen (later the Draughtsmen's and Allied Technicians' Association).

Unemployment amongst professionals and clerks was much lower than the general average:

Percentage unemployment 1931

|                      | Males | Females |
|----------------------|-------|---------|
| All occupied         | 13·3  | 8·9     |
| Higher professionals | 1·8   | 1·9     |
| Lower professionals  | 4·1   | 4·2     |
| Clerical workers     | 5·7   | 4·4     |

For men in religion, law, teaching and medicine, unemployment was almost non-existent in 1931. In occupational class 1A, chemists and metallurgists returned the highest figure, with 5·7 per cent. In the lower professions, 4·0 per cent of laboratory attendants were unemployed, 5·2 per cent of medical auxiliaries and 6·8 per cent of draughtsmen. For women, 4·4 per cent of nurses and midwives were unemployed, 1·6 per cent of teachers and 3·8 per cent of social welfare workers. Actors and musicians formed exceptions, with unemployment high above the overall average.

For twelve industrial groups, unemployment amongst employers and managers averaged 1·9 per cent;[18] for ten industrial groups, it averaged 5·2 per cent for foremen. But for skilled manual workers it was much higher:

|                                |   | Per cent |
|--------------------------------|---|----------|
| Coal hewers and getters        |   | 21·6     |
| Pottery kiln and ovenmen       |   | 13·6     |
| Chemical grinders and mixers   |   | 10·2     |
| Blacksmiths                    |   | 20·8     |
| Fitters, mechanics             |   | 16·1     |
| Tool setters, setter-operators |   | 14·3     |
| Electricians                   |   | 11·3     |
| Spinners, piecers              | M | 25·2     |
|                                | F | 27·3     |
| Weavers                        | M | 24·9     |
|                                | F | 25·5     |
| Bakers and pastry-cooks        | M | 11·7     |
|                                | F | 8·0      |
| Carpenters                     |   | 17·3     |
| Bricklayers                    |   | 13·4     |
| Compositors                    |   | 7·3      |
| Engine drivers                 |   | 3·2      |

But there did not seem to be any clear-cut difference between the rate of unemployment for skilled workers and their associated semi-skilled assistants. The two rates were generally close, with the skilled sometimes above the semi-skilled, sometimes below. The dominant factor was the industry rather than the level of skill. The position of the major groups was as follows:

|  |  | *Per cent* |
|---|---|---|
| Agricultural labourers |  | 8·5 |
| Motor drivers |  |  |
|    goods |  | 10·7 |
|    passenger |  | 6·2 |
| Shop-assistants | M | 8·4 |
|  | F | 8·4 |
| Indoor domestic servants | M | 12·1 |
|  | F | 7·3 |
| Waiters | M | 18·9 |
|  | F | 14·7 |

But it was the unskilled who were most adversely affected:

|  |  | *Per cent* |
|---|---|---|
| Building labourers |  | 19·3 |
| Dock labourers |  | 21·2 |
| Other labourers | M | 32·0 |
|  | F | 22·9 |

The group 'other labourers' included 481,000 unemployed men and 57,000 unemployed women: 24 per cent of all the unemployed in the case of men and 10 per cent in the case of women.

As in the previous period, there is no simple relationship between unemployment and pay. In Table 2.27, we noted a small increase in average pay between 1924 and 1935—4 per cent for men and 3 per cent for women. Amongst the men, the higher skills did better than the lower: an 8 per cent rise for the higher professionals, a 4 per cent fall for the lower; an 8 per cent rise for skilled manual workers, a 1 per cent rise for the unskilled. Perhaps the same influences were at work in causing a 5 per cent rise for male clerks and a 7 per cent fall for female clerks. But between 1928 and 1931, the effect of unemployment seems to assert itself in the rather greater general fall in the pay of manual workers as compared with that of non-manual workers.

## 3. 1935 TO 1955

Between 1931 and 1951 we have noted substantial increases in the numbers of professional workers, managers, clerks and foremen. The number of skilled and semi-skilled workers hardly changed, while unskilled workers fell by 13 per cent. In pay, on the other hand, professionals, higher and lower, suffered a drastic relative reduction. There was also some reduction for male clerks and foremen, and, to a smaller extent, female clerks and forewomen. Skilled men lost a little ground, but managers, semi-skilled and unskilled men improved their positions. In general, white-collar workers (excluding managers) lost considerable ground to manual workers.

By 1935, prices were rising, after having reached their trough in 1933 and 1934; unemployment had fallen to 15 per cent after the 22 per cent of 1932; the fall in wage rates was at last reversed.

### PAY MOVEMENTS

From 1935, there was a significant contrast in the behaviour of manual and non-manual pay. We noted a fall in manual earnings between 1928 and 1931. By 1935, the level of 1928 had been more or less regained and between 1935 and 1938 there was a rise of 8 per cent.

Manual earnings

|  | Percentages of 1928 | |
|---|---|---|
|  | *Oct. 1935* | *Oct. 1938* |
| Pottery, bricks, glass, chemicals | 97·5 | 104·1 |
| Metal manufacture, engineering and ship-building | 99·1 | 111·2 |
| Textiles | 94·2 | 98·1 |
| Clothing (including laundries) | 101·3 | 101·3 |
| Food, drink and tobacco | 101·3 | 106·2 |
| Wood products | 98·4 | 99·7 |
| Paper and printing | 92·1 | 95·7 |
| Building and contracting | 95·1 | 102·2 |
| Gas, electricity and water | 99·3 | 105·3 |
| Weighted average | 99·2 | 107·3 |

Civil servants, manual and non-manual, had their pre-1931 rates restored in 1935 and 1936, but ended the decade generally a little below the level of 1928, while most salaries in the Marley–Campion series got back in 1936 and 1937 to pre-depression levels and remained there until 1940. By contrast, manual earnings rose by 30 per cent between 1938 and 1940. Year-to-year increases for manual workers were then as follows:

|              | *Per cent* |
| ------------ | ---------- |
| 1940 to 1941 | 10         |
| 1941 to 1942 | 14         |
| 1942 to 1943 | 7          |
| 1943 to 1944 | 5          |
| 1944 to 1945 | −2         |

It was only after 1942 that salaries rallied and regained some of their lost differentials. We calculated that the median pay of male clerks in 1929 was 128 per cent of average manual earnings; in 1942, it was 111 per cent. For females, the relevant percentages were 68 and 60. By 1946, the clerks had more than recovered their lost ground; but by 1952, the males had slipped back to their 1942 position and the females had again lost some ground.[19]

|               | *Percentage of manual average* | | | |
| ------------- | ------ | ------ | ------ | ------ |
|               | *1929* | *1942* | *1946* | *1952* |
| Male clerks   | 128    | 111    | 135    | 110    |
| Female clerks | 68     | 60     | 70     | 66     |

We can get a year-by-year picture of what was happening in the Civil Service, and this may serve to fill in some of the gaps. With 1938 = 100, pay indexes moved as shown on page 155.

While differentials are narrowing between related classes in the Civil Service, all are declining in relation to manual earnings. The decline reaches a trough about 1944, then reverses itself in 1945 or 1946, then resumes its downward drift.

The pattern is repeated in the case of engineering draughtsmen (p. 155):[20]

Indexes of Civil Service Pay, 1940–50
1938 = 100

| | 1940 | 1941 | 1942 | 1943 | 1944 | 1945 | 1946 | 1947 | 1948 | 1949 | 1950 |
|---|---|---|---|---|---|---|---|---|---|---|---|
| Administrative class | 100 | 101 | 101 | 102 | 105 | 108 | 112 | 112 | 116 | 116 | 128 |
| Executive class | 100 | 102 | 104 | 108 | 113 | 116 | 122 | 122 | 132 | 132 | 132 |
| Clerical officers | 102 | 108 | 111 | 116 | 120 | 124 | 131 | 140 | 140 | 140 | 154 |
| Women clerks | 100 | 106 | 109 | 113 | 117 | 120 | 135 | 135 | 138 | 138 | 143 |
| Postmen and sorters | 114 | 122 | 126 | 133 | 136 | 141 | 171 | 171 | 184 | 194 | 194 |
| PO engineers, professional and supervisory | 102 | 105 | 106 | 111 | 117 | 119 | 124 | 128 | 128 | 129 | 140 |
| PO engineers, manual | 115 | 122 | 128 | 135 | 138 | 144 | 155 | 188 | 196 | 196 | 207 |
| Weekly earnings, all in earnings census | 130 | 142 | 160 | 176 | 182 | 180 | 182 | 198¼ | 217 | 226¼ | 236¼ |

Engineering Draughtsmen

| | 1940 | 1941 | 1942 | 1943 | 1944 | 1945 | 1946 | 1947 | 1948 | 1949 | 1950 |
|---|---|---|---|---|---|---|---|---|---|---|---|
| 1. Section leaders | 109 | 115 | 118 | 126 | 131 | 140 | 148 | 153 | 161 | 163 | 168 |
| 2. All men over 30 | 109 | 116 | 122 | 129 | 134 | 141 | 151 | 155 | 163 | 166 | 170 |
| 3. 1 as per cent of manual earnings index | 82 | 80 | 72 | 72 | 71 | 77 | 79 | 75 | 72 | 71 | 69 |
| 4. 2 as per cent of manual earnings index | 83 | 81 | 74 | 74 | 73 | 78 | 79 | 76 | 73 | 72 | 70 |

Here again, the decline is reversed in 1945 and 1946 and then resumed.

The year 1944 seems to have been the time when non-manual pay reached its lowest point in relation to manual earnings. In the case of Civil Service clerical officers, 66 per cent of the decline had taken place by 1940; for draughtsmen aged over 30, 63 per cent of the decline had taken place by that year. Indeed between 1938 and 1940, a major shift in income in favour of manual workers seems to have taken place: compared with their 30 per cent rise, that for all employees, according to the national income estimates, was only 14 per cent.[21] This is certainly true as regards the Civil Service where the pay of manipulative and manual engineering grades rose 15 per cent between 1935 and 1940, while that of the non-manual classes hardly moved at all.

It is also supported by a comparison of draughtsmen's pay with that of the engineering craftsmen. Between July 1938 and July 1940, hourly earnings of the engineering craftsmen rose by 25·5 per cent. Engineering draughtsmen are a group of non-manual workers with close links with engineering craftsmen, yet the average rate for section leaders and draughtsmen over 30 rose only 9 per cent. One would expect the effect of the rise in manual pay to be still further diluted in more remote non-manual groups.

The relation between the national income estimates of changes in wages and salaries per head for those in civil employment and changes in manual weekly earnings indicates that, in subsequent years, there were fluctuations about the 1940 relationship and no further radical changes. From 1944, a series is available relating pay-as-you-earn income and the number of earners concerned. The resulting average actually rose faster than average manual weekly earnings from 1944 to 1947; then fell relatively in 1947, then resumed an upward course. This is not just a result of fluctuations in industrial hours: the pay-as-you-earn average and hourly earnings show a similar relationship, the former rising relatively to 1946 and 1947, dipping in 1948, then rising again.

We have calculated that average earnings in the higher professions in 1955/6 were 256 per cent of their level of 1935/6.[22] We get a glimpse of their level between these two years from the evidence before the Danckwerts Tribunal,[23] which showed that professional income (as indicated by tax returns) was in 1949/50 188 per cent of the level of 1937. In this year, earnings in earnings census industries were 230 per cent of the level of 1938 and 249 per cent of the level of 1935. Interpolation by means of the index of wage rates[24] would show 1949 to be 241 per cent of 1937. We get this picture of the relative progress of manual and professional earnings.

|                     | 1937 | 1949 |     | 1955/6 |
|---------------------|------|------|-----|--------|
| Manual earnings     | 100  | 241  | 100 | 160    |
| Higher professions  | 100  | 188  | 100 | 136    |
| Percentage gap      |      | 22   |     | 15     |

Thus the erosion of manual/professional differentials must have had a second period of activity after it had spent itself about 1944.

Average earnings for all employees moved in step with those for manual workers between 1944 and 1950 or 1951. Then followed further narrowing:

|                              | Nos. 000s | Average earnings, 1955 as per cent of 1950 |
|------------------------------|-----------|-------------------------------------------|
| 1.  All employees[a]         | 19,850    | 138                                       |
| 2.  Manual earnings[b]       | 10,500    | 147                                       |
| 3.  Coal                     | 700       | 143                                       |
| 4.  Agriculture              | 660       | 141                                       |
| 5.  Railways                 | 418       | 147                                       |
| 6.  1 minus 2 to 5           | 7572      | 124                                       |

[a] From PAYE tax tables.
[b] Ministry of Labour earnings census (*Ministry of Labour Gazette*).

Those in lines 2 to 5 were, in 1955, getting 353 per cent of their earnings of 1938; the residue 244 per cent. The inclusion of professional individuals and partnerships, as shown in the Schedule D analysis of the tax reports, would widen the gap fractionally.

UNEMPLOYMENT

The drastic reduction in the differential between manual and non-manual workers occurred in a period when unemployment amongst the former remained high. Unemployment was falling between 1932 and 1937, but in 1938, when it was once more on the increase, wage rates continued to rise.

Per cent unemployment, insured males

| 1935 | 17·5 |
|------|------|
| 1936 | 14·6 |
| 1937 | 12·0 |
| 1938 | 13·5 |

It is curious that employers should have found it necessary to increase the pay of their manual workers in these years when, at best, one in eight of the male work force was unemployed; what is still more curious is that rates for the unskilled should generally have risen more than those for skilled workers, for, as in 1931, unemployment was much heavier amongst the former. An analysis for the Special Areas in 1937 showed that of the unemployed in coalmining, shipbuilding, engineering and building, 63 per cent were unskilled.[25] In March 1940, when unemployment was still high by modern standards, nearly half the unemployed were labourers: 295,000 out of 631,000.[26]

Unemployment remained extraordinarily low after the war, even allowing for the fact that the insured population of which it is expressed as a percentage is no longer limited to manual workers. In April 1951, only 253,000 work-seekers were registered with employment exchanges, who had been notified of 437,000 vacancies. The registered unemployed represented 1·9 per cent of all civilian employees. The census, however, listing all unemployed and not only those who were registered, shows them to have been 2·3 per cent of all employees. Again, rates for non-manual workers were lower than those for manual workers:

Percentage unemployment, 1951

|  | Males | Females |
| --- | --- | --- |
| All occupied | 2·2 | 2·0 |
| Higher professionals | 0·7 | 1·8 |
| Lower professionals | 1·4 | 2·0 |
| Clerks | 1·2 | 1·2 |

For skilled and semi-skilled manual workers, unemployment was above average for coal hewers and getters (3·9 per cent), indoor domestic servants (males, 8·6; females 2·5) and waiters (males, 7·2; females 4·5). Again, it is amongst the unskilled that unemployment is highest:

Percentage unemployment, 1951

| Building labourers |  | 5·1 |
| --- | --- | --- |
| Dock labourers |  | 3·4 |
| Other labourers | M | 5·1 |
|  | F | 2·5 |

## 4. 1956 TO 1960

PAY MOVEMENTS

This period was characterised by a widening of differentials. Table 2.29 showed a pronounced relative decline for semi-skilled and unskilled men and for all women manual workers, while clerks and professionals enjoyed a relative advance. However, the lower professions did better than the higher professions and managers did no better than manual workers (though they did no worse).

In manufacturing industry the narrowing process seems to have been reversed about 1956 or 1957. There, average wages rose in relation to average salaries between 1950 and 1956 and fell thereafter:[27]

Average wages as per cent of average salaries

| | |
|---|---|
| 1950 | 59·6 |
| 1956 | 68·0 |
| 1957 | 66·3 |
| 1958 | 66·0 |
| 1959 | 65·3 |
| 1960 | 64·8 |

The Ministry of Labour's indexes of average weekly earnings and average salary earnings show a similar relationship:[28]

| | *Average weekly earnings* | *Average salary earnings* |
|---|---|---|
| 1955 | 100·0 | 100·0 |
| 1956 | 108·0 | 107·3 |
| 1957 | 113·0 | 114·8 |
| 1958 | 116·9 | 118·5 |
| 1959 | 122·2 | 126·3 |
| 1960 | 130·6 | 133·4 |

There are various other traces of this reversal of trend in the pay history of the period. On the railways, station-masters and clerks gained relatively to the manual grades.[29] In various industries, grade D clerks lost relatively to manual earnings between 1952 and 1954, remained steady between 1954 and 1956 and gained between 1956 and 1958.[30]

From 1955 to 1957, the manual earnings of boys, women and girls all improved *vis-à-vis* those of men in manufacturing industry, then lost ground again. Between related grades of manual workers, too, differentials reached their narrowest about 1953 or 1954, then fluctuated about the level or widened slightly. Table 3.7 illustrates this in respect of the engineering industry.[31]

UNEMPLOYMENT AND UNFILLED VACANCIES BY OCCUPATION

From 17 March 1958, the Ministry of Labour has given a quarterly analysis of unemployment and unfilled vacancies for adult men and women on a broad occupational basis.[32] Again, this refers to people registered for employment and vacancies notified to employment exchanges, so is not exhaustive either of unemployment or vacancies. However, it gives a useful indication of the state of demand and supply relating to the occupations cited. The tables that follow average the data for June and December 1958, 1959 and 1960.

On average, there has been an excess demand for all skilled craftsmen except painters and shipwrights. The occupations listed contributed 4·6 per cent to the unemployed and 19·3 per cent to the vacancies. For tool-setters, setter-operators, the demand has been particularly acute: nearly four vacancies for each applicant.

For the semi-skilled men, excess supply was the rule, with the exception of bus drivers and conductors, for whom there were, on average, more than eight vacancies for each applicant. But for drivers of goods vehicles, the reverse applies: nearly six applicants for each vacancy. On balance, the semi-skilled supplied a lower proportion of unemployed (11 per cent) than of vacancies (17 per cent).

It is again amongst the labourers that unemployment is most highly concentrated. They supplied 56·5 per cent of the unemployment and had only 14 per cent of the vacancies: eleven applicants for each job.

In the case of women, general clerks were substantially in excess supply, while the reverse applied to shorthand typists and typists. On balance, office workers supplied just about the same percentage of unemployed as there were office vacancies.

There was a comfortable excess demand for skilled and semi-skilled process workers (except in textile spinning), while semi-skilled service workers were in excess supply, though they contributed equal proportions to the totals of unemployed and vacancies.

The contrast in the case of unskilled women is not as great as in the case of the men. There are nearly two for every vacancy and they supply

TABLE 3.7 Engineering industry: interrelationship of earnings in various occupations, 1950–60

| | 1950 | 1951 | 1952 | 1953 | 1954 | 1955 | 1956 | 1957 | 1958 | 1959 | 1960 |
|---|---|---|---|---|---|---|---|---|---|---|---|
| **Rate** | | | | | | | | | | | |
| Labourers as per cent of fitters | 86·0 | 84·7 | 86·3 | 87·0 | 86·2 | 85·2 | 84·5 | 84·3 | 84·3 | 84·3 | 84·3 |
| Women as per cent of fitters | 62·2 | 63·5 | 66·0 | 67·2 | 67·1 | 67·2 | 67·1 | 67·6 | 67·6 | 67·8 | 67·8 |
| **Earnings (time-workers)** | | | | | | | | | | | |
| Fitters as per cent of toolroom fitters | .. | 90·1 | 89·9 | 88·9 | 91·0 | 90·8 | 92·3 | .. | 90·4 | 90·2 | 90·2 |
| Turners and machinemen, semi-skilled as per cent of fitters | .. | 82·2 | 81·8 | 82·5 | 80·8 | 81·2 | 81·4 | .. | 80·7 | 80·6 | 81·8 |
| Labourers as per cent of fitters | .. | 79·2 | 78·1 | 78·4 | 76·5 | 76·9 | 73·9 | .. | 74·8 | 74·3 | 74·5 |
| Women as per cent of fitters | .. | 47·8 | 48·1 | 48·5 | 47·1 | 46·5 | 46·8 | .. | 46·8 | 48·1 | .. |

TABLE 3.8 Unemployment and unfilled vacancies from employment exchange records, average for 1958, 1959 and 1960, June and December each year.

| | *Unemployed* | *Vacancies* |
|---|---|---|
| **Men** | | |
| A. Skilled | | |
| Carpenters, joiners (construction) | 1552 | 3788 |
| Bricklayers | 1029 | 2477 |
| Painters | 3598 | 2036 |
| Shipwrights | 377 | 92 |
| Electricians | 1177 | 1347 |
| Precision fitters (other than toolroom) | 1743 | 2061 |
| Maintenance fitters, erectors | 835 | 1075 |
| Tool-setters, setter-operators | 877 | 3459 |
| Electronic equipment, installers, testers | 528 | 1005 |
| Vehicle-body-builders | 256 | 464 |
| All the above | 11,972 | 17,804 |
| Per cent of all occupations | 4·63 | 19·33 |
| All occupations | 258,610 | 92,093 |
| B. Semi-skilled | | |
| Manufacturing process workers | 5958 | 4482 |
| Motor drivers (not public passenger) | 12,495 | 2223 |
| Bus drivers, conductors | 458 | 3888 |
| Shop-assistants | 4524 | 2885 |
| Hotel and catering occupations | 4127 | 1932 |
| All the above | 27,562 | 15,410 |
| Per cent of all occupations | 10·7 | 16·7 |
| All occupations | 258,610 | 92,093 |
| C. Unskilled | | |
| Light labourers | 52,784 | 190 |
| Other labourers | 93,333 | 12,908 |
| All the above | 146,117 | 13,098 |
| Per cent of all occupations | 56·5 | 14·2 |
| All occupations | 258,610 | 92,093 |
| **Women** | | |
| D. Office workers | | |
| Clerks | 8963 | 3363 |
| Book-keepers, cashiers | 1946 | 1424 |
| Shorthand typists | 1523 | 4104 |
| Typists | 1097 | 2151 |
| Office machine operators | 650 | 740 |

Table 3.8 (*Contd.*)

|  |  | Unemployed | Vacancies |
|---|---|---|---|
|  | All the above | 14,179 | 11,782 |
|  | Per cent of all occupations | 14·27 | 15·79 |
|  | All occupations | 99,337 | 74,604 |
| E. | Skilled and semi-skilled workers |  |  |
|  | Mechanical and electrical engineering and |  |  |
|  | metal goods manufacture | 3034 | 3514 |
|  | Pottery | 142 | 356 |
|  | Food, drink, tobacco | 1275 | 2074 |
|  | Boot and shoe manufacture | 349 | 367 |
|  | Textile spinning | 539 | 803 |
|  | Textile weaving | 1028 | 846 |
|  | Wholesale heavy clothing | 1211 | 3218 |
|  | Light clothing | 1439 | 4301 |
|  | All the above | 9017 | 15,479 |
|  | Per cent of all occupations | 9·07 | 20·74 |
|  | All occupations | 99,337 | 74,604 |
| F. | Semi-skilled service workers |  |  |
|  | Motor drivers | 291 | 133 |
|  | Bus conductors | 290 | 477 |
|  | Shop-assistants | 11,300 | 7248 |
|  | Hotel and catering service |  |  |
|  | Kitchen staff | 4652 | 4092 |
|  | Barmaids, service hands | 2161 | 2849 |
|  | Waitresses | 3365 | 2854 |
|  | All the above | 22,059 | 17,653 |
|  | Per cent of all occupations | 22·2 | 23·7 |
|  | All occupations | 99,337 | 74,604 |
| G. | Unskilled |  |  |
|  | Kitchen staff | 4652 | 4092 |
|  | Others | 52,183 | 27,212 |
|  | All the above | 56,835 | 31,304 |
|  | Per cent of all occupations | 57·2 | 42·0 |
|  | All occupations | 99,337 | 74,604 |

about the same proportion of the unemployed (57 per cent for the women, 56·5 per cent for the men), but have 42 per cent of the vacancies (compared with only 14 per cent in the case of the men).

## 5.  1960 TO 1970

### PAY MOVEMENTS

Average pay doubled over the ten years. Amongst the men, the lower professions and semi-skilled did exceptionally well, with the unskilled running them close. Skilled manual workers and managers fell a long way behind, foremen did even worse and higher professionals worst of all.

In the case of the women, forewomen, skilled manual and higher professionals did badly, but kept within a few percentage points of one another. The unskilled did best, keeping pace with the unskilled men, and the lower professions came next, but well behind the lower professional men.

Because pay was rising so fast, it was to be expected that patterns would be broken and discrepancies appear, and Table 3·9 gives evidence of this. Of the groups represented, agriculture and coalmining fell behind, and so did non-manual men in banking and insurance, and men and women clerks in banking, insurance and the public sector. In the other groups, only small differences appeared: non-manual males, production industries, ended up just behind the manual men, and non-manual females six percentage points ahead of the manual women.

In the first three years of the decade, non-manual workers forged ahead, but in 1964, the manual workers caught up; they remained level until 1966 and then gradually drew ahead to end up with a lead of 2·6 per cent over the non-manuals.[33]

Examination of the details of each occupational class shows that the convergence between classes 1A and 1B, and between classes, 5, 6 and 7 was due not to a narrowing of differentials in job clusters but to the varying fortunes of some of the dominant professions. Army officers and the clergy did particularly well, but they (especially the clergy) were catching up after years of neglect. Architects did no worse than lawyers nor doctors and dentists than engineers, but all four did much worse than the average for all men. In the men's class 1B, teachers, draughtsmen and lab assistants did very well, thus raising the average for the whole class; amongst the women, nurses moved ahead strongly.

TABLE 3.9 Earnings per week of manual and non-manual workers, men and women, 1960 and 1970, October (pounds)

| | 1960 | 1970 | % of 1960 |
|---|---|---|---|
| **Manual workers** | | | |
| Manual men[a] | 14·53 | 28·05 | 193 |
| Manual women[b] | 7·42 | 13·99 | 189 |
| Agriculture[c] | 10·35 | 19·15 | 185 |
| Coal mining[d] | 16·28 | 28·01 | 172 |
| Railway conciliation grades[e] | 13·93 | 29·26 | 210 |
| Dock labour[f] | 16·52 | 36·28 | 220 |
| **Administrative, technical and clerical workers** | | | |
| Non-manual males, production industries[g] | 19·18 | 36·25 | 189 |
| Non-manual females, production industries | 7·97 | 15·51 | 195 |
| National and local government, males | 18·87 | 36·00 | 191 |
| National and local government, females | 12·30 | 22·78 | 185 |
| Banking and insurance, males | 20·30 | 34·63 | 171 |
| Banking and insurance, females | 8·60 | 16·02 | 186 |
| Transport, males[h] | 17·70 | 37·61 | 212 |
| Transport, females | 10·35 | 21·13 | 204 |
| Clerks in public sector, banking and insurance, males | 13·10 | 22·58 | 172 |
| Clerks in public sector, banking and insurance, females | 9·85 | 17·49 | 178 |

[a] United Kingdom, men twenty-one and over, in manufacturing, construction, gas, electricity, water, transport (not railways), industrial civil servants.

[b] As a, but women eighteen and over.

[c] Average weekly earnings for six months commencing October each year.

[d] Includes sick pay and payments for holidays and rest days.

[e] 1960: average for spring earnings censuses for 1960 and 1961.

[f] 1960: average weekly earnings, October–December 1960.

[g] Manufacturing, mining, quarrying, construction, gas, electricity and water.

[h] British Transport Docks, British Waterways, British Rail, civil air transport. 1970 includes London Transport and British Road Services.

Amongst the semi-skilled men, farm workers did badly, but bus drivers and conductors, shop-assistants and postmen all did very well.

In engineering, there were fluctuations in the relative earnings of skilled, semi-skilled and unskilled men, but no discernible trend. With labourers = 100, semi-skilled men and skilled men were 124·8 and 139·6 respectively in January 1963, and 124·5 and 139·0 in June 1970.[34] Electrical contracting seems to have been unique, with a differential that moved from 13 per cent in June 1964 to 35 per cent in January 1970.[35]

PRICES

From Table 3.1, we may see that prices rose 49 per cent in the decade, so that real income rose about 30 per cent. This was a repetition of the previous decade, when prices also rose by about 50 per cent, earnings by 90 per cent and thus real earnings by nearly 30 per cent. The retail price index rose 4·3 per cent in 1962, 4·8 per cent in 1965 and 4·7 per cent in 1968, with more moderate rises in the intervening years. But after that an ominous acceleration took place: 5·4 per cent in 1969 and 6·4 per cent in 1970, a foretaste of the extraordinary rises that were to come.

UNEMPLOYMENT AND VACANCIES

Unemployment, too, increased in the later years of the decade, reaching levels low by present standards but high compared with those of the preceding twenty years. In 1965, it averaged 1·6 per cent; from 1966 to 1970, 2·5 or 2·6 per cent.

Table 3.8 showed an excess of vacancies over unemployed in the case of skilled and semi-skilled manual workers, and a great excess of unemployment over vacancies for the unskilled. In June 1970, the total of registered unemployed men had increased by 69 per cent over the total shown in Table 3.8 for 1958–60. The total of registered unemployed women, by contrast, had fallen by 34 per cent and the number of vacancies for women risen by 29 per cent.

The number of unskilled unemployed men had risen from 146,000 to 232,000, but because total male unemployment was up (from 259,000 to 437,000) the proportion that they represented of unemployed men had fallen from 56·5 to 53 per cent.[36] There were still some occupations in which the number of vacancies exceeded the number of unemployed men, the principal being:

|  | December 1970 | |
|  | Vacancies | Unemployed |
| --- | --- | --- |
| Coal-miners | 2893 | 426 |
| Turners | 1365 | 615 |
| Machine-tool setters, setter-operators | 4465 | 2056 |
| Bus drivers, conductors | 2072 | 610 |
| Nurses | 1932 | 435 |

INCOMES POLICIES

The sixties were busy years for incomes policy-makers, but it was only in 1973 that a Conservative government introduced an imperative equalising factor into the formula governing increases. Prior to that, restrictions covered rich and poor alike, though, as we shall see, Labour policies did envisage special treatment for the low-paid.[37]

On 25 July 1961, the Chancellor of the Exchequer, Selwyn Lloyd, introduced a 'pay pause' that was to continue for nine months. Over the previous year salaries and wages had risen 8 per cent, other personal income 6·5 per cent, while real national product had risen only 3 per cent. He announced in Parliament, 'In my view there must be a pause until productivity has caught up and there is room for further advances . . . In those areas for which the Government have first responsibility we shall act in accordance with this policy, and the government ask that the same lines should be followed elsewhere . . .'. In April 1962, the 'zero norm' gave way to the 'guiding light', that first prescribed maximum increases of 2·0 to 2·5, and then 3·0 to 3·5 per cent.

Workers in the public sector objected to being made an example of and, in the event, did rather better than those in the private sector:

|  | | *Percentage increases* | |
|  | | *1961–2* | *1962–3* |
| --- | --- | --- | --- |
| Administrative, technical and clerical | | | |
| All | M | 5·4 | 5·3 |
| | F | 6·2 | 5·4 |
| National and local government | M | 7·3 | 6·0 |
| | F | 7·0 | 6·1 |
| Public corporations | M | 5·3 | 8·1 |
| | F | 4·5 | 6·5 |
| Manual workers | | | |
| Manufacturing industries | M | 2·8 | 5·8 |
| Gas, electricity and water | M | 6·7 | 4·5 |
| Public administration | M | 4·5 | 5·1 |

*Source: British Labour Statistics Historical Abstract 1886–1968*, Table 53, pp. 122–3; Table 54, p. 124; and Table 42, p. 102.

In 1964, a Labour government was returned to power and attempted to apply first a voluntary agreement on pay and price rises. In February 1965 a White Paper was published announcing the establishment of the National Board for Prices and incomes;[38] in April 1965 a further White

Paper outlined the general terms of the policy: pay increases should be limited to increases in output per head, estimated at about 3·0–3·5 per cent per year, with additions only where workers make a direct contribution to raising productivity, where such additions are necessary for recruitment purposes, where existing pay levels were generally recognised as being too low or where there was widespread recognition that the pay of a certain group of workers had fallen seriously out of line and needed, in the national interest, to be improved.[39]

The voluntary system having proved disappointing (with an increase in all-industry average earnings between April 1965 and April 1966 of 9·6 per cent for manual men and 10 per cent for manual women), there followed a legally enforced standstill in pay and prices from July to the end of December 1966, to be followed by a further six months of 'severe restraint'.[40] The Prices and Incomes Act 1966 gave the Secretary of State, through the National Board for Prices and Incomes, considerable powers for the control of prices and incomes, and incomes policy went through three more stages of 'zero norm' until 1969, followed by a norm of 2·5 to 4·5 per cent until the demise of the Labour government in 1970. From mid-1967, however, legal enforcement was discontinued.

The period of freeze was effective: from July 1966 to January 1967 basic weekly wage rates moved by less than 1 per cent, while the index of earnings, seasonally adjusted, actually fell fractionally. But after that, though the norm was zero, average earnings rose by about 8 per cent a year.

Despite the provision for special treatment for the low-paid, wages council rates lagged behind the overall average for the rise in wage rates. Wage rates for all manual men rose 32 per cent between April 1965 and April 1970, while the lowest wages council rates for men rose between 18 and 28 per cent.[41] The National Board for Prices and Incomes in their report *General Problems of Low Pay*, found 'that what little improvement took place in the relative position of the low-paid in the earlier years of the prices and incomes policy was later lost'.[42] Whatever intention the policy-makers had of reducing inequality seems to have been lost on the decision-makers.

## 1970 TO 1978

We arrive now at the last stretch of the course. In a setting of industrial stagnation, with unemployment at pre-1914 levels, pay and prices enter into a furious race. We must go back half-a-century to find movements of similar magnitude:

|                | 1920<br>(1914 = 100) | 1976<br>(1970 = 100) |
|----------------|----------------------|----------------------|
| Wage rates     | 260                  | 271                  |
| Cost of living | 251                  | 215                  |

It might be expected that in a race at this velocity the field would be very ragged, but apart from the substantial relative fall in the pay of managers there were no great changes in the men's hierarchy. We saw in Table 2.27 that women had done better than men in the period 1913–24, after which they had tended to lag; but in this last period, they forge ahead with an increase at their average of 227 per cent over 1970, compared with the men's 180 per cent. The Equal Pay Act of 1970 was applied by degrees between 1970 and 1975, when women became legally entitled to equal treatment for performing the same or broadly similar work to men, or work that had been given an equal value to men's jobs in a job evaluation exercise. The Equal Pay Act became fully operative on 29 December 1975, on the same date as the Sex Discrimination Act, in terms of which it is unlawful for an employer to discriminate in the recruitment of new employees or in the treatment of existing employees. A perverse effect of these Acts was that in employment in which equal pay already applied, women received smaller increases than in those in which it did not. The percentage deviations from the average increases for men and women, respectively, were as follows:

|     |                     | M       | F       |
|-----|---------------------|---------|---------|
| 1.  | Professional        |         |         |
|     | A. Higher           | + 1·1   | − 16·5  |
|     | B. Lower            | + 2·8   | − 2·8   |
| 2B. | Managers etc.       | − 15·4  | − 17·1  |
| 3.  | Clerks              | − 1·1   | − 1·6   |
| 4.  | Foremen             | 0·0     | − 3·1   |
| 5.  | Skilled manual      | + 7·9   | + 1·5   |
| 6.  | Semi-skilled manual | + 6·1   | + 11·6  |
| 7.  | Unskilled manual    | + 5·0   | + 14·1  |

Now we have a wealth of detail from the New Earnings Surveys from which to track the course of events.

MEN AND WOMEN

Table 3.10 shows the progress of men's and women's pay according to the New Earnings Surveys. Between 1968 and 1970 the two averages move in step. Then, perhaps in the first careless rapture after the passing of the Equal Pay Act, the women's increase has a lead of two percentage points between 1970 and 1971. There is a back-slide over the next year, followed by two years of modest advance and two years in which women forge ahead. By 1977, the women's average is 65 per cent of the men's, after sixty years during which it has hovered about the level of 55 per cent.[43] After that, strangely enough, there is a reversion, so that the women's average, 64·8 per cent of the men's in 1977, falls to 63·3 per cent in 1978.[44]

TABLE 3.10 Men's and women's average earnings from the New Earnings Surveys, 1968–78

|  | 1968 | 1970 | | 1971 | | 1972 | | 1973 | | 1974 | |
|  | £ | £ | % of 1968 | £ | % of 1970 | £ | % of 1971 | £ | % of 1972 | £ | % of 1973 |
|---|---|---|---|---|---|---|---|---|---|---|---|
| Men | 25·2 | 30·0 | 119 | 32·9 | 110 | 36·7 | 112 | 41·9 | 114 | 47·7 | 114 |
| Women | 13·7 | 16·3 | 119 | 18·3 | 112 | 20·1 | 110 | 23·1 | 115 | 26·9 | 116 |

|  | 1975 | | 1976 | | 1977 | | 1978 | |
|  | £ | % of 1974 | £ | % of 1975 | £ | % of 1976 | £ | % of 1977 |
|---|---|---|---|---|---|---|---|---|
| Men | 60·8 | 127 | 71·8 | 118 | 78·6 | 109 | 89·1 | 113 |
| Women | 37·4 | 139 | 46·2 | 123·5 | 51·0 | 110 | 56·4 | 111 |

(Full-time workers whose pay was not affected by absence.)

There are, of course, many influences at work in determining these averages: the rising proportion of women in the labour force, changes in age and occupational distribution and in the levels of authority to which women advance. There is also the fact that in the public service equal pay for equal work had been established before the advent of the Equal Pay Act, so that the effect of the Act, as registered in the averages for all men and women, would be to that extent reduced. This is not to say that women did not advance in pay in the public service in this period. Women's averages as percentages of average men's pay advanced as follows:

| | Percentages | |
|---|---|---|
| | *1970* | *1978* |
| Primary and secondary school teachers | 79·7 | 86·0 |
| Non-manual workers in | | |
| Medical and dental services | 54·3 | 57·6 |
| Public administration | 57·3 | 61·4 |

But these advances would have been mainly due to advances by women in age and responsibility. Table 3.11 shows the course of events in four occupations from 1970 to 1978 and one from 1973 to 1978 where the full force of the Equal Pay Act was operative.[45]

TABLE 3.11  Women's averages as percentages of men's averages, various occupations, 1970–8

| | *1970* | *1971* | *1972* | *1973* | *1974* | *1975* | *1976* | *1977* | *1978* |
|---|---|---|---|---|---|---|---|---|---|
| Lab technicians | 60·7 | 61·7 | 63·8 | 66·1 | 68·3 | 70·8 | 73·0 | 75·8 | 77·6 |
| Sales | 41·6 | 43·0 | 43·4 | 44·2 | 46·0 | 49·6 | 49·8 | 51·3 | 50·4 |
| Chefs/cooks | 51·4 | 57·6 | 59·1 | 59·3 | 59·6 | 65·7 | 69·9 | 70·7 | 68·9 |
| Packers, bottlers, etc. | 54·2 | 55·1 | 54·6 | 57·1 | 58·0 | 63·8 | 66·1 | 66·9 | 65·9 |
| Machine tool operators, not setters | .. | .. | .. | 56·0 | 55·8 | 61·6 | 70·5 | 72·4 | 67·2 |
| Average of 1st four | 52·0 | 54·4 | 55·2 | 56·7 | 58·0 | 62·5 | 64·7 | 66·2 | 65·7 |
| % change from previous year | — | 4·6 | 1·5 | 2·7 | 2·3 | 7·8 | 3·5 | 2·3 | −0·8 |

In Table 3.10, women's pay was 54·3 per cent of men's in 1970 and 63·3 per cent in 1978: a change of 16 per cent. In Table 3.11, the move is from 52·0 per cent to 65·7 per cent: a change of 26·3 per cent. Thus the change, in those occupations exposed to the Act, has really been quite considerable. The effect was greatest near the beginning and near the end of the period of transition to equal pay and, between 1977 and 1978, the process went slightly into reverse, suggesting that we can look for no further advance from this quarter.

*Incomes Policies*
In 1970, the Labour government was replaced by a Conservative one,

who disposed of the National Board for Prices and Incomes and began by an attempt to persuade those concerned to reduce each successive pay settlement by 1 per cent. In mid-1971, the Confederation of British Industry asked its members to limit price increases to 5 per cent in the ensuing twelve months, and the average rise was indeed reduced to 6·6 per cent, compared with 20 per cent in the twelve months preceding. But government policy was shaken by the mineworkers who, in February 1972, won an increase, backdated to the previous November, of about 22 per cent. Exhortation was plainly inadequate and, on 6 November 1972, the Prime Minister announced a compulsory standstill on prices, rents, dividends and pay for a period of ninety days, subject to a possible sixty-day extension.[46]

The second stage of the programme was announced in January 1973. The standstill would end on 27 February; from then until the autumn, the White Paper explained, 'the total of increases in pay for any group of employees (to run for 12 months from the date of implementation) should not exceed the sum which would result from the payment of £1 a week per head plus 4 per cent of the current pay bill for the group, exclusive of overtime.'[47] The emphasis, it was argued, should be on the lower-paid, and no individual should receive an increase of more than £250. If the negotiating group kept to the formula £1 plus 4 per cent with the £250 maximum, a worker at £1000 a year would get a rise of 9·2 per cent; at £2500, a rise of 6·08 per cent; at £5000, one of 5 per cent. 'The form in which the pay limit is expressed is . . . designed to favour low paid workers . . . The Government attach importance to this and they expect negotiators to pay full regard to it.' A further provision empowered negotiators to decide on increases above the pay limit to women workers to reduce the male–female differential by a third by the end of 1973.[48]

There were other refinements to the regulations: changes in pay should be implemented at not less than twelve-month intervals; those agreed before the standstill but not implemented were subject to delay; 'the current pay bill for the group' required interpretation. To police the application of the policy, a Price Commission and a Pay Board were set up, to whom reports of changes had to be submitted.

But in the third stage, requirements were relaxed. From 1 November 1973, group pay increases of up to 7 per cent were permitted, with a further 1 per cent to remove anomalies 'and obstacles to the better use of manpower'; extra payments for new 'efficiency schemes'; and an optional 'threshold safeguard' in agreements, for a 40 pence per week increase for each 7 per cent increase in the Retail Price Index.[49]

It was again the miners who brought the policy to an end. In January 1974 they struck for an increase far beyond the statutory limits, provoking a general election that resulted in the return of a Labour government. The pattern of events was repeated: voluntary pay policy, pay explosion; the enforcement of limits, though this time by agreement between the Government and the Trades Union Congress, with the possibility of legal sanctions in the background. From August 1975, increases were limited to £6 per week, with no increases on pay of above £8500 a year, and in May 1976 agreement was reached by the government and TUC for a new limit of 4·5 per cent for pay increases in the twelve months from 1 August, 1976. This was to be achieved by fixing a minimum increase of £2.50 and a maximum of £4, with a 5 per cent limit for those in the middle. The twelve-month interval between increases was to continue.[50] The agreement went along with tax-cuts designed to give additional support to purchasing power.

The budget of 1977 contained further tax relief, conditional on a further pay agreement for the year from August 1977.[51] The agreement was not forthcoming, and the Labour government, until it was put out of office in May 1979, had to content itself with exhortations for restraint, the enforcement of cash limits in public expenditure, and threats that the Price Commission would not allow prices to be raised to offset pay increases of more than 5 per cent, while government contracts would not be given to firms that overshot the limits.[52]

Thus we may look in the statistics for the effects of the following:

(1) 6 November 1972 to 27 February 1973: standstill.
(2) 27 February 1973 to 1 November 1973: £1 per week plus 4 per cent with maximum of £250 per year, but additional increases to reduce male-female differential.
(3) 1 November 1973 until the general election of 28 February 1974: group pay increases of up to 7 per cent with further 1 per cent to remove anomalies and possibility of 'threshold agreements' for cost-of-living allowances.
(4) August 1975 to 1 August 1976: maximum increase of £6 per week, with a 'cut off' at £8500.
(5) 1 August 1976 to 1 August 1977: increases of 5 per cent with minimum of £2.50 and maximum of £4.

DIFFERENTIALS

We noted in Table 2.29 that between 1970 and 1978 all the women's classes had improved their position relative to the overall average for men and women, except the higher professionals and the managers. Amongst the men, the managers suffered a considerable relative fall, but the higher professionals maintained their position, with the engineers coming along strongly (hence the superior performance of the men professionals compared with the women). Comparing the men only with the men, we found a fifteen percentage point fall by the managers, and a rise by the manual workers ranging from five points for the unskilled to nearly eight points for the skilled.

By the use of the New Earnings Surveys we may now identify the years in which these changes (or failures to change) took place. As already noted, there was a change in the system of classification in 1973, and an abandonment of the system, so convenient for users of the statistics, of presenting averages for skilled, semi-skilled and unskilled manual workers. Thus Table 3.12 from which the year-by-year changes may be seen, is broken into two: the first part going from 1970 to 1972, with a link with 1973, and the second part, in a somewhat different form, going from 1973 to 1978.

The rift between 1972 and 1973 is discernible, when the pay standstill was followed by a maximum increase of £250 per year. Manual workers were up two percentage points, while white-collar workers, all the way down to clerks, lost ground. In 1975–6 and 1976–7, when flat-rate maxima were also in force, the result is not nearly so marked. The descent of the managers is clearly defined: if we convert their percentage of the average into an index, with 1970 = 100, we get

| | |
|---|---|
| 1970 | 100·0 |
| 1971 | 96·9 |
| 1972 | 95·1 |
| 1973 | 86·4 |
| 1974 | 84·4 |
| 1975 | 81·0 |
| 1976 | 80·3 |
| 1977 | 81·7 |
| 1978 | 82·4 |

There was a considerable fall between 1972 and 1973, and the descent continued until 1976, after which they began making a recovery.

The engineers were on the up-grade until 1972, then took a fall that continued until 1974, and then ascended until 1976. There are other fluctuations to which reference will be made in Chapter 4. But there are

TABLE 3.12 Pay structure, adult full-time men whose pay was not affected by absence (pounds per week or percentage of average for all full-time men)

(a) 1970 to 1973

| | | 1970 | 1971 | 1972 | 1973 |
|---|---|---|---|---|---|
| Engineers, scientists, technologists | £ | 39.6 | 44.1 | 49.5 | 53.9 |
| | % | 132 | 134 | 135 | 129 |
| Medical and dental practitioners | £ | 60.1 | 71.7 | 75.7 | 80.4 |
| | % | 200 | 218 | 206 | 192 |
| Technicians | £ | 31.0 | 34.5 | 37.9 | 41.4 |
| | % | 103 | 105 | 103 | 99 |
| Teachers | £ | 38.9 | 41.4 | 47.5 | 52.2 |
| | % | 130 | 126 | 129 | 125 |
| Managers | £ | 48.7 | 51.8 | 56.6 | 58.6 |
| | % | 162 | 157 | 154 | 140 |
| Clerks | £ | 25.8 | 28.3 | 31.6 | 35.5[b] |
| | % | 86 | 86 | 86 | 85 |
| Foremen | £ | 32.5 | 35.6 | 39.7 | 43.3 |
| | % | 108 | 108 | 108 | 103 |
| Manual workers[a] of whom | £ | 26.8 | 29.4 | 32.8 | 38.1 |
| | % | 89 | 89 | 89 | 91 |
| Skilled | £ | 28.6 | 31.3 | 34.8 | .. |
| | % | 95 | 95 | 95 | .. |
| Semi-skilled | £ | 26.6 | 29.0 | 32.4 | .. |
| | % | 89 | 88 | 88 | .. |
| Unskilled | £ | 23.3 | 25.7 | 28.5 | .. |
| | % | 78 | 78 | 78 | .. |
| Bus conductors | £ | 26.9 | 29.3 | 32.2 | 37.2 |
| | % | 90 | 89 | 88 | 89 |
| Lorry, van drivers | £ | 25.8 | 29.2 | 32.5 | 38.5 |
| | % | 86 | 89 | 89 | 92 |
| Postman, mail sorter, messenger | £ | 25.6 | 27.0 | 31.6 | 34.7 |
| | % | 85 | 82 | 86 | 83 |
| Shop-assistants | £ | 19.5 | 20.9 | 23.7 | .. |
| | % | 65 | 64 | 65 | .. |
| General farm workers | £ | 17.6 | 19.5 | 22.7 | 25.3 |
| | % | 59 | 59 | 62 | 60 |
| All full-time men | £ | 30.0 | 32.9 | 36.7 | 41.9 |
| | % | 100 | 100 | 100 | 100 |

[a] Excluding sales, security, catering, farming, train, bus or truck crew, dockers and stevedores.

[b] The change of classification in 1973 raised the number of supervisors by 330 to 1145. To arrive at the average of £35.50, 330 supervisors at £41.80 have been added to the clerks minus postmen, mail sorters, messengers. This raises the average by £0.25.

Table 3.12 (*Contd.*)

(b) 1973 to 1978

| | | 1973 | 1974 | 1975 | 1976 | 1977 | 1978 |
|---|---|---|---|---|---|---|---|
| Engineers, scientists, tech- nologists | £ | 53.9 | 59.9 | 77.2 | 93.9 | 102.0 | 114.5 |
| | % | 129 | 126 | 127 | 131 | 130 | 129 |
| Medical practitioners | £ | 80.4 | 88.6 | 107.5 | 140.1 | 153.9 | 164.8 |
| | % | 192 | 186 | 177 | 195 | 196 | 185 |
| Judges, barristers, solicitors | £ | 53.7 | ·· | 77.6 | 92.9 | 118.5 | 123.8 |
| | % | 128 | ·· | 128 | 129 | 151 | 139 |
| Accountants | £ | 53.8 | 59.7 | 72.0 | 85.3 | 94.3 | 106.2 |
| | % | 128 | 125 | 118 | 119 | 120 | 119 |
| Architects | £ | 64.2 | 65.8 | 84.8 | 104.2 | 110.0 | 117.5 |
| | % | 153 | 138 | 139 | 145 | 140 | 132 |
| Technicians | £ | 41.4 | 46.7 | 59.0 | 71.9 | 78.5 | 90.8 |
| | % | 99 | 98 | 97 | 100 | 100 | 102 |
| Teachers | £ | 52.2 | 58.3 | 78.2 | 88.9 | 100.7 | 109.4 |
| | % | 125 | 122 | 129 | 124 | 128 | 123 |
| Managers, exc. general management[a] | £ | 52.6 | 58.6 | 71.5 | 84.2 | 93.4 | 106.7 |
| | % | 126 | 123 | 118 | 117 | 119 | 120 |
| Clerks, exc. supervisors | £ | 34.0 | 38.3 | 48.1 | 58.1 | 63.0 | 70.4 |
| | % | 81 | 80 | 79 | 81 | 80 | 79 |
| Foremen[b] | £ | 43.2 | 50.7 | 63.0 | 73.8 | 82.0 | 91.2 |
| | % | 103 | 106 | 104 | 103 | 104 | 102 |
| Carpenters and joiners (building and maintenance) | £ | 41.5 | 45.4 | 57.2 | 63.6 | 69.3 | 76.7 |
| | % | 99 | 95 | 94 | 89 | 88 | 86 |
| Machine tool setter-operators | £ | 41.1 | 47.4 | 58.1 | 68.0 | 75.2 | 86.2 |
| | % | 98 | 99 | 96 | 95 | 96 | 97 |
| Toolmakers, tool fitters | £ | 43.4 | 50.1 | 60.5 | 70.5 | 77.5 | 89.8 |
| | % | 104 | 105 | 99 | 98 | 99 | 101 |
| Electricians (installation and maintenance, plant, etc.) | £ | 44.8 | 51.5 | 64.9 | 76.0 | 82.7 | 95.1 |
| | % | 107 | 108 | 107 | 106 | 105 | 107 |
| Bricklayers | £ | 41.1 | 46.5 | 57.6 | 65.8 | 71.5 | 79.2 |
| | % | 98 | 97 | 95 | 92 | 91 | 89 |
| Face-trained coalminers | £ | 41.8 | 51.3 | 74.5 | 80.7 | 84.9 | 109.7 |
| | % | 100 | 108 | 123 | 112 | 108 | 123 |
| Engine-drivers, motormen | £ | 40.9 | 43.9 | 64.3 | 74.5 | 80.2 | 86.0 |
| | % | 98 | 92 | 106 | 104 | 102 | 97 |
| Compositors | £ | 46.1 | 47.2 | 57.0 | 74.4 | 77.4 | 89.3 |
| | % | 110 | 99 | 94 | 104 | 98 | 100 |
| Postmen, mail sorters, messengers | £ | 34.7 | 41.7 | 54.2 | 67.4 | 70.0 | 74.3 |
| | % | 83 | 87 | 89 | 94 | 89 | 83 |
| Salesmen, shop assistants | £ | 32.5 | 36.0 | 43.6 | 48.9 | 54.5 | 62.4 |
| | % | 78 | 75 | 72 | 68 | 69 | 70 |
| Farmworkers | £ | 25.3 | 33.0 | 37.4 | 46.8 | 51.6 | 57.7 |
| | % | 60 | 69 | 62 | 65 | 66 | 65 |
| Repetitive assemblers (metal and electrical goods) | £ | 38.5 | 43.7 | 53.1 | 62.7 | 69.3 | 78.3 |
| | % | 92 | 92 | 87 | 87 | 88 | 88 |
| Bus conductors | £ | 37.2 | 40.3 | 60.1 | 68.3 | 74.4 | 83.2 |
| | % | 89 | 84 | 99 | 95 | 95 | 93 |
| Goods drivers (3 tons or less) | £ | 34.7 | 38.9 | 49.7 | 54.9 | 59.6 | 67.5 |
| | % | 83 | 82 | 82 | 76 | 76 | 76 |
| Refuse collectors | £ | 31.4 | 35.8 | 49.5 | 58.0 | 64.6 | 70.4 |
| | % | 75 | 75 | 81 | 81 | 82 | 79 |

Table 3.12(b) (*Contd.*)

|  |  | 1973 | 1974 | 1975 | 1976 | 1977 | 1978 |
|---|---|---|---|---|---|---|---|
| Packers, bottlers, canners, | £ | 35.2 | 39.5 | 49.2 | 59.3 | 66.1 | 75.0 |
| fillers | % | 84 | 83 | 81 | 83 | 84 | 84 |
| Goods porters | £ | 32.6 | 36.2 | 49.1 | 56.6 | 60.7 | 72.4 |
|  | % | 78 | 76 | 81 | 79 | 77 | 81 |
| General labourers | £ | 32.3 | 36.8 | 47.7 | 56.3 | 60.1 | 68.6 |
|  | % | 77 | 77 | 78 | 78 | 76 | 77 |
| All full-time men | £ | 41.9 | 47.7 | 60.8 | 71.8 | 78.6 | 89.1 |
|  | % | 100 | 100 | 100 | 100 | 100 | 100 |

[a] There was a break in continuity in NES grade I, Managerial (general management) between 1974 and 1975, so they are omitted from this comparison. Managers include NES group VI plus company secretaries, marketing, sales, personnel and advertising managers and town clerks. Civil servants, administrative and executive are not included. Works foremen are extracted as explained in text, p. 86.
[b] Includes supervisors of clerks and works foremen.
*Source*: *New Earnings Survey.*

also a number of occupations or occupational groups that maintain their place in the earnings hierarchy with very little change.

We have an alternative source of information relating to the year-to-year change in differentials in the Department of Employment survey of manual earnings by occupation in the engineering industry. This relates to June each year and is published in the Gazette for October. To pick out changes in differentials rather than in hours or overtime worked, Table 3.13 expresses skilled and semi-skilled hourly earnings, excluding overtime premia, as percentages of those of labourers.

TABLE 3.13 Average hourly earnings, excluding overtime premia, of skilled and semi-skilled male workers as percentages of labourers' earnings, engineering industry, June each year, 1970–8

|  | 1970 | 1971 | 1972 | 1973 | 1974 | 1975 | 1976 | 1977 | 1978 |
|---|---|---|---|---|---|---|---|---|---|
| Skilled | 144 | 147 | 144 | 141 | 139 | 133 | 130 | 131 | 131 |
| Semi-skilled | 127 | 134 | 131 | 130 | 127 | 123 | 121 | 122 | 121 |
| Labourers | 100 | 100 | 100 | 100 | 100 | 100 | 100 | 100 | 100 |

*Source*: *Department of Employment Gazette*, October each year.

UNEMPLOYMENT AND VACANCIES

1976, 1977 and 1978 were years of unusually high unemployment: higher than had been known since 1939. From December 1972, the Department of Employment began classifying the unemployed and offers of employment in terms of the key occupations for statistical purposes (KOS), so that since that time we have had a statistical statement that matches the occupational earnings recorded in the New Earnings Survey.

We shall do some matching in Chapter 4. In passing, we may note the continued preponderance of unskilled labourers amongst the unemployed:

|               | *Men*   | *Women* |
|---------------|---------|---------|
| December 1972 | 280,634 | 21,286  |
| December 1977 | 391,649 | 68,871  |

The unskilled women constituted 20 per cent of unemployed women in each year; the unskilled men, 47 per cent in 1972 and 41 per cent in 1977.

We may also note a considerable increase in unemployed managers (for men, from 9113 to 24,359) and in unemployed scientists, engineers and technicians (from 10,433 to 17,430 in the case of men, and 788 to 2482 in the case of women).

There are now very few occupations in which the number of notified vacancies exceed the number of registered unemployed: policemen, prison officers, traffic wardens; foremen cleaners, sewage plant attendants; a few specialist jobs in the clothing industry; machine tool setter operators, toolmakers and tool fitters, instrument mechanics; face-trained coalminers; railway guards.[53]

## 7. PERIODS OF CHANGE

We can distinguish nine major states in the pay history of the period:

### 1914 TO 1920

There was a general narrowing of differentials. Money earnings of manual workers increased rapidly, while non-manual earnings lagged behind. The narrowing included related occupations at different levels of skill and the range of earnings in particular professions. These movements were associated with a high rate of inflation and a high demand for labour.

## 1920 TO 1923

Wage rates and manual earnings came tumbling down, in the wake of a drastic fall in prices and heavy unemployment. Non-manual earnings were much more stable, so that the two converged at about twice the money level of 1914.

## 1924 TO 1933

There was a downward drift of money earnings, more pronounced amongst manual than non-manual workers, and more pronounced amongst the unskilled than the skilled. Unemployment again approached the extraordinary levels of 1922 and 1923 and retail prices between 1924 and 1933 fell even more than between 1920 and 1923, but the change is now spread out over a much longer period.

## 1934 TO 1944

Manual earnings moved upward at accelerating pace, with maximum rise between 1938 and 1940. Salaries regained their pre-depression level somewhat later (1936 or 1937) and, by 1940, had failed to improve on it. The change in pay structure was again associated with a substantial rise in prices (nearly 30 per cent between 1935 and 1940; 22 per cent between 1940 and 1944) but, in contrast to the narrowing of 1914 to 1920, with a high level of unemployment. Unemployment was highest amongst those whose relative pay rose most.

## 1944 TO 1950

There was an upward movement of money earnings, with the pay structure generally unchanged; a high level of employment temporarily disturbed in 1946; a somewhat slower rise in retail prices—26 per cent spread over the six years.

## 1951 TO 1955

A further narrowing of differentials accompanied a high level of employment and a somewhat faster rise in prices (30 per cent from 1950 to 1955).

1956 TO 1960

A fairly general widening of differentials, with relative declines for semi-skilled and unskilled manual workers. Employment remained high though it fell slightly in the recession of 1958/9. The rise in prices continued but at a much more moderate pace: 15 per cent between 1955 and 1960.

1960 TO 1970

No discernible narrowing of differentials in job clusters, but some occupations, especially amongst the lower professionals and semi-skilled and unskilled groups, did well. Unemployment ranged between 1·5 and 2·6 per cent; earnings doubled, prices rose nearly 50 per cent, so real earnings were up by 30 per cent. There was a marked decline in the relative pay of the higher professionals.

1970 TO 1978

Prices rose by a factor of 2·7; men's pay, on average by very little more so that real pay hardly changed; women's pay, by contrast, more than tripled. Except for the managers, relative pay held fairly steady. The extraordinary rise in earnings and prices was matched, after 1974, by an extraordinary rise in unemployment.

# 4 Interpretations

We have now tracked movements in pay and employment over nearly three-quarters of a century, not year-by-year but at intervals of ten or twenty years. But we have also produced evidence indicating the course of the variables in the years in between, and, since 1970, we have annual data of occupational earnings, unemployment and job vacancies. There are, too, a number of theories that purport to explain movements in employment and pay, and it will be our task in this chapter to see how well they fit the empirical data, and finally, to present an explanatory hypothesis for further testing.

The most widely accepted theory is that the price of different sorts of labour, like that of different sorts of goods, is determined by the interaction of demand and supply, with equilibrium at that price at which quantity demanded equals quantity offered. A variant of this is the marginal productivity theorem which argues that adjustments take place not at the average but at the margin.

The doctrine of demand and supply was presented in refutation of that of the just wage, which maintained that wages, like all prices, should be determined according to what is fair between buyer and seller. Each occupation had a bundle of attributes that determined the status of those who professed it, and pay should be appropriate to the maintenance of that status. The modern equivalent of this doctrine is the argument relating to custom and usage, the maintenance of traditional differentials and relativities, and the related notion that pay should be based on job evaluation—the nature of the job—rather than on the number of workers offering to do it relative to the number of jobs waiting to be done.

Somewhere in between these theories comes another which is a composite of both but qualitatively different from either: the theory of internal labour markets. In monopolistic competition theory the supplier can, within certain limits, manipulate the demand schedules for his products; so, in internal labour markets, the employer by training and promotion, can manipulate the supply of skills, and need concern himself with external labour markets only at certain ports of entry.

Within the firm, job evaluation and the just wage rule: justice must be done (or at least, seem to be done) and only occasionally need this harmony be disturbed by shocks from the outer world.

Pertinent to all these theories is the question of their degree of determinateness: it may be that we shall find that chance and accidental elements play an important part in the formation of pay structure and its changes, and that we must take account of this, however obnoxious it may be to the human mind.

## 1. SUPPLY AND DEMAND

The doctrine that supply and demand determined price, and that it was right and inevitable that they should do so, was presented in two independently produced pamphlets in the year 1691, one by John Locke and the other by Sir Dudley North.[1] In the eighteenth century, first Richard Cantillon and then Adam Smith suggested that relative pay depended on certain defined attributes of each occupation, including the cost and difficulty of learning it. Malthus accepted the importance of these attributes but argued that they influenced pay not because of any intrinsic value they added to the labour in various professions, but because they 'are causes of a nature to influence the supply of labour in the particular departments in question, and to determine such wages by the demand compared with the supply of the kind of labour required'.[2]

In the last quarter of the nineteenth century, the marginal refinement was added: that each newly employed worker would add to the revenue of the firm but, obedient to the law of diminishing returns, less than the previously engaged worker. The maximising employer would then continue to engage workers, other things being equal, until the revenue added by the employment of the last worker was just equal to the wage. If wages were raised for any reason, equilibrium would be regained by the simple process of dismissing workers until output per marginal worker rose to equal the new wage.

These theories led Ricardo to believe that a rise in unemployment would rapidly reduce wage rates until all who wished were once again employed. 'All general reasoning I apprehend is in favor of my view of this question, and for why should some agree to go without any wages while others were most liberally rewarded.'[3] And Alfred Marshall— '. . . the fluidity of labour is sufficient to make it true that the wages of labour of the same industrial grade or rank tend to equality in different occupations throughout the same western country';[4] the Council on

Prices, Productivity, and Incomes—'We think it most important that the flexibility of relative wages in response to changes in the demand for labour should be preserved, since in a free enterprise economy without direction of labour this is the main means on which we must rely for ensuring the most efficient distribution of the country's labour forces';[5] Sir Henry Phelps Brown—'. . . whatever reduces the supply of labour to a given occupation relatively to the supplies to other occupations tends to raise its relative pay, and whatever extends that supply tends to reduce it; though the tendency may take effect only if and when other changes occur that break up the rule of custom'.[6]

While Marshall and Phelps Brown demonstrate the socioeconomic complexity of the determinants of employment and pay, the views of non-economists, amongst whom may be included some econometricians, remain in thrall to the demand-supply model, though it is far from clear how they imagine the system to work. One difficulty is that theories at the level of abstraction of those outlined above can never be subjected to satisfactory empirical tests. We can, however, see whether the patterns of change seem to be responding to demand and supply as their main determinants. The examples given below suggest that this has not been so for some of the big changes discerned, and that some of the obvious movements in supply and demand have not been reflected in the expected changes in relative pay.

Perhaps the first thing to note is the *stability* of pay structure over certain periods. The price of provisions fluctuates from year to year, Adam Smith remarked, 'But in many places the money price of labour remains uniformly the same sometimes for half a century together.'[7] Phelps Brown and Hopkins observed the same constancy in building wages, including the differentials between craftsmen and labourers.

'In all, there seems to have been no change, of the sustained kind we record, in about 500 years out of 690. It is unlikely that supply and demand remained exactly balanced at the ruling price; rather it must have been that their movements were not wide enough to overcome the inertia of convention . . . The same strength of convention may be seen in the remarkable stability of the differential between the rates of the craftsman and his labourer. Our figures bear out the decline noted by Beveridge and Postan in the hundred years down to about 1410; but after that there was no sustained change until the First World War . . . Here as before, we cannot believe that market forces always worked to keep the equilibrium prices of the two grades of labour in so constant a relation . . .'[8]

W. B. Reddaway noted a much higher degree of stability between earnings in different industries than in changes in employment in those industries. Within the food, drink and tobacco industrial order, for instance, 'The earnings increases were all much the same . . . There is clearly some force which produced the big changes in the distribution of labour, and there seems no reason to look beyond the 'obvious' one, which we have christened job opportunities.'[9]

The OECD report, *Wages and Labour Mobility*, throws further light on this matter.[10] Here a group of distinguished labour economists assembled and analysed a mass of empirical data relating to employment and pay and sought in it a link between pay and mobility. They found a relative stability of pay structures in the face of substantial changes in employment. For inter-industry movements, especially at the more detailed three digit level,[11] the Reddaway thesis is confirmed—'Industries have in general been able to expand their employment as necessary by increasing their interception of new entrants, the unemployed, and employed jobseekers.' By contrast, when an industry is running down, with earnings, employment and profit on the decline, the flow of workers from it is encouraged. But an expanding industry poorly placed to intercept a recruitment stream because of its remoteness or its low level in the earnings structure may have to raise its wages relatively.[12] As for industries, so for occupations: a general lack of correlation between changes in earnings and in employment.

Rodney Crossley found a high level of stability in the ranking of average earnings by industry. Hourly earnings for 132 separate industries in 1948 and 1959 had a rank correlation coefficient of + 0·87. Between 1955 and 1963, 188 wage rates for men in a wide range of industries in different parts of the country had a rank correlation coefficient of + 0·93. At the same time, there were a number of quite striking changes that Crossley attributes to contrasting influences to which different industries were subject in technology or in their product market.[13]

In 1978, Richard Wragg and James Robertson, of the Department of Employment Unit for Manpower Studies, published a paper showing trends in employment, productivity, output, labour costs and prices in eighty-two manufacturing industries and twenty-two retail distributive trades, covering the years 1954–73 for manufacturing and 1950–71 for retail trade.[14] It is clear that the annual average compound rates of growth in earnings per operative are not related to the growth or decline of employment in the industry concerned. For illustration, industries whose operatives enjoyed a compound rate of increase in earnings of 7·0 per cent per year experienced employment changes per year of + 3·2, + 1·7, + 1·4, − 1·0, + 0·2, − 0·8, − 4·5, − 3·5, − 3·3, − 3·6, and − 5·2. Nor were earnings correlated with output per worker: 'Over the long run, earnings increases between industries moved in parallel and were not determined by differential rates of growth in labour productivity.'[15]

Let us now turn to the data assembled in Chapters 1 to 3.

1906 TO 1960

The average pay of men in occupational class 7 (unskilled manual workers) was, in 1924, a little more than double the average for 1914, while that for skilled men had risen by 80 per cent. By 1935, the relative position of these two classes had almost been restored, but between 1935 and 1955, unskilled men again drew ahead. Their average in 1955 was 337 per cent of that for 1935, while for skilled men the 1955 average was only 319 per cent of the 1935 figure.

Over the following five years, 1955 to 1960, the trend was again in favour of skilled workers, whose increase we estimated at 28 per cent, compared with 23 per cent for the unskilled.

The net result was a skilled average in 1960 equal to 800 per cent of that of 1914; an unskilled average equal to 850 per cent of that of 1914.

Can these changes be explained in terms of changing demand and supply schedules? The absolute numbers of skilled workers in each census year show an extraordinary constancy, while the absolute numbers of unskilled workers fluctuate, rising between 1911 and 1931, then falling by 13 per cent between 1931 and 1951.

We know that in 1916, 1917 and 1918, unemployment was below 1 per cent of the insured population. This may conceivably have placed unskilled men in a more favourable bargaining position than skilled men (though this seems unlikely), but both before the war and in the economic collapse that followed the post-war boom, we have estimated that unemployment was considerably higher amongst the semi-skilled and unskilled than amongst the skilled.

In particular, the Ministry of Labour investigations of 1923 and 1924 showed a much lower rate of unemployment amongst the apprenticed (approximating to occupational class 5) and the trained (approximating to occupational class 6) than amongst the untrained (occupational class 7). The apprenticed constituted 21 per cent of the unemployed and (including foreman) 42 per cent of the manual work force, while the unskilled constituted 20 per cent of the manual work force and 40 per cent of the unemployed. With an overall rate of unemployment of 10 per cent, this would mean that the rate of unemployment was 5 per cent amongst the skilled and 20 per cent amongst the unskilled. Thus the differential increase for the unskilled is the reverse of what demand-supply relations would suggest.

There is a similar contradiction between demand and supply theory and the relative changes in the period including the Second World War. We estimated that in 1955, the unskilled men's average was 337 per cent of their average in 1935, compared with 319 per cent for the skilled men (Table 2.29). Yet by 1940, when the major narrowing had taken place, there was still substantial unemployment amongst unskilled workers. Even in 1951, when overall unemployment according to the population census, was down to 2·2 per cent, for unskilled workers it was 5·1 per cent.

Movements in the relative pay of manual and non-manual workers have also contradicted the prognostications of the theory of demand and supply. Between 1935 and 1955, there were substantial relative reductions for all the non-manual classes except managers (Table 2.30), with the greatest reduction between 1935 and 1940. This was brought about by a high degree of stability in non-manual pay, juxtaposed with large increases in pay for manual workers, which were paid in the face of heavy unemployment of manual workers.

In Table 3.8, we assembled data about the state of demand and supply in respect of various occupations in the years 1958, 1959 and 1960. This shows great variation between occupations, which demand and supply theory postulates should be equalised by changes in relative pay, yet there was little correlation between excess demand or supply, on the one hand, and pay on the other.

This lack of correlation is illustrated by the following:

| Occupation | Unfilled vacancies per unemployed worker, 1958/60 | Pay in 1960 as % of 1955 |
|---|---|---|
| Men | | |
|  Bricklayers | 2·4 | 133 |
|  Engineering fitters | 1·2 | 128 |
|  Bus drivers | 8·5 | 115 |
|  Bus conductors | 8·5 | 122 |
|  Shop-assistants | 0·6 | 125 |
|  Unskilled workers | 0·1 | 123 |
| Women | | |
|  Clerks | 0·4 | 135 |
|  Waitresses | 0·8 | 115 |
|  Shop-assistants | 0·6 | 124 |

One may cite two occupations in which there was a consistent and exceptionally high degree of excess demand: tool-setters, setter-operators, with an average of 877 unemployed for 3459 vacancies (that is 4 vacancies for each applicant) and shorthand typists, with 1523 unemployed for 4104 vacancies (2·7 vacancies for each applicant). Far from increases in pay moving the demand for and supply of tool-setters towards equilibrium, the state of disequilibrium had become more pronounced by 1960 when (averaging the figures for June and December) there were 463 applicants for 5679 vacancies (more than twelve vacancies per applicant). We can watch the progress of their pay, relative to that of other engineering workers, from the earnings inquiries of the Engineering and Allied Employers' National Federation. Between September 1954 and June 1960, the earnings of this grade (designated skilled turners and machinemen) rose 46·9 per cent for time-work and 49·4 per cent for payment by results. In the same period, fitters' earnings rose by 43·3 and 45·8 per cent respectively. But even this slight lead fluctuated: fitters made up some lost ground between 1958 and 1959, then lost it again between 1959 and 1960. Thus the very great excess demand for tool-setters, setter-operators, compared with the very modest excess demand for fitters, is reflected in an irregularly dispersed increase of a little more than half of a percentage point per year.

The Ministry of Labour's analysis of unemployment and unfilled vacancies has shown an excess supply of women clerks, book-keepers and cashiers (for 1958–60, an average of 12,656 unemployed for 7678 vacancies) and an excess demand for shorthand typists and typists. But this overall shortage has been concentrated in the London and south-eastern region.

The Institute of Office Management distinguished typists from other clerks in their report for 1960. In grades C, D and E, in London, median pay for typists was between 8 and 15 per cent more than that for female clerks. In north-western England, the range was between 0 and 10 per cent: in the south-east Lancashire conurbation, minus 6 to 4 per cent.[16]

The setter-operators and the shorthand typists present two cases of persistent excess demand, calculated in the conventional theory to activate the equilibrating mechanism. Pay should rise as employers sort out the urgency of their wants, with demand falling accordingly and supply coming to meet it half way; but this does not happen.

## 1960 TO 1978

Crossley, as mentioned above, found a rank correlation coefficient of

+ 0·87 for earnings in 132 industries in 1948 and 1959; now the rate of pay increases has accelerated and the degree of correlation fallen: for men manual workers in 124 industries in 1960 and 1975 it was + 0·617. Between 1960 and 1970, semi-skilled and unskilled men and women gained on the skilled. But this, as indicated in the last chapter, was due to the peculiar success of certain occupational groups rather than to a narrowing of differentials in job clusters. In engineering, differentials between skilled, semi-skilled and unskilled men hardly changed between 1963 and 1970. Then, as we saw in Table 3.13 there was a widening between 1970 and 1971, followed by five years of narrowing to 1976. Why should the labourers have been able to make gains when the employment position was deteriorating between 1974 and 1976? In March 1976, there were 379,000 general labourers registered at employment offices as unemployed, 41 per cent of all unemployed men, compared with 150,000 'craft and similar occupations, including foremen, in processing, production, repairing, etc.'.[17]

Let us now look at the fate of women workers in this period when their relative pay was making substantial gains. The proponents of demand and supply have maintained that equal pay for equal work must have been established long since, for rational maximising employers would not have paid men more unless their superior output justified it. Thus a legally enforced rise in women's pay would result in a displacement of women by men. Table 3.10 shows the women's relative rise of 1970–1 cancelled out in 1971–2, but after that an accelerating relative rise for women so that between 1972 and 1977 their average rose by a factor of 2·5, compared with 2·1 for men. In the former year, their average was 54·8 per cent of the men's, in the latter 64·9 per cent. In this period, employment, seasonally adjusted, moved as follows:

|         | *Thousands* | |
|---------|------------|------------|
|         | *March 1972* | *March 1977* |
| Males   | 13,298     | 13,099     |
| Females | 8327       | 9040       |

In 1972, women constituted 38·5 per cent of employees in civil employment; in 1977, 40·8 per cent.[18]

Lastly, let us consider the decline in the relative pay of managers between 1970 and 1976 observed in Table 3.12. Could this be a reflection of a changed ratio of demand and supply? It is true that the number of managers who had registered at employment exchanges as unemployed rose substantially between 1970 and 1976. In December 1970, the total for male administrative, professional and technical workers as 30,697; in March 1976 we are given, according to the List of Key Occupations for Statistical Purposes (KOS):

Group I Managerial (general management) 1588
Group VI Managerial (exc. general management) 20,324

The total of registered unemployed managerial and professional men had risen to 57,000.[19] But in the same period, the total for all unemployed men had almost doubled. We have another measure of the state of the market for managers: that is the index constructed by MSL International on the basis of managerial and technical vacancies advertised in *The Times, Daily Telegraph, Guardian, The Economist, The Observer* and *The Sunday Times*. This shows a fall from 160 in the first quarter of 1970 to 80 in the third quarter of 1971, followed by a rise to 160 in the third quarter of 1973 and a fall to 80 in the last quarter of 1975, followed by a rise to 98 in the third quarter 1976. But in earnings, the descent was continuous from 1970 to 1976 (April each year), with a fall in (relative) pay of 11 per cent between 1971 and 1973 (when demand was rising) and of 7 per cent from 1973 to 1976, when it was falling.[20]

## 2. NON-COMPETING GROUPS

Adam Smith, following Cantillon, identified those characteristics of occupations that were effective in determining their differences of pay, one of them being the 'easiness and cheapness or difficulty and expense of learning it'.[21] Cantillon remarked on the connexion between this and occupational class: 'As the Handicraftsmen earn more than the Labourers they are better able to bring up their children to Crafts; and there will never be a lack of Craftsmen in a State when there is enough work for their constant employment.'[22] Despite the length and expense of his education, a curate was paid less than a mason, because, Smith explained, 'It has been considered of so much importance that a proper number of young people should be educated for certain professions, that sometimes the public and sometimes the piety of private founders have established many pensions, scholarships . . . etc., for this purpose, which draw many more people into those trades than could otherwise pretend to follow them.' If, in other professions, an equal proportion were educated at public expense,

> . . . the competition would soon be so great, as to sink very much their pecuniary reward. It might then not be worth any man's while to educate his son to (law or physick) at his own expense. They would be entirely abandoned to such as had been educated by those publick charities, whose numbers and necessities would oblige them in general to content themselves with a very miserable recompence, to the entire degradation of the now respectable professions of law and physick.[23]

That might explain why curates and chaplains were so miserably paid despite their expensive education, but why did disagreeableness of employment seem to go with low pay instead of being made up for by high pay, as Cantillon and Smith had prescribed? John Stuart Mill thought out a most plausible explanation.

> These inequalities of remuneration, which are supposed to compensate for the disagreeable circumstances of particular employments, would, under certain conditions, be natural consequences of perfectly free conpetition: and as between employments of about the same grade, and filled by nearly the same description of people, they are, no doubt, for the most part, realized in practice. But it is altogether a false view of the state of facts, to present this as the relation which generally exists between agreeable and disagreeable employments. The really exhausting and the really repulsive labours, instead of being better paid than others, are almost invariably paid the worst of all, because performed by those who have no choice . . . The more revolting the occupation, the more certain it is to receive the minimum of remuneration, because it devolves on the most helpless and degraded, on those who from squalid poverty, or from want of skill and education are rejected from all other employments[24].

Mill's pupil, J. E. Cairnes, developed these ideas still further and thus laid the foundation for subsequent investigations into social class stratification and inter-class mobility. Once trained, labour became somewhat immobile as between different occupations, so that changes in demand had to be met largely from the constantly emerging stream of young workers (the equivalent of liquid capital) who could direct themselves into the most profitable occupations. There was, however, an important limitation to this process: each individual could choose his employment only 'within certain tolerably well defined limits', set by the qualifications required for each occupation. Thus the sons of unskilled workers would have all forms of mere unskilled work open to them, but beyond this they were practically shut out from competition. 'The barrier is his social position and circumstances, which render his education defective, while his means are too narrow to allow of his repairing the defect, or of deferring the return upon his industry till he has qualified himself for a skilled occupation.' The sons of artisans suffered from similar limitations of choice, and so on up the occupational scale:

> The limits imposed are not such as may not be overcome by extraordinary energy, self-denial, and enterprise; and by virtue of these qualities individuals in all classes are escaping every day from the bounds of their original position, and forcing their way into the ranks of those who stand above them . . . But such exceptional phenomena do not affect the substantial truth of our position. What we find, in effect, is, not a whole population competing indiscriminately for all occupations, but a series of industrial layers, superposed on one another, within each of which the various candidates for employment possess a real and effective power of selection, while those occupying the several strata are, for all purposes of effective competition, practically isolated from each other . . . so . . . that the average workman, from whatever rank he be taken, finds his power of competition limited for practical purposes to a certain range of occupations, so that, however high the rates of remuneration in those which lie beyond may rise, he is excluded from sharing them. We are thus compelled to recognise the existence of non-competing industrial groups as a feature of our social economy; and this is the fact which I desire here to insist upon[25]

Wicksteed, while applying marginal analysis to the labour market, came to rather similar conclusions. There are many factors that interfere with 'the flow of undifferentiated human talent in the direction which would best minister to the want highest on the collective scale . . . . Thus, those occupations which require an elaborate and expensive preparation will, so long as present conditions remain, always be recruited from a small section of society; and the talent which exists in the great mass of people will be either undetected or left untrained[26].

He then states the conditions that would be required for the fulfilment of Adam Smith's formula for the determination of pay by job-content. The educational system would have to play the part of a 'great sorting machine for adjusting opportunities to capacities throughout the whole population'[27]. A flow would follow from less pleasant, less highly paid, occupations, to pleasanter and more highly paid ones, so that the marginal productivity of the latter would be lowered and that of the former raised. The utopian ideal would then be approached 'of a higher payment for the more monotonous services rendered to society by the manual workers, than for the more varied and pleasant ones rendered by the exercise of the artistic and intellectual powers'.[28]

Marshall shares these ideas, but adds another, relating to bargaining strength, that may help to explain differences in occupational pay. The unskilled labourer is in the weakest position, because his wages leave him very little margin for saving, and because if he stops work, there are large numbers who are capable of replacing him. It is also more difficult for unskilled workers to form 'strong and lasting combinations' and thus bargain on equal terms with their employers. At the other extreme are the professional classes who 'are richer, have larger reserve funds, more knowledge and resolution, and much greater power of concerted action with regard to the terms on which they sell their services, than the greater number of their clients and customers'.[29]

In more recent years, sociologists have collected data to measure social stratification and mobility. Lipset and Bendix note that

> . . . before World War II, studies of social mobility were usually limited to investigations of the social origins of different occupational groups, employees of single factories, or inhabitants of single communities. Since World War II there have been at least fifteen different national surveys in eleven countries which have secured from representative samples of the population information that relates the occupations of the respondents to the occupations of their fathers. In addition, there have been a number of studies conducted in different cities of various countries. Taken together, these investigations permit the comparison of current variations in occupational mobility, as well as some estimate of differences during the past half century.[30]

After examining the results of these investigations, Lipset and Zetterberg cautiously concluded:

In effect, the principal impression which may be derived from the summary of mobility studies around the world is that no known complex society may be correctly described as 'closed' or static. Although the paths of mobility and the extent to which the mobile may enter or leave different strata are not the same in all such societies, the number of persons in each who are able to rise above the position of their parents is large enough to refute the statement that 'class barriers are insurmountable'.[31]

Lipset and Zetterberg use only three broad classifications to delineate their classes: non-manual occupations, manual occupations and farm occupations. Generally, though, a more detailed system is used. Pitirim A. Sorokin defines social class as a coalescence of occupational and economic bonds associated with a totality of social and legal rights and duties:

> We have seen that economic and occupational bonds taken separately exert a powerful influence on the body and mind, the behavior and way of life of an individual. Their combined influence, re-enforced by similarity of status in the stratified pyramid of the population, is still greater. Persons having essentially similar occupations, economic position, and rights and duties cannot fail to become similar in a great many other ways, physical, mental, moral and behavioral.[32]

The Department of Sociological Research at the London School of Economics investigated the social origins, education, occupation, marriage and fertility of a random sample of 10,000 adults. The findings show a high (though changing) degree of social stratification in Britain. This stratification was by no means completely rigid, and there was, in fact, a fair degree of mobility between classes, 'nevertheless the general picture is of a rather stable social structure, and one in which social status has tended to operate within, so to speak, a closed circuit. Social origins have conditioned educational level, and both have conditioned achieved social status. Marriage has also to a considerable extent taken place within the same closed circuit.'[33]

The facts seem to lend themselves to interpretations in the way suggested by Cairnes and the others: an occupational distribution and occupational pay structure supported by class stratification, not completely rigid and yet set enough to limit severely competition for higher-paid jobs. We have noted Adam Smith's and Wicksteed's conditions for the break-up of this system: public education for higher occupations, with the educational system as a sorting machine to adjust opportunities to capacities.

Since the war, the education system has been more and more adapted to serve this end and, as we have seen, between 1935 and 1955, higher professional pay fell from 395 to 269 per cent of the all-class average; lower professional pay from 188 to 114 per cent. This was associated with a substantial increase in the proportion of full-time university students and in the number receiving public grants for full-time study.

Teachers give an example of this process. Between 1913 and 1924, they increased their pay lead over the averages for all men and women respectively, but between 1936 and 1955, they suffered a substantial relative reduction. Despite this reduction, it was possible to make up for the wartime fall in the number of teachers and then to increase their numbers, between 1949 and 1956, by over 20 per cent.[34] By 1955, there were more qualified applicants than places in the training colleges. This the government had been able to do by, in effect, paying entrants from the date their specialised training commenced and thus relieving them (or their parents) of the expense of fees, maintenance and wages forgone.

In order to examine more closely the extent of upward mobility between occupational classes, we conducted an inquiry into the social origins of engineering draughtsmen and design technicians. This, it seemed, might be one of the gateways to the professions. If there were a high degree of exclusiveness in the recruitment of draughtsmen, that is, if son followed father in this occupation or if father's occupation was predominantly also in the lower professions, this would indicate a restriction of supply that might well serve to maintain class differentials. On the other hand, if this were in fact a 'gateway occupation', it would suggest that there were facilities for adequate supplies of professional labour.

Table 4.1 summarises the results of this inquiry in so far as it relates to fathers' occupational class.[35] The first line shows the percentage distribution of respondents classified according to their father's occupational class. The second line of figures shows the occupational class distribution of all occupied men in Great Britain in 1931. If there had been equal chance for all to become draughtsmen then, by the laws of probability, the percentage distribution in both lines would have been similar. But in fact there are great differences. It is only in the case of the sons of clerks that there are neither more nor less than a random distribution would suggest. Proportionately, the sons of foremen are five times more numerous than would have been expected, of higher professionals two and a half times; skilled workers, one and a third

TABLE 4.1 Distribution of draughtsmen by fathers' occupational class, 1960, and distribution of occupied men by occupational class, 1931

| | Professional | | | | | Manual workers | | | |
|---|---|---|---|---|---|---|---|---|---|
| | Higher | Lower | Mana-gerial | Clerical | Foremen | Skilled | Semi-skilled | Un-skilled | All |
| Draughtsmen's fathers | 3·8 | 3·5 | 14·1 | 5·6 | 10·0 | 40·6 | 17·4 | 4·9 | 100 |
| Occupied males, 1931 | 1·5 | 2·0 | 12·0 | 5·5 | 2·0 | 30·0 | 29·0 | 18·0 | 100 |

times. But sons of semi-skilled workers have only 60 per cent of the places equal opportunity would have given them, and those of unskilled workers only 27 per cent.

This is in keeping with the findings of other inquiries: the great underrepresentation of the sons of semi-skilled and unskilled manual workers; much talent is going to waste; there is great inequality of opportunity. But at the same time, 70 per cent of the entrants to this profession were the sons of foremen or manual workers; 43 per cent of them had in fact entered draughtsmanship after a craft apprenticeship, that is, had themselves switched from a manual to a non-manual occupation.

There were two other indications that the occupation is associated with high mobility: it is a 'young' occupation, not only because the rate of intake is accelerating, but because it offers a favourable stepping-stone to promotion; secondly, the children of draughtsmen are in a favourable position to enter the professions. So, in 1931, in England and Wales, there were 15,380 draughtsmen in the age group 25–34. But in 1951 in the range 45–54, there were only 9086, despite the fact that in the intervening years the total number of draughtsmen had more than doubled. Draughtsmen in the sample had fifty-five sons who were at work and sixty daughters. Their occupational distribution is shown in Table 4.2.

TABLE 4.2 Occupational classes of draughtsmen's children

| | Professional | | | | | Manual workers | | | |
|---|---|---|---|---|---|---|---|---|---|
| | Higher | Lower | Mana-gerial | Cleri-cal | Foremen | Skilled | Semi-skilled | Un-skilled | All |
| Boys | 23 | 12 | 5 | 5 | — | 9 | 1 | — | 55 |
| Girls | — | 25 | 2 | 28 | — | 2 | 3 | — | 60 |

Even though the sons of semi-skilled and unskilled manual workers are hardly in the running for the higher professions and get much less than their share of the others, a great increase of supply may be brought about simply by easing the way for the children of other classes, and not least for those of professional workers themselves. In the sample study of 1949, 38.8 per cent of the sons of fathers who had been professional men and high administrators were employed in the same class; 15.5 per cent of the sons of managers and executives had become professional men or high administrators[36]. There was thus some scope for an increase in recruitment from these classes themselves.

In 1960, class 1A (higher professions) would have required nearly 20,000 new male entrants to provide for its growth and to make up for deaths and retirements[37]. On the same basis, 3500 women would have been needed. A calculation based on the age and number of married men in census order XIX (the professions) and mean family size for socio-economic group 3 suggests that in 1960, sons and daughters of higher professional fathers must have been coming off the educational assembly line at the rate of seventeen or eighteen thousand a year. Potentially, this class could thus supply a high proportion of men and a superabundance of women.

However, the children of fathers in occupational classes 1B (lower professions), 3 (clerks) and 4 (foremen) and in the lower divisions of class 2 (managers and proprietors) are in one respect in an even more favourable position: parents' incomes here would not be so high as to disentitle them to public grants, so that their higher education would not involve their parents in much financial sacrifice. At the same time, their home environment is not unfavourable to social and educational advancement.

The relative shortage of certain professional workers is now due rather to limitations of the educational system than to a shortage of boys and girls with the basic education and financial resources to undertake the required training. We have indeed achieved the state where the majority of those educated for the learned professions are educated at public expense: have they, as Adam Smith predicted, 'to content themselves with a very miserable recompence, to the entire degradation of the now respectable professions of law and physick'? Their relative pay fell during the periods of the two world wars, but the falls took place *before* the passage of the Education Act of 1944. Though they suffered a substantial fall between 1960 and 1970, they held their own in the previous and subsequent periods distinguished in Table 2.27. Their recompense remains more than twice that of the average man. It may be that the non-competing group hypothesis, plausible as it may seem, does not apply to the pay of occupational classes in the way suggested.

## 3. AN EXPLANATORY HYPOTHESIS

A mass of new evidence has become available since the first edition of this book, and much new thought has been presented to encompass it. But I repeat this section from the first edition with only minor changes, and add a fourth section to take account of the new material.

The outstanding characteristic of the national pay structure is the rigidity of its relationships. Adam Smith remarked upon this nearly two hundred years ago.[38] The price of provisions fluctuated but nominal wages did not, so that if workers could subsist when prices were high, they were well off when they were low. Regional differences, too, persisted. Wages might be 25 per cent higher in a great town that in the surrounding countryside, though the price of necessities in the town was no higher and was frequently lower.

> Such a difference of prices, which it seems is not always sufficient to transport a man from one parish to another, would necessarily occasion so great a transportation of the most bulky commodities, not only from one parish to another, but from one end of the kingdom, almost from one end of the world to the other, as would soon reduce them more nearly to a level. After all that has been said of the levity and inconstancy of human nature it appears evidently from experience that a man is of all sorts of luggage the most difficult to be transported.

Changes in occupational distribution have been markedly sluggish: the number of skilled and semi-skilled manual workers has fluctuated, but in 1951 was little different from the number in 1921; the *proportion* of employers and managers hardly varied from 1911 to 1951, while that of professional workers moved through only a few percentage points.

In the relative pay of occupations and occupational classes, too, the constancy has been more striking than the change.

This is not to say that relationships between class averages and between various occupations do not fluctuate: they do. But they seem to have the capacity to regain previous shapes, sometimes after lapses of many years. Thus class relations were similar in 1935 to those of 1913, and, as between managers, foremen, skilled, semi-skilled and unskilled manual workers, the structure was not much different in 1960 from what it had been in 1913. Coalminers and agricultural workers suffered relative declines after the First World War, but regained their previous position after the second. The relative pay of railwaymen and Civil Servants was allowed to deteriorate during and after the Second World War and was then restored by drastic upward revisions in the middle or late 1950s.

It is not perhaps very surprising that those who share a common occupation should be dedicated to the maintenance of its status relative to other occupations; the misteries of the Middle Ages were so engaged, as are the trade unions and professional bodies of the present day. St Thomas Aquinas justified this phenomenon in the thirteenth century in a system of thought that was further developed by subsequent scholastic thinkers.[39] The test of justice was whether or not income was adequate to maintain the recipient in his due social status:

> The things that can be said without reservation to be necessary to a state of life are those without which a man would be forced to lower his status. He might have to change from living as a nobleman to practising a trade, or to make a notable cut in his domestic staff, in the liberality of his entertainment, or in his sons' education or his provision for them. The goods necessary to a state of life include provision for contingencies such as sickness. All these things also contribute to the decency of a state in life, and can be provided for according to custom, and within the limits of an honourable liberality. And in so far as a man's current status is inferior, he can also count as one of the requirements of decency the acquisition of the goods he needs for a moderate rise in status.[40]

Elliott Jaques, using psycho-analytic techniques, identified in workers what he regarded as an intuitive knowledge of what their pay ought to be, having regard to the work that they were doing.

> Payment at the equitable level is intuitively experienced as fair relative to others . . . Deviations in payment below the equitable level are accompanied by feelings of dissatisfaction which become stronger the greater is the deviation . . .
> Deviations above the equitable level are accompanied by feelings of being *relatively* well off as compared with others; at the 10 to 15 per cent level of deviation there is a strong sense of receiving preferential treatment, whfch may harden into bravado, with underlying feelings

of unease about how long the relatively advantageous position can be maintained.[41]

We can accept the existence of this intuitive knowledge (or something answering to that description) without accepting Dr Jaques's ascription of it to a single variable—the 'time span of discretion'. In practice, workers seize on to scraps of information pertaining to the pay of others in their occupation and in other occupations of similar status, the Ministry of Labour conducts an elaborate service for publicising pay rates, levels of earnings and their rate of change and the collection and interpretation of such data is a major preoccupation of trade unions and professional organisations, large firms belong to networks for the exchange of information, the Civil Service has its Pay Research Unit and at employment exchanges there is readily available information relating to a multitude of vacancies and their rates of pay.

It then becomes extraordinarily difficult to gain anything more than a temporary improvement in the pay of any occupation. In the words of Lady (then Professor) Wootton,

> Change—always, everywhere—requires justification: the strength of conservatism is that it is held to justify itself. It is not therefore surprising that the maintenance of standards, absolute or comparative, should be woven as warp and woof into the texture of wage discussions; or, to change the metaphor, that history should be summoned to fill the void when moral actions must be performed without moral principles to guide them.
>
> This lack of guiding principle affects, moreover, equally those who pay and those who receive wages. Conservatism does duty on both sides. On the one side, the unions, as we have seen, appeal to precedent, and defend their proposals as necessary to restore the *status quo*—if not literally *ante bellum*, at least before some selected date-line; whilst employers, on the other hand, take their stand on the simple rule of 'no change'. The dispute between them turns, not so much on the choice of the direction in which to move, as on rival interpretations of what is meant by standing still.[42]

There is something elemental in this attachment of a person to his level of income, measured in terms of its purchasing power (the maintenance of a standard of living) and in terms of the earnings of other occupations, that is not unlike the attachment of an animal to its young. It applies to the individual and leads individuals to act in concert with or without trade union organisation; a sense that their work has been devalued can turn a disciplined work force into a surly, disgruntled mob. In the phrase of Adam Smith, they are 'desperate men'.

And there is justification for this frame of mind, for the devaluation of a man's labour, through no fault of his own, is a form of confiscation of property.

The *status quo* is constantly being disturbed, however, by trade unions or professional associations getting better terms for the occupations they represent or by employers unilaterally or by individual bargaining raising the pay of all or some of the occupations or individuals they employ. This is a never-ending process, though the speed at which it operates may show great variation from time to time, and, since there are always some occupations whose members feel aggrieved or that they deserve upgrading in the pay structure, it is unlikely that equilibrium can ever be attained. So the process draws its energy from an endless stock of hope and envy, of which trade unionism is in part an expression. But trade unionism is only the outward expression of a general tendency for people with common interests to ally themselves for their mutual advancement. In non-union shops or unorganised sectors, discontent will show itself if they are left behind; and if rising activity is at the same time increasing profits and the need of the employer for his workers, he will have to raise his rates as well, simply to keep his workers happy.

Thus it would be quite mistaken to regard the pay structure as unchanging: it is in an almost constant state of change. It is by its nature incapable of reaching a state of rest, because it is made up of a multitude of units (that is, units for purposes of determining rates of pay) who have different ideas as to what their relationships to one another should be. Group A may claim parity with group B, which may claim a differential of $x$ per cent over group A. Both groups cannot then be at rest at the same time.[43]

From Chapter 3, we can describe the circumstances in which major changes in pay structure are brought about. There were three periods between 1913 and 1960 when this occurred, in the form of a general narrowing of differentials: 1914 to 1920, 1934 to 1944 (in particular, 1938 to 1940) and 1951 to 1955. Between 1920 and 1924, there was a drastic widening of differentials so that, by the latter year, the pre-war position had generally been regained. After 1955, there was again a reversal of the narrowing process.

The common characteristic of the periods of narrowing differentials is their high rate of inflation. For the period 1914 to 1920, the average annual rise in the cost of living index was nearly 17 per cent; for 1935 to

1942, 6·2 per cent; for 1950 to 1955, 5·1 per cent. In the periods 1944 to 1950 and 1956 to 1960 when dispersion was stable or widening, the rise in prices was more moderate: 3·7 per cent and 2·7 per cent per year, respectively.

What is the connexion between rapidly rising prices and reduced differentials? Sometimes it is felt that the change is temporary and that, pending a general reassessment that must be postponed until a new period of stability is reached, lower-paid workers should be compensated in whole or in part so that they may avoid real hardship. This, at any rate, was the basis of cost of living bonuses in the public service in the two wars, when the degree of compensation for price rises diminished as the income range ascended.

Another cause is the frequency of claims for flat-rate rather than percentage increases during periods of rapidly rising prices; and even when the increase is in percentage form, it is generally a percentage of the standard rate so that it forms a lower percentage for those whose rates are above the standard. In periods of rapid change, with social relationships under strain, flat-rate claims are made because they express and generate a sense of solidarity between occupations at different levels in the same union or federation of unions. The employers are offered a package deal: the proportions of skilled and unskilled labour are fixed by technique or custom and, though they could buy their unskilled labour more cheaply, they are prevented from doing so by the fact that the craftsmen stipulate not only their own rate, but that for their helpers.

For the reductions in differentials between manual and non-manual workers, the greater stability of salaries appears to be the immediate cause. We noted in Chapter 3 that their rise began later and moved more slowly between 1914 and 1920 and that, when wages tumbled in 1921 and 1922, salaries remained almost unscathed. Part of this greater stability may stem from the difference in social relationships between non-manual workers and their employers, part from the greater stability of their employment (for revisions of pay tend to be delayed until new appointments are made) and part from the fact that they are frequently on incremental scales so that inflation is mitigated by the annual rise.

From the contrasting pay history of the years 1921 to 1923 and 1924 to 1934, we may deduce some of the conditions necessary for a reduction in wage rates. The reductions of 1921 and 1922 were achieved in a period in which retail prices were halved and unemployment reached 23 per cent and did not fall below 12 per cent. More than half the reductions in 1921 and nearly 40 per cent of those in 1922 were brought about 'automatically' in terms of cost of living sliding scale agreements, but even so, there was great industrial unrest and the loss, through strikes, of more than a hundred million man-days.

Between 1924 and 1934, we have noted an almost equal fall in retail prices and rise in unemployment, but these were accompanied by a fall in wage rates of only 6 per cent, compared with 38 per cent in 1921 and 1922. For the 'ratchet effect' to be overcome, then, it is not enough for a price fall and unemployment to be substantial: they must be both drastic and sudden.

What is the role of the trade unions in the process of change? There has been considerable controversy on this subject, some writers conceding them great power to reshape pay structure, others an ability merely to rubber-stamp what would have happened anyway.[44] To some extent, this controversy has been caused by a misconception, by the notion that pay structure is static instead of in a constant state of movement. As with Alice, it is sometimes necessary to run faster and faster to stay in the same place; the object of the race is not to win, for it is one without an end, but to get closer to those ahead or farther away from those behind; the unions then act as agents for hurrying things along.

In the race, transient advantages may be of considerable importance to the parties concerned, and may give groups of workers advantages that are obscured in long-term comparisons.[45] Their neglect by those theorists who stress the self-defeating nature of wage increases is one reason why their arguments fail to get across. An increase in pay may give real and immediate relief to those who get it, even though in due course it will work its way round to retail prices and they will be no better off than they were before.

It is possible that trade unions may be responsible for the upward movement of money wage rates in the face of high unemployment at the upward turn in the trade cycle. Why do employers raise rates when there are still large numbers of unemployed workers who would be delighted to take employment at prevailing rates? Part of the reason may be found in the relationship of the employer to his workers: profits are rising, orders accumulating, the losses of the depression are being recouped. But his employees have also suffered in the depression and feel they have a right to some share in the new prosperity. The avoidance of ill-feeling might in itself be sufficient reason for granting increases, but the existence of a union that might close the factory at this crucial moment, when customers have alternative sources of supply, is likely to hasten and augment the share-out.

The proximity of foremen and managers to the manual workers

whom they control may explain their immunity from the sort of reductions, relative to manual pay, from which professional workers have suffered. An increase for manual workers necessitates one for foremen, which sends the impulse up the hierarchy. Managers have a second source of increase: if profits rise, the pay of directors and general managers will tend to follow and this movement will tend to be transmitted downward.

It is a mistake to imagine that there is a sharp division between unionized and un-unionised workers, for trade unions cannot do much more than institutionalize and direct drives and aspirations that are already present in the individual workers. Unions protect individual workers against arbitrary acts; they give collections of workers more control over their own destiny than they would have as individuals and present the possibility of pursuing social ends that might not otherwise be attainable. It is in pursuit of such ends that unions set about reducing differentials by extracting flat-rate increases from employers for different levels of skill. It does not follow that they always succeed in changing established patterns. For example, we may watch the movement of negotiated increases and earnings in the engineering industry when, between 1934 and 1940, flat-rate increases were claimed and conceded regardless of skill:[46]

| | Changes in standard hourly rate Pence | Change in hourly earnings | | |
|---|---|---|---|---|
| | | Skilled Pence | Semi-skilled Pence | Unskilled Pence |
| October 1934–October 1935 | 0·50 | 0·81 | 0·76 | 0·65 |
| October 1935–October 1936 | 0·50 | 0·94 | 1·02 | 0·58 |
| October 1936–October 1937 | 0·625 | 1·16 | 0·86 | 0·84 |
| October 1937–July 1938 | 0·375 | 0·58 | 0·43 | 0·36 |
| July 1938–October 1939 | 0·50 | 2·17 | 1·41 | 1·08 |
| October 1939–July 1940 | 1·25 | 3·51 | 3·02 | 2·11 |

*Notes:* Time-workers and payment by results workers combined. Skilled includes skilled fitters (not toolroom), turners, machinemen rated at or above fitters' rate, platers, riveters and caulkers, moulders, sheet metal-workers. Semi-skilled: machinemen rated below fitters' rate. Unskilled: labourers.

Although, between October 1934 and July 1940, standard hourly rates for all classes had risen by 3·75*d.*, hourly earnings for skilled workers had increased by 9·17*d.*, for the semi-skilled by 7·50*d.* and for the unskilled by 5·62*d*. It was union policy to extract the same increases for all and, *ipso facto*, to narrow differentials, but resistances were such that the end result was a stalemate, with unskilled hourly earnings 66·0 per cent of skilled in October 1934 and 64·4 per cent in July 1940.

By June 1959, the differential in standard rates had narrowed still further: the labourer's rate was 84·25 per cent of the fitter's. But the hourly earnings differential for time-work was almost identical: the labourer 73·7 per cent of the fitter in July 1940 and 73·6 per cent in June 1959.[47] Both fitters and labourers had developed an earnings gap,[48] but while this was 11·8 per cent for labourers in June 1959, it was 18·6 per cent for fitters.

Of course, the above is only an hypothesis; but it appears to make the facts intelligible, whereas demand and supply theory does not. It suggests that attempts to formulate a national pay policy or to manipulate pay structure are misconceived if they are based on a belief in the effectiveness of price in the regulation of supply and demand. Bishops, judges and cabinet ministers have had their real pay drastically reduced in the last fifty years, yet there is still no shortage of candidates for those positions; the substantial increases paid in recent years to civil servants, police and railwaymen to restore their place in the pay hierarchy are a demonstration of the fact that these services could continue for a considerable time with levels of pay inferior to those of comparable workers elsewhere.

Pay structure cannot easily be varied by design nor undermanned industries manned up by a simple increase in pay, for if one class of workers is advanced beyond their conventional position, forces will be generated that in due course will be likely to restore the former position. It seems that it is easier, on the whole, to correct great inequalities in pay by more extensive education, by training people for higher jobs rather than raising the pay for the lower ones and by the improvement of non-pecuniary conditions, including job security and holidays.

A change in pay structure, to have lasting effect, would require careful preparation, much public education, support of trade unions and employers, and consent of those to whom it was to apply.

## 4. AN ALTERNATIVE PRESENTATION

In the previous section, I presented a new paradigm through which to interpret the phenomena of labour markets, as conceived in the first edition of this book.[49] Orderly patterns were maintained through the tensions of perpetual disequilibrium, the system powered by *moral energy*: the pursuit of what is right and fair.[50] Opposed to this is the orthodox vision, invented in the seventeenth century, established in the eighteenth, that views economies as orderly systems in which market equilibria are established between supply and demand through the medium of price.[51] In the days when people believed in the intercession of God in the affairs of man, this state of holy harmony in an apparently unholy and disorderly world was accredited to a miracle and sold to the world under that label.[52]

After three centuries of this doctrine, it is difficult for modern man and woman not to believe that demand-and-supply are beavering away out there, tirelessly regulating rewards, optimising allocation and maximising profits and utility. The difficulty is that, because these ideas have been so long accepted, the onus has been placed on those who reject them to prove that they are wrong. So Richard Lester's paper of 1946 is held to have been rebutted by Fritz Machlup's of the same year, not by Machlup amassing evidence of cases where marginal productivity determined pay, but by his criticising Lester's evidence of cases where it did not.[53]

It is popularly held that every person has his or her price and, to complete the symmetry, that no one will buy the services of another if it does not pay to do so. But this is not enough: the model specifies that excess demand will raise price, so stimulating an increase in supply whilst simultaneously moving back the margin of demand to the point where the marginal product is once more equal to price. Resources are thus reallocated, factors reproportioned, equilibrium re-established.[54] During the early years of research for this book, I searched for cases that would illustrate this process. I followed up many false clues. Some led to cases of inelastic supply of labour where pay was bid up, not in such a way as to restore equilibrium, but merely to ration between employers those talents that were available. Employers were reluctant to respond to shortages by raising pay, partly for that reason, and partly because of its repercussions amongst the rest of their staff.[55] Likewise, when there is an excess supply of labour to any occupation, workers prefer to ration jobs rather than cut rates in the hope that employment will thereby be increased.[56] But a phenomenon still more indigestible is the lavish raising of rates of pay in the face of high unemployment: this is so serious a breach of the rule as to bring the rule itself into doubt. I am not so optimistic as to imagine it will be easy to separate from these ideas those who are attached to them, for there are powerful interests vested in their perpetuation: in textbooks, lecture notes, and the application of skills in econometrics that demand determinate solutions for their sets of equations.[57]

We may, if we wish, call workers' willingness to work 'supply' and employers' willingness to employ 'demand'. What contributions does this make to explaining the puzzles of pay? In Cairnes's words, simply none at all, or next to none at all—what we want to know is what it is which governs supply and demand in each case.[58]

If we are not to get lost with our very next step, we must stop for a moment and survey the scene. Each morning the rise of the sun brings millions of workers from their beds and sends them streaming off to work, each to what he regards as his own job. The employer also regards it as the worker's own job, and is piqued if he does not appear to occupy it. These workers are not in the labour market nor are their jobs in the job market nor is their pay a matter of contention. They constitute what Clark Kerr calls the 'hard core of the employed'. 'They were attached to their jobs or their areas as in a "marriage contract," as Boulding put it. There was no single labor market but many labor markets, each with its own characteristics and rules for entry and movement within.'[59]

> Although the majority of the workers are vaguely conscious of the job market, they cannot be said to be actively in it. They are sufficiently satisfied with their current jobs or fearful of the un-certainties to be encountered in movement so that they are not weighing the advantages of other jobs as against their own. Unless ejected from their current jobs they are only passive participants in the market. Not only by choice but also by necessity is this the case, for many employers, as demonstrated by a current study of employer hiring practices in the San Francisco Bay Area, prefer not to hire persons employed elsewhere. From the point of view of the smooth functioning of the job market, they are the hard core of the employed.[60]

These findings conform closely with those of a study of the mobility of Brighton households conducted in 1971. Interviewers gathered data about 1017 households. Of these 442 had moved into Brighton or had moved back to Brighton after having moved away, or at least one of the partners had done that during his or her adult life. The rest (575) had been born in Brighton or brought there by their parents and had never moved away. Of the movers, 140 had at some time moved for reasons connected with their jobs, but having moved, most of them had relapsed into immobility. Of the 575 who had never moved, 453 appeared to be

totally ignorant of and indifferent to job opportunities and pay in other
towns. They appeared to find positive satisfaction in remaining where
they were, undisturbed by thoughts of the possibility of doing better by
being somewhere else.[61]

But how, in these circumstances, does pay structure retain so regular a
form, a phenomenon attested to by the evidence presented above? We
know that collectively negotiated settlements keep fairly well in step. Or
perhaps a more appropriate simile would be a platoon of infantry, ill-
disciplined but heading in the same direction so that the tail keeps fairly
near the front. Changes per head in rates negotiated for manual workers
have averaged as follows:[62]

| Year | £ per week |
|------|------------|
| 1967 | 0·78 |
| 8 | 0·89 |
| 9 | 0·98 |
| 1970 | 1·74 |
| 1 | 1·64 |
| 2 | 2·49 |
| 3 | 2·33 |
| 4 | 6·56 |
| 5 | 7·34 |
| 6 | 3·97 |
| 7 | 3·13 |
| 8 | 7·73 |

How do these changes in pace occur? It appears to have been the
London dustmen who ushered in the new era at the end of 1969, by
winning their (for those days) high increase of £2 a week. In August and
September, 1972, the change of pace was introduced by engineering,
with a £3 rise for skilled men at the end of August, and building and civil
engineering with £6 for craftsmen and £5.20 for labourers from 18
September. In 1974, came the miners' settlement effective on 1 March,
with increases ranging from £6·71 to £11·21.

Aubrey Jones, from his considerable experience as chairman of the
National Board for Prices and Incomes, was able to observe the
mechanisms by which this phenomenon was sustained. He contrasts the
ways of the world with those attributed to it in conventional economic
thought:

> An inherited body of thought retains a powerful hold over the minds of men long after the moment of utterance . . . It is, however, at odds with what we observe in contemporary society, because it would be more realistic to say that the present-day phenomenon is one of 'wage leadership'. In other words a 'leading' sector grants wage increases which set the pace for other sectors to follow. Let us suppose that this leading sector is the one in which the growth in productivity is fastest; then if similar wage increases follow in the sectors in which productivity is growing more slowly, wages in these will be rising faster than productivity, and prices will accordingly need to be raised if the rate of profit is to remain unchanged. Thus the leading sector could be an important force in the inflationary process, particularly if it is a fast-growing sector.[63]

There were many possible initiating causes, including the accession to power of a more militant trade union leader. The inspiration is social and political: ' . . . each feels entitled to the increase which others, particularly those near him, are seen to be getting'. Mergers lead to claims that pay be levelled up to that of the highest-paying firm; 'automobile firms in the southern part of the United Kingdom are under pressure to pay earnings equivalent to those obtained in the Midlands— even though employment conditions generally may vary from one location to another'.[64]

If demand and supply are at work, their influence is but dimly discerned. In the words of H. A. Turner, 'Taking one consideration with another, the "zone of indeterminacy" in the operation of market forces appears so substantial that one could well argue that the latter's apparent dominance, in historical and comparative observation, results only from the various and conflicting directions in which other forces have pressed.'[65]

This leads to a conclusion of the highest importance for policy purposes, that leads Clark Kerr to distinguish between the job market and the wage market, which are 'substantially disjointed and can and sometimes do go their own separate ways'.[66] If the link between employment and earnings increases is a figment of the theorists' imaginations, then governments need no longer refrain from promoting employment for fear of intensifying inflation; and far less need they pursue deflation, knowing that it will increase unemployment, in the hope that the rise in prices will be thereby diminished.

Ironically, all we need do to observe the low correlation between the level of unemployment and changes in wage rates is to consider the data

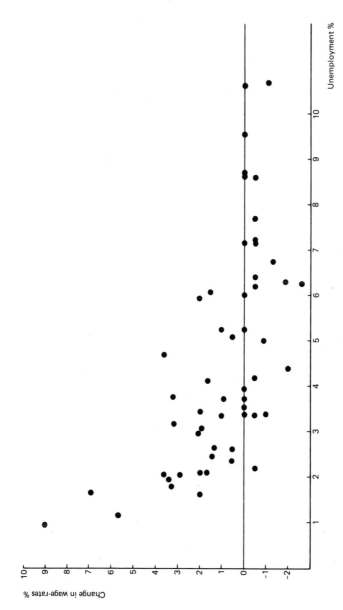

FIGURE 4.1 Unemployment and the changes in money wage rates, 1861–1914

upon which the well-known Phillips curve was based.[67] These are shown in Figure 4.1, in which the co-ordinates of each point are given by the change in wage rates (the vertical axis) and the rate of unemployment (the horizontal axis) in the years 1861 to 1913. It takes only a moment to see that, for any given level of unemployment, there is a wide range of possibilities for wage rates, and vice versa. But Phillips submitted the data to econometric torture, creating the appearance of relations of which it was innocent.[68] If, as in a change of paradigm, we could convert the unthinkable into the obvious, we might persuade our rulers to engineer an expansion of employment, free from the fear that they will thereby be promoting inflation. The promotion of output may be a surer way of reducing inflation than the promotion of unemployment. If money earnings are going to rise in any case, each percentage rise in output will reduce price rises by an equal amount. If the rise in employment is in house-building, purchasing-power will be absorbed without much increase in imports.[69]

PAY DETERMINATION IN PRACTICE

Before 1914 and between 1924 and 1939 there was a high degree of stability in pay rates in the United Kingdom. The influence of national negotiation was widespread, and it was from this that increases in pay were expected, and decreases resisted. But nowadays, plant bargaining is of much more importance, encouraged, no doubt, by the recommend-ations of the Donovan Commission.[70] In 1979, William Brown and others reported, following a nation-wide survey, that for 45·9 per cent of the manual workers and 40·6 per cent of the establishments in the sample the most important level of manual pay bargaining was the single establishment, while corporate multi-plant agreements covered 21·0 per cent of the manual workers and 11·2 per cent of the establishments. For non-manual pay bargaining, the percentages were 45·5 of employees for single establishment agreements and 39·5 per cent of establishments, and 26·8 per cent for corporate multi-plant agreements and 14·6 per cent of establishments.[71] Workers are playing a much more active role in the determination of their rates of pay. What is the nature of the resulting decision-making process? To gather data on this subject, Geoffrey Walker conducted interviews with 60 full-time trade union officials, 496 shop stewards, 333 rank-and-file trade unionists and 83 wives of trade unionists.[72]

Rank and file members had no precise view of what the amounts of their pay claims should be. Determining factors were figures that they had heard or read in the media in the three weeks or so before focusing their minds on the claim; any ceiling imposed by government restrictions; expectations derived from trade union journals or local shop stewards' news sheets; a vague notion to which they gave the label 'cost of living' but which bore little relation to the official index; employers' profits, unlikely to be known except in terms of being 'up' or 'down' on the previous year; an intrusion of unavoidable housekeeping expenses into the member's 'disposable income'—the residual funds whose presence makes all the difference to a man's life.

Transcending all the above questions of size and timing of claims was one circumstance in which the rank and file had very clear views of magnitude, size and immediate necessity for a claim, and this circumstance arose where a cherished relativity with a well-known immediate and clearly perceived comparator was changed. This situation, it cannot be emphasised too strongly, was the one which exercised the imagination and determination of all trade union members at all levels, and indeed it might be said that the rank and file level was that which perceived most keenly such a change.

A particularly revealing part of Walker's study relates to pay determination at Crawley. Informal gatherings of shop stewards planned the strategy and selected the next firm to be tackled according to 'criteria of vulnerability'. Personnel managers on the industrial estate knew what was going on, but were unable to do much to counteract it. 'The only hope would be if we could all hold out together but each one of us has his own particular pressures and if the firm has a contract to fulfil there are no thanks to be had in standing firm and fighting to the last drop of your own blood for the other companies.'

In these circumstances one would expect differences and fluctuations to reveal themselves between different firms that might be avoided in centralised, national negotiations, and this is the question that we shall consider next.

DISPERSION WITHIN OCCUPATIONS

We must now consider a feature of pay structure that may cause us to reconsider the assumptions upon which much of Chapter 2 has depended: that is, the demonstration in the NES of the very wide dispersion of earnings between people in the same occupation. As presented in Table 2.27, the pay structure by occupational class seems to make moral and economic sense: the higher professions are paid more than the lower professions, skilled manual workers more than the unskilled, and so on. But that is because we have compressed what is a great range of earnings for each occupation into a single average. When we were working on our calculations in the late 1950s and early 1960s it seemed that averages really could be taken as representative of the class as a whole, that each class was united by social and educational bonds and could have a price ticket attached to it. Consider the data shown in Table 4.3. Here are a group of linked occupations representing workers engaged in engineering. If we knew only their median pay, the arrangement would seem sensible enough: the general manager gets £133, the engineering maintenance manager £107. We might criticise the differentials as being too wide or too narrow, but at least the occupations seemed to be ranked in the right order, except, perhaps, for the women who are still getting relatively little despite the Equal Pay Act.

Figure 4.2 puts the data in diagrammatic form. The vertical axis measures the medians—no trouble with ranking. The horizontal axis measures the dispersion, the left-hand dot being the lowest decile (Q10), the middle dot the median (Q50) and the right-hand dot the highest decile (Q90). Now turn the diagram on its side. You will see that, over a wide range, many workers doing these different jobs are paid exactly the same. At £76 a week, you could hire any of them, and run your factory with equal pay for all, if it were 'demand-and-supply' that determined willingness to give or accept a price.

TABLE 4.3 Dispersion of earnings between and within certain occupations within the engineering industry, full-time workers, April 1978 (pounds)

|  | *Q10* | *Median* | *Q90* |
|---|---|---|---|
| General managers[a] | 76·00 | 133·30 | 310·00 |
| Engineering maintenance managers | 73·60 | 106·70 | 153·90 |
| Foremen, engineering machining | 74·70 | 97·20 | 125·70 |
| Maintenance fitters (non-electrical) | 61·70 | 86·00 | 125·60 |
| Repetitive assemblers (metal and electrical goods) | 55·00 | 76·00 | 104·90 |
| Storekeepers[a] | 53·00 | 68·70 | 96·80 |
| Clerks, production and materials control[a] | 53·90 | 65·80 | 85·60 |
| Personal secretaries, shorthand typists (women)[a] | 42·20 | 54·80 | 69·40 |
| Repetitive assemblers (metal and electrical goods) (women) | 40·60 | 52·80 | 68·50 |

[a] Mechanical engineering. *New Earnings Survey 1978*, part D, pp. D41 and D46.

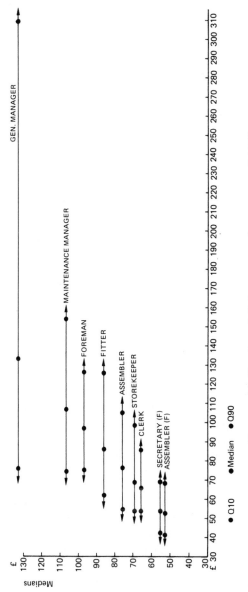

FIGURE 4.2 Earnings, full-time men and women, April 1978

Sir William Petty argued that people were not so much interested in their absolute incomes as in their income relative to other people, for it was on this that their station in society depended;[73] George Bernard Shaw, by contrast, maintained that there was only one sensible way of dividing wealth—and that was to give everyone the same.[74]

The spread of earnings within each occupation greatly weakens the claim of any occupation to a 'representative rate of pay', or of the theorist to have identified such a thing. It is a chastening thought that Adam Smith had arrived at this conclusion two hundred years ago. 'The price of labour, it must be observed, cannot be ascertained very accurately any where, different prices being often paid at the same place and for the same sort of labour, not only according to different abilities of the workmen, but according to the easiness or hardness of the master.'[75]

The range of pay for people in the same professions is clearly very wide: is it increasing or diminishing? A much-admired table presented in the *British Labour Statistics Year Book* shows that for men manual workers included in official earnings censuses there has been little change in dispersion since 1886 if the earnings of all grades of workers are averaged together.[76] So we have, for instance,

|      | Q10  | Q25  | Q50   | Q75   | Q90   |
|------|------|------|-------|-------|-------|
| 1886 | 68·6 | 82·8 | 100·0 | 121·7 | 143·1 |
| 1974 | 68·6 | 82·2 | 100·0 | 121·0 | 144·1 |

suggesting something splendidly immutable about the distribution of pay, at least as far as men manual workers covered by official enquiries are concerned. Yet this is at variance with what we know about the narrowing of differentials since 1914.[77]

The solution to this mystery appears to be a simple one: that while differentials *between* linked occupations have been contracting, dispersion *within* occupations has been expanding so that overall dispersion has remained fairly stable. For example, while differentials between bricklayers, fitters, and their labourers narrowed substantially between 1906 and 1971, the upper quartile of bricklayers and fitters pay was 188 per cent of the lower quartile of their labourers pay in 1906, and 186 in 1971.[78]

I am not laying down a pay version of the le Chatelier principle: that pressure applied to pay in one direction will generate an equal pressure in another. If there is a connexion between narrowing differentials and widening dispersion it will reveal itself to empirical reasearch, not to flights of imagination. Indeed, one may cite an immediate counter-instance: between 1970 and 1978, differentials narrowed in the engineering industry, as we saw in Table 3.13, but so did dispersion as measured by the relation of lowest and highest deciles.

Of course one must bear in mind the multitude of differences between jobs even when they bear the same occupational name. The more closely the job was defined, the less one might suppose the dispersion would be. There are also personal differences between those who perform them. Alfred Marshall blandly ascribed differences in pay for the same job to the 'efficiency wage' (measured by differences in output per worker in a specified time) or 'net advantages': non-pecuniary benefits or disadvantages that must be taken into account when jobs are compared.[79] How did he know this? He deduced it by concluding it *must* be so, according to his preconceived principles.

It was in order to standardise comparisons that we submitted detailed job descriptions to the companies who participated in the job rating exercises mentioned above.[80] The mean deviations as percentages of the mean for each job ranged from 15·0 for the personal secretary to 22·75 for the production manager. These are in fact rather similar to the dispersions shown in the NES and measured by the semi-interquartile range expressed as a percentage of the median. The deviations compared as follows:

|  | Job-rating exercise 1964 % | NES 1970 % |
|---|---|---|
| Production manager | 22·75 | 23·1 |
| Electrical engineer | 19·00 | 20·4 |
| Personal secretary | 15·00 | |
| Secretary, shorthand typist | | 17·4 |

While the breadth of dispersion within occupations seriously dilutes the meaning that can be attached to any absolute average, or any other expression of central tendency, for an occupation, let alone an occupational class, the relative pay of occupations and occupational classes does fit into the pattern of internal labour markets about which much has been written in recent years, and it is in this context that the data will now be considered.

There is one other aspect of pay that should be mentioned first, however, that throws further doubt on the solidity of pay structure, and that may be compared with the difference between a substance seen with the naked eye and then under an electron microscope. I mean the variability of individual earnings from year to year. The NES identifies its sample by taking the last two digits of national insurance numbers, which of course gives a sample of 1 in 100. If the same last two digits are taken over a series of years, then a high proportion of the sample in these years will represent the same individuals, so that the computer can then compare the earnings of an individual over several years. The comparisons show considerable variations, both up and down, from year to year. David Marsden has presented a description and analysis of these curious and perplexing movements.[81] These variations are not due simply to the fact that the NES takes each year the earnings in only one week for weekly-paid workers, and one month for monthly-paid, for annual earnings, too, show considerable upward and downward fluctuations.[82]

Whether one takes weekly or annual earnings, wide dispersion within occupations is confirmed. This is illustrated in data relating to the United States, where information about annual earnings by occupation is collected in conjunction with the decennial population census. For example:

Semi-interquartile range as % of median

|  | United States | | | |
|  | *1939* | *1949* | *1959* | *1969* |
| --- | --- | --- | --- | --- |
| Electrical engineers | 30·0 | 21·0 | 19·0 | 20·5 |
| Electricians | 23·0 | 18·5 | 19·0 | 33·0 |
| Machinists | 20·5 | 14·5 | 15·5 | 24·0 |
| Labourers | 27·5 | 22·0 | 27·0 | 32·5 |

*Sources*: Herman P. Miller, *Income Distribution in the United States* (US Bureau of Census, 1966); Bureau of Census, *Special Reports 1970 Census of Population, Earnings by Occupation and Education* (US Department of Commerce, 1973).

One may note from the same sources that average earnings reach their maximum in the 35–54 year age group, but that within each age group, dispersion is very wide.

## INTERNAL LABOUR MARKETS

I expressed doubt about the operational significance of national pay averages for occupational groups. Within the firm or employing organisation, however, they take on the highest significance, for here the *relative* levels of the national class averages are reflected and it is here that the decisions are taken which, in the aggregate, come through to the national figures.

In the twenties and thirties and in the earlier years of this century, more solidarity was manifested amongst employers in the face of the united front of their workers. At first, the trade unions adopted their 'rate' and enjoined their members not to work for less; later, employers' associations were persuaded to accept these rates as the minima that their members would pay. This resulted in the narrow dispersion within occupations manifest in the Board of Trade earnings survey of 1906. After 1958, there was a marked divergence between movements in earnings (as reported by employers) and the index of nationally negotiated wage rates, with earnings forging ahead. Was it then that the break-up of the traditional system began?[83]

Along with in-plant or organisation bargaining has come the spread of job evaluation, a manifestation of the initiative available to firms in establishing and managing their own pay structure.[84] It may be because plant bargaining was the normal method of unions in the United States that attention there was focused on internal labour markets earlier than in the United Kingdom. This focus required empirical investigation if the theorists were to be able to say anything intelligent about the real world, so that the American literature is full of material derived from interview and observation. We are indebted to Doeringer and Piore for building on to the earlier empirical studies in their own pioneering work in this field.[85] They distinguish the *internal labour market* as an administrative unit, such as a manufacturing plant, where the price and allocation of labor is governed by a set of administrative rules and procedures. 'The internal labor market, governed by administrative rules, is to be distinguished from the *external labor market* of conventional economic theory where pricing, allocating, and training decisions are controlled directly by economic variables.'[86]

Communication with the external market (or markets) is through certain ports of entry, so that, provided the flow through these ports remains adequate, the inhabitants of the organisation can go their own way.

Research on similar lines was done by a group of social anthropologists at the University of Manchester, in conjunction with groups of economists at Oxford and Glasgow.[87] They brought their research together at a seminar in March 1970. Derek Robinson reported,

> Discussion of the various seminar papers confirmed the view that there were many examples of pairs of plants in the same locality engaged on very similar engineering work where the higher-paying firm, which also had the better fringe benefits and physical surroundings, had a lower rate of productivity. It has not been possible to test this relationship in any systematic and quantifiable way, but there are strong general impressions that the money and effort bargains of members of the same occupation in the same industry in the same town are by no means similar. Indeed, the relationship is often reversed, so that lower-paying firms may have a higher rate of productivity.[88]

Robinson and his colleagues arrive independently at a conclusion remarkably similar to that of Doeringer and Piore:

> While this study does not make a general claim that economic forces coming from the external labour market exert no pressure on an internal wage structure, it does seem to be the case that in certain situations external economic pressures are weaker than the internal institutional pressures coming from within the company. This suggests that the firm, rather than being a helpless victim of economic forces beyond its control, has a margin of opportunity within which it can adjust its internal position and take independent decisions regarding its wage structure and wage levels. This margin of opportunity may be considerable in scope and extent. For internal labour markets are by definition as well as in observed fact to some extent isolated from the external labour market. Labour does not switch employment continually in order to maximise net advantages. There is labour mobility but there is much less than a comparison of different rates of pay for the same occupation in the same locality would suggest.[89]

Donald Mackay and his colleagues report similar findings from their study of the personnel records of 75,000 manual workers employed by 66 engineering plants over the years 1959–66.[90] Wage differences were not compensated by non-pecuniary factors or efficiency.

> Because employees do respond to wage differentials where these are accompanied by job opportunities, a plant cannot set wages without

regard to the actions of other establishments in the relevant market. At the same time, the plant is far from being a price-taker, merely rubber-stamping a wage set by impersonal market forces. Particularly if it is a high-wage unit, it has more freedom of action than the competitive model suggests. High-wage units will pay a money wage greater than that 'justified' by the higher quality of its labour force. What we are suggesting is that the labour force will benefit in the form of higher wages if the plant enjoys high profitability, economies of scale, efficient management or methods of production, monopoly elements in the product market which allow higher earnings to be passed on, and so forth.[91]

And they quote Sumner H. Slichter, 'wages, within a considerable range, reflect managerial discretion, (so) that where managements can easily pay high wages they tend to do so, and where managements are barely breaking even, they tend to keep wages down'.[92]

So it is that, within the employing organisations, where the decisions are made, we at last witness the assertion of sentiments and beliefs, hopes and convictions, of what is right and proper, just and fair, with the meting out of some sort of rough justice. As soon as we apply the magic of averages, a pattern is seen to appear. In the company salary enquiries of 1962 and 1964, the eighty-eight companies of 1962 and the forty-five of 1964, showed a remarkably similar pay structure for the twelve jobs— when their returns were averaged.[93]

Mid-points of scales as percentages of the average for the twelve jobs

|  | | 1962 | 1964 |
|---|---|---|---|
| 1. | Chief accountant | 169 | 169 |
| 2. | Production manager | 166 | 173 |
| 3. | Production superintendent | 111 | 109 |
| 4. | Divisional sales manager | 147 | 150 |
| 5. | Area sales manager | 104 | 104 |
| 6. | Customer service manager | 91 | 93 |
| 7. | Electrical engineer | 96 | 93 |
| 8. | Maintenance shift manager | 83 | 79 |
| 9. | Research scientist | 98 | 95 |
| 10. | Junior research scientist | 62 | 61 |
| 11. | Filing supervisor | 38 | 37 |
| 12. | Personal secretary | 35 | 36 |
|  | | 100 | 100 |

Had the forty-five of 1964 cribbed from the report covering the eighty-eight of 1962? Not at all, for, as already reported, dispersion about the mean was wide in both years, mean deviations averaging 17 or 18 per cent of the mean, while increases in pay of 7, 8 or 9 per cent had been applied. But more important, there was some diversity even in the ranking of the jobs and considerable variation from the pay pattern suggested by the averages.

CONCLUSION

I must now bring this discourse to an end, with a great deal left unsaid and even more left undone. A commentator on the first edition of this book complained that the material did not lend itself to econometric treatment because it had been drawn from various sources. But in this, it reflects the nature of labour and pay. Anyone wanting determinacy, predictability and continuity must find a different medium to exercise his talents.

Because we are dealing with human institutions in which people have combined for the sake of power, profit or security, we must draw on psychology, politics, sociology, social anthropology, law and philosophy as well as economics to seek insight into what is going on. These greater insights may well inform us that justice, equality and order will remain beyond the reach of policy as long as present ideas and institutions persist.

*of Ideas – Hymum Social Values & 2R.*

*Institutions    Donovan Report*

*Can you therefore reform one without the other?*

# Occupational Composition of the Occupational Classes

For a complete list of occupations in each occupational class reference must be made to the *Census 1951: Classification of Occupations.*[1] From the 'Alphabetical index of occupational terms' contained in that volume, the classification of any of a great multitude of occupations can be found.[2]

The classification also shows the Registrar General's allocation of the occupations to five social classes and it is on this, in general, that our allocation to occupational classes has been based. But social classes II and III have been further subdivided in the present study, so that the line-up is as follows:

| Description | Social class | Occupational class |
|---|---|---|
| Higher professional | I | 1A |
| Lower professional | II | 1B |
| Employers and proprietors | II | 2A |
| Managers and administrators | II | 2B |
| Clerical workers | III | 3 |
| Foremen, supervisors, inspectors | III | 4 |
| Manual | | |
|   Skilled | III | 5 |
|   Semi-skilled | IV | 6 |
|   Unskilled | V | 7 |

The rules are simply applied: a professional worker allocated in the census to social class I goes to our occupational class 1A; one in social class II goes to occupational class 1B. All employers and proprietors[3] have been put in occupational class 2A, except those following one of the professions of occupational class 1A or 1B to which *all* professionals, of whatever industrial status, have been allocated. Likewise, all managers and administrators go to occupational class 2B, all clerical workers to class 3, all foremen and supervisors to class 4.

Manual workers in social class III go to occupational class 5, those in social class IV to occupational class 6, those in social class V to occupational class 7.

There are some exceptions to these rules, however, and in the list that follows these have been indicated by placing the social class number in brackets after the relevant occupation.

The list that follows is not exhaustive but shows the general scope of each class, those occupations whose allocation might otherwise be in doubt and those whose occupational class and social class do not line up in the way described above. (Figures in brackets denote the Registrar General's social class where this does not align with the occupational class as suggested in the rules stated above.)

### OCCUPATIONAL CLASS 1A (HIGHER PROFESSIONS)

Accountants (professional)
Architects and town planners
Authors, editors, journalists
Clergy, priests, nuns
Engineers (professional)
Lawyers, judges, stipendiary magistrates
Medical and dental practitioners
Officers in the armed forces
Scientists

### OCCUPATIONAL CLASS 1 B (LOWER PROFESSIONS)

Actors (III)
Aircrew (III)
Artists
Draughtsmen
Engineering officers and electricians on board ship
Librarians

Medical auxiliaries, including chiropodists (III), opticians and
   physiotherapists
Musicians (III)
Navigating officers and pilots
Nurses, including assistant (III), student (III) and nursery (III) nurses
Officials of associations
Pharmacists
Sportsmen (professional) (III)
Teachers, including university teachers

## OCCUPATIONAL CLASS 2A (EMPLOYERS AND PROPRIETORS)

All employers except those in the professions (Occupational classes 1A
   and 1B)
Proprietors, as defined above
Farmers
Restaurant, boarding-house, hotel and public house proprietors
Retail and wholesale traders
Road transport proprietors

## OCCUPATIONAL CLASS 2B (ADMINISTRATORS AND MANAGERS)

Managers and administrators in mining, manufacturing, trade, transport, finance, and public administration, including the following:

Auctioneers, estate agents, appraisers, valuers
Bankers, inspectors (I)
Bus and tram managers (I)
Civil Service administrative and other higher officers (I)
Civil Service and local government executive and higher clerical officers
Clerks of works
Company directors (business not specified) (I)
Government officials n.e.s. (not clerks) (III)
Inspectors and superintendents in gas, water and electricity distribution
   (III)
Insurance managers, underwriters (I)
Police inspectors, superintendents, chief constables

Railway officials
Secretaries and registrars of companies, institutions and charities
Shipbrokers, agents, managers (I)
Stockbrokers (I)

## OCCUPATIONAL CLASS 3 (CLERICAL WORKERS)

Clerks n.e.s.
Costing, estimating and accounting clerks, including book-keepers (II)
Insurance agents and canvassers
Office machine operators
Typists and shorthand typists

## OCCUPATIONAL CLASS 4 (FOREMEN, SUPERVISORS, INSPECTORS)

All foremen, supervisors and inspectors, including the following:

Farm bailiffs
Haulage and cartage contractors, master carmen (employees)
Inspectors, viewers, testers
Overmen, coalmining

## OCCUPATIONAL CLASS 5 (SKILLED MANUAL WORKERS)

All craftsmen and skilled process workers in social class III, as well as the following:

Fire brigade officers and men
Hairdressers
Photographers
Police, other ranks
Radio operators
Railway transport: engine drivers, guards, signalmen, pointsmen and
    level crossing men
Sea transport: petty officers, seamen and deckhands; pursers, stewards
    and domestic staff
Warehousemen
Stationary engine drivers

## OCCUPATIONAL CLASS 6 (SEMI-SKILLED MANUAL WORKERS)

Semi-skilled process workers in social class IV, as well as the following:

Agricultural workers
Armed forces, other ranks (III)
Conductors, bus and tram
Domestic servants, including chefs (III) and kitchen hands (V)
Drivers of self-propelled passenger and goods vehicles (III)
Laundry workers
Machine minders
Packers
Postmen and sorters (III)
Railway engine firemen, running-shed workers, ticket collectors
Salesmen, shop-assistants (III)
Storekeepers (III)
Telephone and telegraph operators (III)
Waiters (III)

## OCCUPATIONAL CLASS 7 (UNSKILLED MANUAL WORKERS)

Boiler firemen and stokers (IV)
Builders' labourers and navvies
Charwomen, office cleaners
Door-keepers (IV)
Labourers and other unskilled workers n.e.s.
Porters
Watchmen

## APPENDIX B

# Occupational Groups by Industry, England and Wales, 1951

| Order | Industry | | Occupational class | | | | | | | | |
|-------|----------|---|-----|-----|---------|--------|--------|---------|---------|--------|---------|
| | | | 1A | 1B | 2 | 3 | 4 | 5 | 6 | 7 | Total |
| I | Agriculture, forestry, fishing | M | 239 | 708 | 256,984 | 2094 | 17,496 | 73,384 | 510,507 | 1943 | 863,355 |
| | | % | 0·03 | 0·08 | 29·77 | 0·24 | 2·03 | 8·50 | 59·13 | 0·23 | 100 |
| | | F | 44 | 123 | 18,585 | 4849 | 167 | 492 | 75,310 | 375 | 99,945 |
| | | % | 0·04 | 0·12 | 18·60 | 4·85 | 0·17 | 0·49 | 75·35 | 0·38 | 100 |
| | | Total | 283 | 831 | 275,569 | 6943 | 17,663 | 73,876 | 585,817 | 2318 | 963,300 |
| | | % | 0·03 | 0·09 | 28·61 | 0·72 | 1·83 | 7·67 | 60·81 | 0·24 | 100 |
| II | Mining and quarrying | M | 4791 | 2609 | 6671 | 15,744 | 42,183 | 295,278 | 353,308 | 14,684 | 735,268 |
| | | % | 0·65 | 0·35 | 0·91 | 2·14 | 5·74 | 40·16 | 48·05 | 2·00 | 100 |
| | | F | 45 | 320 | 118 | 7659 | 18 | 95 | 2775 | 1118 | 12,148 |
| | | % | 0·37 | 2·63 | 0·97 | 63·05 | 0·15 | 0·78 | 22·84 | 9·20 | 110 |
| | | Total | 4836 | 2929 | 6789 | 23,403 | 42,201 | 295,373 | 356,083 | 15,802 | 747,416 |
| | | % | 0·65 | 0·39 | 0·91 | 3·13 | 5·65 | 39·52 | 47·64 | 2·11 | 100 |
| III | Treatment of non-metalliferous mining products other than coal | M | 1447 | 3437 | 11,296 | 8309 | 7831 | 77,956 | 42,807 | 68,019 | 221,102 |
| | | % | 0·65 | 1·55 | 5·11 | 3·76 | 3·54 | 35·26 | 19·36 | 30·76 | 100 |
| | | F | 39 | 500 | 511 | 11,386 | 822 | 32,623 | 13,739 | 10,829 | 70,449 |
| | | % | 0·06 | 0·71 | 0·73 | 16·16 | 1·17 | 46·31 | 19·50 | 15·37 | 100 |
| | | Total | 1486 | 3937 | 11,807 | 19,695 | 8653 | 110,579 | 56,546 | 78,848 | 291,551 |
| | | % | 0·51 | 1·35 | 4·05 | 6·76 | 2·97 | 37·93 | 19·39 | 27·04 | 100 |

| | | | | | | | | | | Total |
|---|---|---|---|---|---|---|---|---|---|---|
| IV Chemicals and allied trades | M | 14,385 | 14,577 | 26,628 | 22,620 | 12,879 | 58,121 | 70,249 | 70,773 | 290,232 |
| | % | 4·96 | 5·02 | 9·17 | 7·79 | 4·44 | 20·03 | 24·20 | 24·38 | 100 |
| | F | 805 | 5121 | 1268 | 40,960 | 1333 | 2722 | 36,896 | 17,473 | 106,578 |
| | % | 0·76 | 4·80 | 1·19 | 38·43 | 1·25 | 2·55 | 34·62 | 16·39 | 100 |
| | Total | 15,190 | 19,698 | 27,896 | 63,580 | 14,212 | 60,843 | 107,145 | 88,246 | 396,810 |
| | % | 3·83 | 4·96 | 7·03 | 16·02 | 3·58 | 15·33 | 27·00 | 22·24 | 100 |
| V Metal manufacture | M | 6080 | 7798 | 13,547 | 22,549 | 23,942 | 188,223 | 82,491 | 105,900 | 450,530 |
| | % | 1·35 | 1·73 | 3·01 | 5·00 | 5·31 | 41·78 | 18·31 | 23·51 | 100 |
| | F | 171 | 1628 | 350 | 22,418 | 3291 | 7038 | 11,686 | 10,258 | 56,840 |
| | % | 0·30 | 2·86 | 0·62 | 39·44 | 5·79 | 12·38 | 20·56 | 18·05 | 100 |
| | Total | 6251 | 9426 | 13,897 | 44,967 | 27,233 | 195,261 | 94,177 | 116,158 | 507,370 |
| | % | 1·23 | 1·86 | 2·74 | 8·86 | 5·37 | 38·48 | 18·56 | 22·89 | 100 |
| VI Engineering, shipbuilding and electrical goods | M | 25,114 | 54,934 | 62,382 | 69,207 | 77,290 | 604,290 | 191,413 | 155,016 | 1,239,646 |
| | % | 2·03 | 4·43 | 5·03 | 5·58 | 6·23 | 48·75 | 15·44 | 12·50 | 100 |
| | F | 425 | 7797 | 2229 | 108,522 | 24,185 | 39,125 | 105,290 | 35,730 | 323,303 |
| | % | 0·13 | 2·41 | 0·69 | 33·57 | 7·48 | 12·10 | 32·57 | 11·05 | 100 |
| | Total | 25,539 | 62,731 | 64,611 | 177,729 | 101,475 | 643,415 | 296,703 | 190,746 | 1,562,949 |
| | % | 1·63 | 4·01 | 4·13 | 11·37 | 6·49 | 41·17 | 18·98 | 12·20 | 100 |
| VII Vehicles | M | 7892 | 20,374 | 41,893 | 38,722 | 50,223 | 428,199 | 122,810 | 89,844 | 799,957 |
| | % | 0·99 | 2·55 | 5·24 | 4·84 | 6·28 | 53·53 | 15·35 | 11·23 | 100 |
| | F | 197 | 2546 | 1852 | 51,896 | 6434 | 9498 | 31,662 | 12,711 | 116,796 |
| | % | 0·17 | 2·18 | 1·59 | 44·43 | 5·51 | 8·13 | 27·11 | 10·88 | 100 |
| | Total | 8089 | 22,920 | 43,745 | 90,618 | 56,657 | 437,697 | 154,472 | 102,555 | 916,753 |
| | % | 0·88 | 2·50 | 4·77 | 9·88 | 6·18 | 47·74 | 16·85 | 11·19 | 100 |
| VIII Metal goods not elsewhere specified | M | 1751 | 1228 | 20,343 | 11,854 | 15,915 | 145,583 | 53,167 | 41,405 | 291,246 |
| | % | 0·60 | 0·42 | 6·98 | 4·07 | 5·46 | 49·99 | 18·26 | 14·22 | 100 |
| | F | 34 | 900 | 1093 | 26,384 | 7285 | 18,375 | 73,455 | 22,317 | 149,843 |
| | % | 0·02 | 0·60 | 0·73 | 17·61 | 4·86 | 12·26 | 49·02 | 14·89 | 100 |
| | Total | 1785 | 2128 | 21,436 | 38,238 | 23,200 | 163,958 | 126,622 | 63,722 | 441,089 |
| | % | 0·40 | 0·48 | 4·86 | 8·67 | 5·26 | 37·17 | 28·71 | 14·45 | 100 |

| Order | Industry | | | 1A | 1B | 2 | 3 | 4 | 5 | 6 | 7 | Total |
|---|---|---|---|---|---|---|---|---|---|---|---|---|
| | | | | | | | | | *Occupational class* | | | |
| IX | Precision instruments, jewellery, etc. | M | | 1255 | 2724 | 7896 | 4110 | 4820 | 61,081 | 10,445 | 5626 | 97,957 |
| | | % | | 1·28 | 2·78 | 8·06 | 4·20 | 4·92 | 62·35 | 10·66 | 5·74 | 100 |
| | | F | | 61 | 605 | 599 | 11,513 | 2027 | 13,775 | 11,197 | 4801 | 44,578 |
| | | % | | 0·14 | 1·35 | 1·34 | 25·83 | 4·54 | 30·90 | 25·12 | 10·77 | 100 |
| | | Total | | 1316 | 3329 | 8495 | 15,623 | 6847 | 74,856 | 21,642 | 10,427 | 142,535 |
| | | % | | 0·92 | 2·34 | 5·96 | 10·96 | 4·80 | 52·52 | 15·18 | 7·32 | 100 |
| X | Textiles | M | | 2781 | 4112 | 26,111 | 15,717 | 22,736 | 155,961 | 95,110 | 70,589 | 393,117 |
| | | % | | 0·71 | 1·05 | 6·64 | 4·00 | 5·78 | 39·67 | 24·19 | 17·96 | 100 |
| | | F | | 107 | 2548 | 1798 | 28,892 | 3893 | 282,152 | 106,097 | 49,087 | 474,574 |
| | | % | | 0·02 | 0·54 | 0·38 | 6·09 | 0·82 | 59·45 | 22·36 | 10·34 | 100 |
| | | Total | | 2888 | 6660 | 27,909 | 44,609 | 26,629 | 438,113 | 201,207 | 119,676 | 867,691 |
| | | % | | 0·33 | 0·77 | 3·22 | 5·14 | 3·07 | 50·49 | 23·19 | 13·79 | 100 |
| XI | Leather, leather goods and fur | M | | 267 | 263 | 4561 | 1293 | 1829 | 29,646 | 2008 | 6876 | 46,743 |
| | | % | | 0·57 | 0·56 | 9·76 | 2·77 | 3·91 | 63·42 | 4·30 | 14·71 | 100 |
| | | F | | 12 | 94 | 412 | 3093 | 245 | 18,382 | 1239 | 2315 | 25,792 |
| | | % | | 0·05 | 0·36 | 1·60 | 11·99 | 0·95 | 71·27 | 4·80 | 8·98 | 100 |
| | | Total | | 279 | 357 | 4973 | 4386 | 2074 | 48,028 | 3247 | 9191 | 72,535 |
| | | % | | 0·38 | 0·49 | 6·86 | 6·05 | 2·86 | 66·21 | 4·48 | 12·67 | 100 |
| XII | Clothing | M | | 281 | 590 | 24,418 | 7001 | 6577 | 119,722 | 56,639 | 9697 | 224,925 |
| | | % | | 0·12 | 0·26 | 10·86 | 3·11 | 2·92 | 53·23 | 25·18 | 4·31 | 100 |
| | | F | | 19 | 543 | 4774 | 25,241 | 7078 | 126,889 | 267,182 | 16,550 | 448,276 |
| | | % | | 0·00 | 0·12 | 1·06 | 5·63 | 1·58 | 28·31 | 59·60 | 3·69 | 100 |
| | | Total | | 300 | 1133 | 29,192 | 32,242 | 13,655 | 246,611 | 323,821 | 26,247 | 673,201 |
| | | % | | 0·04 | 0·17 | 4·34 | 4·79 | 2·03 | 36·63 | 48·10 | 3·90 | 100 |

| | | | | | | | | | |
|---|---:|---:|---:|---:|---:|---:|---:|---:|---:|
| **XIII Food, drink and tobacco** | | | | | | | | | |
| M | 3191 | 2218 | 41,868 | 26,497 | 18,389 | 127,060 | 96,749 | 90,886 | 406,858 |
| % | 0·78 | 0·55 | 10·29 | 6·51 | 4·52 | 31·23 | 23·78 | 22·34 | 100 |
| F | 427 | 2453 | 2925 | 43,017 | 3095 | 40,582 | 102,099 | 44,058 | 238,656 |
| % | 0·18 | 1·03 | 1·23 | 18·02 | 1·30 | 17·00 | 42·78 | 18·46 | 100 |
| Total | 3618 | 4671 | 44,793 | 69,514 | 21,484 | 167,642 | 198,848 | 134,944 | 645,514 |
| % | 0·56 | 0·72 | 6·94 | 10·77 | 3·33 | 25·97 | 30·80 | 20·90 | 100 |
| **XIV Manufactures of wood and cork** | | | | | | | | | |
| M | 365 | 1718 | 13,504 | 5779 | 8138 | 159,468 | 17,594 | 32,599 | 239,165 |
| % | 0·15 | 0·72 | 5·65 | 2·42 | 3·40 | 66·68 | 7·36 | 13·63 | 100 |
| F | 6 | 248 | 763 | 10,339 | 504 | 22,382 | 7539 | 5516 | 47,297 |
| % | 0·01 | 0·52 | 1·61 | 21·86 | 1·07 | 47·32 | 15·94 | 11·66 | 100 |
| Total | 371 | 1966 | 14,267 | 16,118 | 8642 | 181,850 | 25,133 | 38,115 | 286,462 |
| % | 0·13 | 0·69 | 4·98 | 5·63 | 3·02 | 63·48 | 8·77 | 13·31 | 100 |
| **XV Paper printing** | | | | | | | | | |
| M | 14,153 | 4525 | 29,608 | 19,899 | 9195 | 152,262 | 38,299 | 34,508 | 302,449 |
| % | 4·68 | 1·50 | 9·79 | 6·58 | 3·04 | 50·34 | 12·66 | 11·41 | 100 |
| F | 2139 | 1486 | 2205 | 37,624 | 3688 | 55,326 | 26,085 | 31,832 | 160,385 |
| % | 1·33 | 0·93 | 1·37 | 23·46 | 2·30 | 34·50 | 16·26 | 19·85 | 100 |
| Total | 16,292 | 6011 | 31,813 | 57,523 | 12,883 | 207,588 | 64,384 | 66,340 | 462,834 |
| % | 3·52 | 1·30 | 6·87 | 12·43 | 2·78 | 44·85 | 13·91 | 14·33 | 100 |
| **XVI Other manufacturing industries** | | | | | | | | | |
| M | 1961 | 5085 | 14,471 | 8228 | 6528 | 66,764 | 15,112 | 25,388 | 143,537 |
| % | 1·37 | 3·54 | 10·08 | 5·73 | 4·55 | 46·51 | 10·53 | 17·69 | 100 |
| F | 104 | 1421 | 1029 | 18,560 | 1840 | 34,783 | 21,134 | 18,892 | 97,763 |
| % | 0·11 | 1·45 | 1·05 | 18·98 | 1·88 | 35·58 | 21·62 | 19·32 | 100 |
| Total | 2065 | 6506 | 15,500 | 26,788 | 8368 | 101,547 | 36,246 | 44,280 | 241,300 |
| % | 0·86 | 2·70 | 6·42 | 11·10 | 3·47 | 42·08 | 15·02 | 18·35 | 100 |
| **XVII Building and contracting** | | | | | | | | | |
| M | 15,028 | 4707 | 46,227 | 22,351 | 46,712 | 711,425 | 51,582 | 304,509 | 1,202,541 |
| % | 1·25 | 0·39 | 3·84 | 1·86 | 3·88 | 59·16 | 4·29 | 25·32 | 100 |
| F | 48 | 290 | 1699 | 25,976 | 62 | 1121 | 2299 | 2106 | 33,601 |
| % | 0·14 | 0·86 | 5·06 | 77·31 | 0·18 | 3·34 | 6·84 | 6·27 | 100 |
| Total | 15,076 | 4997 | 47,926 | 48,327 | 46,774 | 712,546 | 53,881 | 306,615 | 1,236,142 |
| % | 1·22 | 0·40 | 3·88 | 3·91 | 3·78 | 57·64 | 4·36 | 24·80 | 100 |

| Order | Industry | | 1A | 1B | 2 | 3 | 4 | 5 | 6 | 7 | Total |
|---|---|---|---|---|---|---|---|---|---|---|---|
| | | | | | | Occupational class | | | | | |
| XVIII | Gas, electricity and water | M | 12,018 | 4794 | 15,865 | 30,688 | 7639 | 90,996 | 56,362 | 82,871 | 301,233 |
| | | % | 3·99 | 1·59 | 5·27 | 10·19 | 2·54 | 30·21 | 18·71 | 27·51 | 100 |
| | | F | 56 | 585 | 252 | 20,755 | 64 | 217 | 3889 | 3275 | 29,093 |
| | | % | 0·19 | 2·01 | 0·87 | 71·34 | 0·22 | 0·75 | 13·37 | 11·26 | 100 |
| | | Total | 12,074 | 5379 | 16,117 | 51,443 | 7,703 | 91,213 | 60,251 | 86,146 | 330,326 |
| | | % | 3·66 | 1·63 | 4·88 | 15·57 | 2·33 | 27·61 | 18·24 | 26·08 | 100 |
| XIX | Transport and communication | M | 5023 | 25,462 | 60,849 | 115,325 | 47,812 | 297,036 | 569,783 | 221,974 | 1,343,264 |
| | | % | 0·37 | 1·90 | 4·53 | 8·59 | 3·56 | 22·11 | 42·42 | 16·52 | 100 |
| | | F | 83 | 1239 | 8496 | 84,232 | 5533 | 3279 | 69,848 | 13,701 | 186,411 |
| | | % | 0·04 | 0·66 | 4·56 | 45·19 | 2·97 | 1·76 | 37·47 | 7·35 | 100 |
| | | Total | 5106 | 26,701 | 69,345 | 199,557 | 53,345 | 300,315 | 639,631 | 235,675 | 1,529,675 |
| | | % | 0·33 | 1·75 | 4·53 | 13·05 | 3·49 | 19·63 | 41·81 | 15·41 | 100 |
| XX | Distributive trades | M | 3471 | 17,421 | 556,623 | 81,793 | 11,389 | 108,941 | 474,094 | 124,493 | 1,378,225 |
| | | % | 0·25 | 1·26 | 40·39 | 5·93 | 0·83 | 7·90 | 34·40 | 9·03 | 100 |
| | | F | 248 | 7555 | 166,480 | 214,558 | 613 | 24,144 | 568,108 | 39,941 | 1,021,647 |
| | | % | 0·02 | 0·74 | 16·30 | 21·00 | 0·06 | 2·36 | 55·61 | 3·91 | 100 |
| | | Total | 3719 | 24,976 | 723,103 | 296,351 | 12,002 | 133,085 | 1,042,202 | 164,434 | 2,399,872 |
| | | % | 0·15 | 1·04 | 30·13 | 12·35 | 0·50 | 5·55 | 43·43 | 6·85 | 100 |
| XXI | Insurance, banking and finance | M | 5181 | 475 | 72,009 | 151,586 | 796 | 9058 | 9072 | 15,477 | 263,654 |
| | | % | 1·97 | 0·18 | 27·31 | 57·49 | 0·30 | 3·44 | 3·44 | 5·87 | 100 |
| | | F | 89 | 186 | 4324 | 117,344 | 98 | 123 | 6544 | 10,052 | 138,760 |
| | | % | 0·06 | 0·13 | 3·12 | 84·57 | 0·07 | 0·09 | 4·72 | 7·24 | 100 |
| | | Total | 5270 | 661 | 76,333 | 268,930 | 894 | 9181 | 15,616 | 25,529 | 402,414 |
| | | % | 1·31 | 0·16 | 18·97 | 66·83 | 0·22 | 2·28 | 3·88 | 6·34 | 100 |

| | | | | | | | | | | |
|---|---|---|---|---|---|---|---|---|---|---|
| **XXII Public administration and defence** | M | 75,602 | 31,225 | 104,776 | 146,103 | 17,938 | 157,863 | 582,914 | 204,550 | 1,320,971 |
| | % | 5·72 | 2·36 | 7·93 | 11·06 | 1·36 | 11·95 | 44·13 | 15·48 | 100 |
| | F | 2756 | 15,317 | 19,150 | 140,079 | 598 | 2921 | 38,666 | 27,973 | 247,460 |
| | % | 1·11 | 6·19 | 7·74 | 56·61 | 0·24 | 1·18 | 15·63 | 11·30 | 100 |
| | Total | 78,358 | 46,542 | 123,926 | 286,182 | 18,536 | 160,784 | 621,580 | 232,523 | 1,568,431 |
| | % | 5·00 | 2·97 | 7·90 | 18·25 | 1·18 | 10·25 | 39·63 | 14·83 | 100 |
| **XXIII Professional services** | M | 150,465 | 195,071 | 26,694 | 57,889 | 1721 | 33,304 | 81,875 | 19,504 | 566,523 |
| | % | 26·56 | 34·43 | 4·71 | 10·22 | 0·30 | 5·88 | 14·45 | 3·44 | 100 |
| | F | 22,202 | 414,659 | 12,417 | 130,941 | 211 | 2777 | 161,618 | 45,252 | 790,077 |
| | % | 2·81 | 52·48 | 1·57 | 16·57 | 0·03 | 0·35 | 20·46 | 5·73 | 100 |
| | Total | 172,667 | 609,730 | 39,111 | 188,830 | 1932 | 36,081 | 243,493 | 64,756 | 1,356,600 |
| | % | 12·73 | 44·95 | 2·88 | 13·92 | 0·14 | 2·66 | 17·95 | 4·77 | 100 |
| **XXIV Miscellaneous services** | M | 5508 | 28,994 | 129,192 | 16,690 | 1969 | 98,132 | 305,036 | 38,810 | 624,331 |
| | % | 0·88 | 4·64 | 20·69 | 2·67 | 0·32 | 15·72 | 48·86 | 6·22 | 100 |
| | F | 1209 | 26,569 | 112,556 | 69,544 | 263 | 58,274 | 899,306 | 59,178 | 1,226,899 |
| | % | 0·10 | 2·17 | 9·17 | 5·67 | 0·02 | 4·75 | 73·30 | 4·82 | 100 |
| | Total | 6717 | 55,563 | 241,748 | 86,234 | 2232 | 156,406 | 1,204,342 | 97,988 | 1,851,230 |
| | % | 0·36 | 3·00 | 13·06 | 4·66 | 0·12 | 8·45 | 65·06 | 5·29 | 100 |
| **ALL** | M | 358,249 | 435,049 | 1,614,416 | 902,048 | 461,947 | 4,249,753 | 3,889,426 | 1,835,941 | 13,746,829 |
| | % | 2·61 | 3·16 | 11·74 | 6·56 | 3·36 | 30·91 | 28·29 | 13·35 | 100 |
| | F | 31,326 | 494,733 | 365,885 | 1,255,782 | 73,347 | 797,095 | 2,643,663 | 485,340 | 6,147,171 |
| | % | 0·51 | 8·05 | 5·95 | 20·43 | 1·19 | 12·97 | 43·01 | 7·90 | 100 |
| | Total | 389,575 | 929,782 | 1,980,301 | 2,157,830 | 535,294 | 5,046,848 | 6,533,089 | 2,321,281 | 19,894,000 |
| | % | 1·96 | 4·67 | 9·95 | 10·85 | 2·69 | 25·37 | 32·84 | 11·67 | 100 |

# Income Distribution, 1911–12 and 1975–6 (Table 2.1)

Schedule E income is deducted by the pay-as-you-earn system (PAYE). The related income distributions may be found in the Inland Revenue 'Surveys of Personal Incomes': that for 1974–5 will be found in Board of Inland Revenue, *Inland Revenue Statistics 1977* (London: HMSO 1978), Tables 43 to 48, pp. 50–5. The figures for 1975–6 were kindly provided by the Inland Revenue.

In 1911/12 only 451,000 employees out of a total of 16,658,000 paid income tax, so that the income distribution for those below this level (£160 per year) had to be constructed from earnings data from other sources. These were:

(a) The Board of Trade earnings and hours inquiry of 1906,[1] embracing manual workers in the following industries: textiles; clothing; building and woodworking; public utility services; agriculture (1907); metal, engineering and shipbuilding; railways, paper and printing; pottery, bricks, glass and chemicals; food, drink and tobacco; miscellaneous trades. For all of these except agriculture, earnings were analysed by sex, adult and juvenile in shilling ranges, so that there was no obstacle to the construction of a frequency distribution. For agriculture, only average earnings for men by county were given. This gives a fairly wide dispersion about the average, but the effect must be to compress the range of earnings.

(b) The dispersion of coalminers (who were not included in the earnings census) was estimated from the data for occupational earnings per shift for June 1914 given by Finlay A. Gibson.[2]

(c) Domestic servants were allocated to income ranges on the basis of the information presented by W. T. Layton, supported by what scraps of information can be collected from household accounts, government estimates and the Booth and Rowntree surveys.[3]

(d) For other occupations below the tax level, representative of a group of about 1,730,000 employees, we use the estimates presented in a report to the British Association for the Advancement of Science in 1910.[4]

The numbers in each range for each industry were raised so that the total equalled that given in the census industry tables for 1911.[5] The aggregates for the industries included in the 1906 earnings inquiry, with agriculture and coal, were then raised again so that, together with domestic servants, shop-assistants, clerks and others included in the Cannan Committee investigation, the totals for males and females equal those shown for employees in the 1911 Population Census.

The 1906 earnings were raised by 4 per cent to approximate to the level of 1911/12, this being about the average rise in industrial wage rates. Agricultural earnings were raised by 2·66 per cent (the approximate rise in rates between 1907 and 1911/12). Coal earnings were reduced to 91·18 per cent of their 1914 level (to offset the rise in rates between 1911/12 and 1914).

But the data for 1975/6 represent actual earnings of individual employees for the year, so they include payments for overtime and are net of deductions for short-time and periods of unemployment.

The tax figures for 1911/12 are, of course, directly comparable with those for the later year; clerks, domestic servants, agricultural workers and shop-assistants enjoyed stability of employment, so that their annual average was probably not far from 52 times their weekly average; but the same did not apply to manual workers in other industrial sectors.

Allowance for overtime and short-time presents no difficulty, for the 1906 reports present two sets of tables; one refers to workers who worked the full standard week, and the other to all workers, however many hours they worked in the week. It is the latter that we have used in compiling the income distribution.

Unpaid holidays present a greater difficulty. Most employers, the 1906 reports tell us, paid their foremen for public or annual holidays; some, especially in the printing, soap and candle, food, drink and tobacco industries, paid all their workers; but the general rule was that holidays were unpaid. They amounted, in all, to about two weeks out of fifty-two. In calculating annual income, weekly earnings were thus multiplied by 50 and not by 52.

The final adjustment concerned unemployment. Trade union unemployment benefit funds returned an average rate of 3·56 per cent for the period April 1911 to March 1912, which is reduced to 2·9 per cent if the effect of the coal stoppage of March 1912 is eliminated. Unemployment for all insured workers was calculated only from September 1912.[6] For the last four months of that year, it was 2·17 times the trade union rate. In Chapter 3 we saw that the rate for all insured workers approximates to that for semi-skilled workers while, in 1931, the rate for the unskilled is 1·78 times that for the semi-skilled.

These ratios give an approximation adequate for this rough calculation. According to them, unemployment in 1911 would have been:

|                      | *Percentages* |
| -------------------- | ------------- |
| Skilled workers      | 3·0           |
| Semi-skilled workers | 6·5           |
| Unskilled workers    | 11·5          |

The income ranges for those covered in the 1906 inquiries were then reduced by 11·5 per cent for the first range; 6·5 per cent for the next range for women and for the next two ranges for men and 3 per cent for the remaining ranges.

In all relevant cases, the money equivalent of board and lodging or payment in kind was included in earnings.

# Derivation of Professional Earnings Data (Table 2.4)

## 1. BARRISTERS, SOLICITORS, DENTISTS, GENERAL MEDICAL PRACTITIONERS

For 1913/14 and 1922/3, we have material derived by the department of Inland Revenue from tax returns. Initially, this was collected for the Committee on Pay, etc. of State Servants (Anderson Committee), whose report was made in July 1923.

The analysis was based on all the assessments for each profession in selected areas without distinction between Schedule D (income of independent practitioners) or Schedule E (salaries).[1]

One difficulty in using income tax returns for pre- and post-World War I comparisons is the comparitively high exemption limit of the first period, so that the group represented in the tax returns of 1913/14 is from a higher segment of the pay hierarchy than that of the post-war years. Thus a comparison of median, quartiles, etc., gives the impression that rates have risen less than they really have. The Inland Revenue statistician accordingly made a further calculation: he compared the incomes at particular points of rank order, correcting the figure of rank for the post-war year only by the percentage increase in male population. Thus he compared the income 200th in rank in 1913/14 (in the selected areas) with the 206th in rank in 1922/3 (in the same area) and so on.

The occupation tables of the 1921 census would not have been available at that time, but a finer adjustment can now be made by using the change in numbers for each profession instead of in the male population as a whole. The number of doctors increased from 26,086 in 1911 to 26,264 in 1921. The median would have come at 13,043/4 in 1911 and 13,132/3 in 1921. Likewise, the 1000th (from top or bottom) in 1911 would be appropriately paired with the 1007th in 1921. The other professions were treated similarly.

In using the material, thus adjusted, for 1913/14 and 1922/3, we assume that numbers did not change much, or changed *pari passu*, between the census years and the tax years, and that numbers in the relevant professions in the sample areas did not change much as a result of migration to other areas.

We have sufficient data to construct frequency distributions for both years. This was plotted on a semi-logarithmic graph and from this the readings shown in Table 2.3 were made.

For 1955/6, we have the survey conducted for the Royal Commission on Doctors' and Dentists' Remuneration, 1957–1960, and described in Appendix A of the *Report*. A detailed statistical analysis is given in the *Supplement to Report: Further Statistical Analysis*, Cmd. 1064 (London: HMSO, 1960). Like the earlier figures, these represent income net of expenses as accepted by the tax authorities.

For medical and dental practitioners we have, in addition, information for the years 1935–7. See 'Tables and Notes Extracted from the Report Made to the British Medical Association by Professor A. Bradford Hill', Appendix II, p. 17, of the *Report of the Inter-Departmental Committee on Remuneration of General Practitioners*, Cmd. 6810 (London: HMSO, 1946) and the *Report of the Inter-Departmental Committee on the Remuneration of General Dental Practitioners*, Cmd. 7402 (London: HMSO, 1948).

## 2. THE CLERGY

For the Church of England, a sample of 300 taken from *Crockford's Clerical Directory* (the first 100, the last 100 and 100 whose names began with the letter L).

For the Presbyterian Church of Scotland, a sample of 700 taken from the *Church of Scotland Year-Book* for 1912, 1926 and 1957, and *Reports of the General Assembly of the Church of Scotland* for 1936. The sample consisted of the first 300, the last 300 and 100 from the middle.

Comparisons over time of the income of the parochial clergy also require some qualifications. Until 1927 a retired clergyman of the Church of England could claim up to a third of the income of his last living and an incumbent might be in the unfortunate position of having to pay a pension to one (or possibly more!) retired predecessors. However, not all those who were entitled to a pension in fact claimed it, and not all those who claimed would necessarily have claimed the full amount. As there were approximately 900 retired clergymen in 1912[2] to something over 12,000 in office, a deduction of 2 per cent from the 1912 stipend would probably be adequate to cover this item. The figure for 1912 shown in Table 2.4 is therefore 2 per cent below the estimate from *Crockford*, while figures for 1924 are given in *Crockford* net of pension payments.

The figures for 1957 were net of dilapidation payments, those for the other years were not. Up to 1924 every incumbent was responsible for repairs to his parsonage house and was supposed to leave it in a good state of repair. This arrangement was replaced by a scheme whereby a five-yearly survey was carried out by the diocesan surveyor who assessed the cost of the work needing to be done. The parson then paid an annual amount based on this assessment. Basically the same scheme operates today but in about three cases out of four the parochial church councils make good the outlay to their clergy. In order to make the 1957 figures more nearly comparable with the figures for the other years in this respect the sum of £45[3] has been added to the average income figure derived from the sample from *Crockford's Directory*.

For purposes of inter-professional comparison, a further adjustment must be made for business expenses—stationery, postage, travelling, official hospitality, etc.—that a vicar must pay from his own income. The Church Assembly estimate these expenses to have amounted, in 1958/9, to about £122 for a vicar in the suburbs of London and £156 for a country vicar.[4] Estimates for the earlier years are not available, and the best that can be done is to deflate the 1958/9 figures by the cost of living index[5] assuming for that year a weighted average for town and country of about £135.[6] The *Crockford* figures for the various year have been reduced as follows:

|      | £   |
| ---- | --- |
| 1912 | 32  |
| 1924 | 56  |
| 1935 | 46  |
| 1957 | 131 |

For 1970, the procedure for the Church of Scotland was repeated, but the Church of England now mercifully has a Central Stipends Authority that fixes stipends and mobilises the funds to pay them. See, e.g., Central Stipends Authority, *Sixth Report by the Church Commissioners, July 1977 to September 1978* (Church Information Office). For an historical record and expression of the considerations by which stipends should be regulated, see Central Stipends Authority, *Differentials* (Church Information Office, 1977). Table III, p. 39, shows average stipends for each year from 1963–4 to 1976–7.

## 3. ARMY OFFICERS

Ten-year scale averages for those living in, with major-generals, majors and lieutenants weighted as follows:

| | | | | | | |
|---|---|---|---|---|---|---|
| 1913 | 1 | : | 15 | : | 45 |
| 1924 and 1936 | 1 | : | 11 | : | 49 |
| 1955 and 1960 | 1 | : | 30 | : | 30 |

## 4. ENGINEERS

For 1923, from an inquiry by the Society of Technical Engineers reported in the International Labour Office, *Engineers and Chemists: Status and Employment in Industry*.[7] Average salaries are shown at 15 age points in the range 22 to 50. 1913/14; the average for those aged under 45 and 45 to 54 for 1923, reduced *pari passu* with the average for executive engineers in the Post Office Engineering Department and Lloyd's engineering surveyors.

For 1955/6, average from the Royal Commission on Doctors' and Dentists' Remuneration (the Pilkington Commission). For 1959/60, from the *Professional Engineer*, January 1961. The arithmetic mean is not given for this year, so the same relationship has been assumed between it and the average of the quartiles and median and this raised accordingly to represent the arithmetic mean.

## 5. CHEMISTS

The average for 1955/6 as shown in the Pilkington Report. This has been reduced for earlier years *pari passu* with relatives for those aged 20 to 40. Earlier years are from censuses of the Royal Institute of Chemistry for 1938/9 and 1930/1.[8] 1913/14: average for 1930/1 reduced *pari passu* with Civil Service analysts, 2nd class.

# Derivation of Managers' and Administrators' Earnings

For the years 1913/14 and each year from 1920/1 to 1924/5, we have the extracts from tax returns made by the Inland Revenue initially for the Anderson Committee.[1] This enables us to compare the income of employees in various industries who were receiving £200 and £500 in 1913/14 with employees in the same rank order (by level of pay) in the same collections of companies in the later years.[2] For example, in coal, metals and engineering, the individual at £500 in 1913/14 was ranked 1982nd in the salary hierarchy. In the same companies in 1924/5, the 1982nd highest paid employee was getting £1195.

In the returns we are given additional information, including the average income of those in the sample who were getting more than £2000 in 1913/14 and the average pay for the same number (counting from the top) in 1924/5; and also the rank position of individuals at £2000 and £1000 in 1913/14 and the income of the individuals in the same rank positions in the later years.

## CURRENT SURVEYS

The British Institute of Management, in association with Remuneration Economics Ltd produces the *National Management Salary Survey*. The 1979 report includes information relating to 27,000 managers employed in 361 organisations. A special section is devoted to 1878 full-time boardroom directors. There is a matched sample measuring the movement over twelve months based on 241 companies common to the 1978 and 1979 surveys.

Nine levels of management are included, from middle management to chief executives. Medians, upper and lower quartiles and averages are shown, analysed by age and length of service. Data is given on the numbers employed at each level, pensions and fringe benefits. The British Institute of Management runs an Executive Remuneration Service to advise its collective subscribers on questions of executive pay.

Hay Management Consultants produce the annual *Hay Remuneration Comparison*. The report for 1978, based on information drawn from 295 companies, with jobs standardised by the Hay job evaluation system, included directors and managers, supervisory, professional, technical and administrative staff, within a pay range of £2400 to £62,000. Base salary, total cash (basic pay plus bonus) and total remuneration including all benefits are shown, with medians, quartiles and highest and lowest levels of remuneration represented against standard job evaluation units. Comparisons with previous years are given, and information on profit-sharing, bonus and productivity payments and fringe benefits.

Inbucon/AIC Salary Research produce various annual surveys, including *Executive Salaries in the UK*, of which the seventeenth number, 1978, covered 7605 executives in 611 companies, with salaries ranging from £4000 to £57,000 and an average of a little under £9000. Remuneration levels are given for the twenty-eight most common executive jobs in sales, production, accounts, research, personnel and administration, by size of company, rank, industry and location.

# Notes

NOTES TO INTRODUCTION

1. Since 1801, when the first population census was held in Great Britain, questions have been included to enable those gainfully employed to be classified by occupation and/or industry. The Registrar General began his decennial investigations into occupational mortality in 1851 and into occupational fertility in 1911.
2. The British Medical Association assumed its present title in 1856; the National Union of Teachers in 1889.
3. We should have liked to extend our investigation to the United Kingdom by including Northern Ireland, but the difficulties were insuperable. The population census of 1911 covered all Ireland; none was held there in 1921.


NOTES TO CHAPTER 1

1. See *Census 1951: Classifaction of Occupations* (HMSO, 1956).
2. General Register Office, *Classifications of Occupations, 1960* (HMSO, 1960).
3. General Register Office, *Census 1961, England and Wales: Occupation and Industry National Summary Tables* (HMSO, 1965), p. iii.
4. Economically active (or gainfully employed) people are classified by status as employers, self-employed, unpaid family workers, employees or unemployed. Employees are further divided into managers, foremen and supervisors, and other employees.
5. Before reading further, it would be a good idea to look at Appendix A, 'Occupational composition of the occupational classes'.
6. I have not incorporated census data for 1961 and 1966 in the tables that follow, though some reference is made to it in the text, partly because the tables would have become too cumbersome and partly because the arduous task of allocation for these years has happily been performed by George Sayers Bain and Robert Price, from whom the percentages for 1961 in the above table have been taken. See 'Union Growth and Employment Trends in the United Kingdom, 1964–1970', *British Journal of Industrial Relations*, vol. 10, no. 3 (November 1972), pp. 368–9. See, too, Rose Knight, 'Changes in the Occupational Structure of the Working Population', *Journal of the Royal Statistical Society Series A*, vol. 130, no. 3, (1967), p. 408.
7. From the ILO *Yearbook of Labour Statistics 1977*. The composition of the

groups may be found in ILO, *International Standard Classification of Occupations* (ISCO) (Geneva, 1969).

8. Which may be easily discerned by consulting ISCO, pp. 25–33. Note that *Major Group 2: Administrative and Managerial Workers* is more narrowly defined in ISCO than occupational class 2B used in this book.

9. Manchester Statistical Society, *Occupational Patterns in the USSR and Great Britain: Some Comparisons and Contrasts*, paper read 10 January 1962, p. 11.

10. United States Bureau of the Census, *Comparative Statistics for the United States, 1870 to 1940, 16th Census of the United States, 1940, Population* (Washington, Government Printing Office, 1943), Part III, and *Historical Statistics of the United States, Colonial Times to 1957* (Washington, D.C.: Government Printing Office, 1960), pp. 75–8. For more recent years, *Employment and Training Report of the President* (Washington, D.C.: Government Printing Office, 1978), Table A-15, p. 206.

11. Perhaps harking back to the days of the Wild West when a train conductor was more like a captain of a ship than a ticket-collector.

12. US Department of Commerce, *1970 Census of Population Subject Reports, Occupational Characteristics* (Washington, D.C., 1973).

13. The data include cashiers and book-keepers; stenographers, typists and secretaries; office machine operators; shipping and receiving clerks; bank tellers; dispatchers and starters, vehicle; clerical and kindred not elsewhere classified.

14. They are taxed under Schedule D, but doctors are *de facto* employees engaged on task work, while dentists are paid by the piece.

15. I had better try to clarify this point for those who may not have understood me. I am trying to determine whether or not there is a trend for professionals to leave independent practice to become employees of employers, public or private, with end-products other than the rendering of the relevant professional service.

16. Professional accountants were given a class of their own in 1951 and 1971; in 1961, they were pooled with secretaries and registrars of companies. In this calculation I have estimated the number of company secretaries and registrars by interpolation (34,690) and extracted them to get the number of accountants in 1961.

17. But the distinction between an employer and a manager is one in law rather than economics, for an employer becomes a manager as soon as his business is incorporated, and, however interesting the distinction may be, we cannot, from the census material, distinguish between a manager who depends for his position in a business on his ownership of shares and one who does not.

18. There is no precise distinction between a manager and an administrator; the exercise of authority is an attribute of both. But while the manager exercises it over subordinate employees, the administrator may be vested with power, by law or regulation, to exercise it over members of the public.

19. The census of employment distinguishes 'employment units', each of which is generally a separate business, but may be a branch of another business. The criterion is whether the branch maintains its own payroll.

20. By dividing the industrial totals by the number of employers and managers

listed in the census occupation tables for the relevant industry. In fact, the two classifications do not match, even though the managers are divided industrially. A manager listed in engineering in the occupation tables may be managing a department counted as being, for example, in the chemical industry in the industry tables if it is part of a chemical firm. Nevertheless, this method gives a rough guide to the proportion of managers to all employed.

21. Which is described more fully in Chapter 2. It is a random sample of nearly 1 per cent of the employee population.
22. Occupational groups of less than 100 are not shown separately.
23. They have been separated by estimates based on official reports and railway returns.
24. Including employers.
25. See Appendix B, p. 230.
26. See *Department of Employment Gazette*, vol. 86, no. 7 (July 1978), p. 801.
27. You are reminded that an occupational classification has regard to the sort of work done, and an industrial classification to the end-product.
28. *Census 1951: Classification of Occupations* (London: HMSO, 1956), p. x.
29. This is not an industrial classification, for all skilled metal-makers and metal-workers, for example, are included under that head without regard to the industry in which they are employed.
30. Occupational groups, that is, without regard to the industry in which they are employed. The self-employed have been excluded from this calculation.
31. So-called because they get their pay in a lump, free from the usual deductions.
32. This analysis is made possible by the introduction of a complete industry–occupation cross tabulation for England and Wales in 1951 (Table 7 of the *Census 1951, England and Wales: Industry Tables* [London: HMSO 1957]). For previous years, and for Scotland in 1951, there are only tables, similar in scope to Table 8 of the 1951 *England and Wales Industry Tables*, showing the numbers in the more important occupations in each industry.

    Census Industry Table 7 shows no status divisions, however, so that the numbers derived from it do not represent quite the same allocation of employers and self-employed as the tables that have appeared in this study. The discrepancy has been partly overcome by the combination of classes 2 A and 2 B. There is also an occasional deficiency in the numbers on which the percentages have been based, due to the omission of sub-orders and groups when no figure of 10 or more would appear in the line to which they referred. For 1971, see *Census 1971, Great Britain: Economic Activity Part III* (10 per cent sample) (London: HMSO, 1975), Table 19.

NOTES TO CHAPTER 2

1. Department of Employment, *New Earnings Survey 1978 Part D Analysis by Occupation* (London: HMSO, 1979) pp. D6 and D7. Earnings are shown per week, but are here multiplied by 52 to give an annual equivalent.
2. See, e.g., *Report No. 4, Second Report on the Standing Reference* (London: HMSO, 1976) Table 4, p. 12.

3. Income from self-employment of individuals or partnerships is assessed for tax purposes under Schedule D. This covers all sorts of unincorporated businesses, with or without employees. When a business is incorporated (e.g., a shop or hotel is registered as a company), the proprietor becomes an employee, taxed under Schedule E (pay-as-you-earn) and the business is subject to corporation tax.

4. Its collection would make a difficult and dangerous, but rewarding, project for a research team.

5. The price index and its derivation are shown on pp. 134–5.

6. Department of Employment, *New Earnings Survey 1975 Part D Analysis by Occupation* (London: HMSO, 1976) Table 93, p. D17.

7. Ibid., Table 97, p. D27.

8. Ibid., Part F, Table 178, p. F54.

9. For an identification of the low-paid, see Frank Field (ed.), *Low Pay* (London: Arrow Books, 1973).

10. Many of the higher-paid workers subscribed to trade union health and unemployment schemes, but these were voluntary payments.

11. See, e.g., Board of Inland Revenue, *Inland Revenue Statistics 1976* (London: HMSO, 1977), Table 30, p. 37.

12. See, e.g., *Social Trends*, No. 8, 1977 (London: HMSO, 1977), pp. 108–9.

13. Surtax was a supplementary levy imposed on incomes above (in 1971–2 and 1972–3) £3000. It has since been abolished. See *Inland Revenue Statistics 1975*, Table 23, pp. 28–9.

14. See *The Times*, 3 July 1976, p. 1.

15. *Report No. 1, Initial Report on the Standing Reference* (London: HMSO, 1975), Table 27, p. 73.

16. The Commission does not exaggerate when it says, 'Our knowledge of the distribution of wealth is less detailed than our knowledge of the distribution of income, reflecting a serious shortage of reliable statistical information.' (Ibid., para. 175, p. 69.)

17. Estimates will be found in *Inland Revenue Statistics 1975* tables 105–10, pp. 116–29. The onset of the slump in 1973, with its fall in share prices, caused a reduction in the wealth of the upper echelons, but a slow recovery in their position followed after 1974. See A. L. Dunn and P. D. R. B. Hoffman, 'Ownership of Wealth', *Economic Trends*, no. 301 (November 1978).

18. According to the Commission, ordinary shares in UK companies constituted 8 per cent of the total assets of the personal sector in 1973.

19. They explain why: 'The first problem is the sheer size of the task. At the end of 1973 there were about 600,000 registered United Kingdom companies, of which 3,000 were quoted on the Stock Exchange. The number of shareholdings in a company ranges up to half a million for the largest . . . many shares are held in the names of nominee or trustee companies . . .' (paras. 27 and 29, p. 6).

20. Royal Commission on the Distribution of Income and Wealth, *Report No. 1*, Table 27, p. 73. The estimates fluctuated with share prices from £22,682 million for 1971 to £26,010 million for 1972 to £16, 538 for 1973.

21. 'Inheritance and the Characteristics of Top Wealth Leavers in Britain,' *Economic Journal*, vol. 83, no. 331 (September 1973), p. 832.

22. *Higher Incomes from Employment* (London: HMSO, 1976).
23. Ibid., p. 10.
24. Ibid., p. 116.
25. Note that in Report No. 3 the Royal Commission dealt only with employees, while this estimate includes the self-employed.
26. Weekly or hourly paid workers are in fact often paid by the minute, with *pro rata* deductions for lateness or absence.
27. Thus the standardised mortality ratio, 1949–53, of the owners of retail shops, aged 20–64, was well above the average; that for shop-assistants well below. The highest rate was scored by company directors (so returned). See *The Registrar General's Decennial Supplement, England and Wales, 1951: Occupational Mortality* Part II, vol. 2 (London: HMSO, 1958) p. 14.
28. Earnings censuses for manual workers have generally been confined to a particular week. In the NES, even monthly salaries are reduced to equivalent weekly earnings. Here, we multiply the week's earnings by 52.
29. Now 'new' only in the sense that it is freshly conducted each year.
30. For the first two years, information is drawn from the Inland Revenue reports to the committee appointed to inquire into the standard of remuneration and other conditions of employment of state servants (see *Report of Committee on Pay, etc. of State Servants* [Anderson Committee] [London:HMSO, 1923]); for 1955/6, from the *Report of the Royal Commission on Doctors' and Dentists' Remuneration, 1957–60*, Cmnd. 939 (London: HMSO, 1960). The nature of the material and the methods used are described in Appendix D.
31. See tables and notes extracted from the report made to the British Medical Association by Professor (now Sir) Austin Bradford Hill: *Report of the Inter-departmental Committee on Remuneration of General Practitioners*, Cmd. 6810 (London: HMSO, 1946), Appendix II, p. 17. Specialists and assistants were excluded from the inquiry. Returns were received from 3008 respondents in 1946, relating to accounts accepted by the Inspector of Taxes for the years 1935, 1936 and 1937. This lapse between the event and the inquiry results in some distortion of age distribution and this has been corrected by weighting the age ranges in accordance with age distribution shown in the 1931 census.
32. The main omissions are architects, surveyors, authors, editors and journalists, who constituted 18 per cent of the men in the class in 1951. Requests to the national daily papers for information on editors' pay were unanimously refused—in the interests of personal privacy.
33. But then they were given an increase of 57 per cent that would have raised their pay to about 135 per cent of the barristers' upper quartile.
34. Higher-paid white collar workers are as a rule not paid for overtime and do not have their pay reduced for absence. Manual workers not infrequently depend on overtime to make up for inadequate wages, and thus these deductions and additions make up an important element of pay that must be taken account of when comparisons are made.
35. *New Earnings Survey 1970*, Table 34, p. 89.
36. Ibid., Table 30, p. 81; numbers in each occupation, Table 28, p. 78.
37. Royal Commission in Doctors' and Dentists' Remuneration, 1957–60. A

survey was conducted for the Commission into professional pay (including self-employed income) for the tax year 1955–6. The average is £1835 for doctors, dentists, accountants, barristers, solicitors, architects, surveyors and engineers, with weights according to their numbers in the population census of 1951.

38. The index of average earnings of salaried employees (administrative, technical, professional, clerical and analogous grades) was 243 in 1970 with 1955–6 = 100. See Department of Employment and Productivity, *Statistics on Incomes, Prices, Employment and Production*, No. 28 (March 1969), Tables B. 16 and B. 17, pp. 34–5, and *British Labour Statistics Year Book 1970*, Table 20, p. 68.

39. The NES 1970 collected usable results for 1 in 127 of the male employee population.

40. Employers are asked in the questionnaire to state what the employee's job is called in their organisation, to give a brief description of his main duties, and to select from the DEP's list of occupations the one that most nearly describes what the employee is doing. The list gives various branches of engineering for those 'performing work normally requiring university degree or equivalent'.

41. Surveys were conducted jointly by the CEI and the Ministry of Technology in 1966 and 1968, then by the CEI in 1971 and 1973 'with the support and co-operation of its fifteen chartered institutions'. Questionnaires were distributed through the journals of the fifteen institutions. The analysis for 1973 was based on 27,137 satisfactorily completed forms from corporate or graduate members of one or other of the institutions. Thus the chance of the inclusion of non-professional engineers is ruled out. A bias of unknown magnitude is incorporated due to the fact that only those sufficiently interested or energetic would have responded. See the *1973 Survey of Professional Engineers* (London: Council of Engineering Institutions, 1973), p. 27.

42. For 1970, see Board of Inland Revenue, *Inland Revenue Statistics 1974* (London: HMSO, 1975).

43. *Report of the Inter-Departmental Committee on Remuneration of General Practitioners.*

44. *Report of the Royal Commission on Doctors' and Dentists' Remuneration, 1957–60*

45. An investigation into company salaries by the National Institute of Economic and Social Research showed a wide dispersion of rates for similar occupations, for example, in the case of chief accountants, there was an average deviation from the average of 18 per cent. For production managers, it was 22 per cent (see pp. 79–80).

46. The calculations are explained in Appendix E.

47. *102nd Report of the Commissioners of H.M. Inland Revenue*, Cmnd. 922 (London: HMSO, 1960), Table 59.

48. The Royal Commission on the Distribution of Income and Wealth estimated that managers constituted 70 per cent of employees receiving £10,000 or more in 1975–6. See *Report No. 3*, para. 256, p. 116.

49. From a table of schedule E income kindly supplied by the Department of Inland Revenue.

50. See Royal Commission on the Distribution of Income and Wealth, *Report No. 3*, Table 49, p. 97. This is much higher than the £187 suggested as the cost of fringe benefits for main board members by the National Board for Prices and Incomes in 1969. See their *Report No. 107, Top Salaries in the Private Sector and Nationalised Industries* (London: HMSO, 1969), Table B, p. 7. But it is of the same order as the 26 to 34 per cent found in 1978 for average salaries of £22,575 and £30,864, respectively, by the Review Body on Top Salaries in their *Report No. 10, Second Report on Top Salaries*, Cmd. 7253 (London: HMSO, 1978), Table 8, 84. This suggests that fringe benefits were being increased because of the obstacles in the way of salary increases.

51. E.G., an item in the *Guardian* of 4 April 1979 telling us that Mr I. R. Postgate of Alexander Howden, an insurance group, has received a rise in pay of £98,000 a year to bring his salary up to £143,000.

52. Data from company accounts is presented and analysed in Appendix F of the Royal Commission *Report No. 3*, and in A. Cosh, 'The Remuneration of Chief Executives in the United Kingdom', *Economic Journal*, March 1975, pp. 75–94. Earlier works contributing to the discussion are J. A. Brittain, 'Some Neglected Features of Britain's Income Levelling', *American Economic Review*, vol. 50, no. 2 (May 1960), p. 593; H. F. Lydall, 'The Long-Term Trend in the Size Distribution of Income', *Journal of the Royal Statistical Society*, series A, vol. 122, part 1 (1959), p. 1, and *The Structure of Earnings* (Oxford: Clarendon Press, 1968); and Richard Titmuss, *Income Distribution and Social Change* (London: Allen and Unwin, 1962).

53. Excluding those in the public service, and brokers and agents working on their own account. See Table 1.7, above.

54. 1922–3: from the Inland Revenue figures. The presentation for 1924–5 does not enable the calculation to be made for that year. 1938–9, from J. G. Marley and H. Campion, 'Changes in Salaries in Great Britain, 1924–39', *Journal of the Royal Statistical Society*, vol. 103, part 4 (1940), p. 524. Miss Marley (now Mrs Cox) kindly made available to us the cards on which the data were abstracted.

55. Further data from the inquiry is given on pp. 90–91.

56. Bowley and Stamp (1924) show for various industries the numbers of men and women getting above and below the tax exemption limit and a dispersion by income ranges for those below: see A. L. Bowley and Sir Josiah Stamp, *The National Income, 1924* (Oxford: Clarendon Press, 1927), reprinted in Bowley and Stamp, *Three Studies on the National Income* (London School of Economics and Political Science, 1938). From the Inland Revenue, we have a dispersion by income ranges for those above.

57. Published in three reports: Ministry of Labour, *Report on an Inquiry into the Rates of Wages, Hours and Degree of Industrial Organisation in the Wholesale and Retail Grocery and Provisions Trade*, etc. (London: HMSO, 1926).

58. Marley and Campion, 'Changes in Salary in Great Britain'.

59. Further information will be found below on p. 215.

60. Institution of Works Managers, *The Works Manager and his Responsibilities: Report of a Membership Survey* (London, 1954) and

'Remuneration Survey', *Works Management*, n.s., vol. 13, no. 3 (March 1960), p. 21.

61. The information related to 7,466 graduates in twenty large industrial and commercial undertakings. See the Commission's *Report* (Cmnd. 939), presented in Feb. 1960, p. 299.

62. 'Where Are the Top Salaries?', *Business*, vol. 89, no. 12 (December 1959), p.68.

63. Institute of Personnel Management, *Personnel Management Salaries* (London, 1961).

64. The means or medians of 68 per cent of such samples would probably lie within one standard error of that given by the sample in point, while 95 per cent would lie with in two standard errors.

65. Until, that is, the problem is empirically researched.

66. I.e., excluding agriculture, the distributive trades, the catering trades and private employment in services and transport.

67. These may be found, *inter alia*, in *British Labour Statistics*, beginning with the *Historical Abstract 1886–1968* (London: HMSO, 1971), Table 53, pp. 122–3.

68. Ibid., Table 54, pp. 124–5.

69. *The Financial Times*, 28 June 1965. Information about managerial salary surveys will be found in Appendix E.

70. As already remarked, the maximum is the more important figure, for while the incumbent will be on the minimum for only about a year, he may be on the maximum for a number of years.

71. See 'The Salary Concertina', *The Financial Times*, 9 October 1970.

72. We suggested a range of £1800 to £1900 for 1960; on the basis of the above calculations, this would have widened to £3323 to £3475 in 1970. An increase of 33 per cent for 1960–4 on £1850 would have resulted in £3544 in 1970, an overall rise of 91·6 per cent.

73. See Royal Commission on the Distribution of Income and Wealth, *Report No. 3*, Table 25, pp. 25–6.

74. Ibid., p. 57, and *The Financial Times*, 28 June 1965.

75. Department of Employment, *Classification of Occupations and Directory of Occupational Titles* 3 vols. (London: HMSO, 1972).

76. The total in 1973 was 1426.

77. Ibid., Table 25, pp. 55–6, and Table 17, p. 46.

78. Ibid., Table 26, p. 57.

79. 'The Amount of Distribution of Income (Other Than Wages) below the Income-Tax Exemption Limit in the United Kingdom: Report of the Committee, Consisting of Professors E. Cannan (Chairman), A. L. Bowley (Secretary), F. Y. Edgeworth, and H. B. Lees Smith and Dr. W. R. Scott', *Report of the 80th Meeting of the British Association for the Advancement of Science, Sheffield, 1910*, p. 170. For 'commercial and industrial clerks' (those not in banking, insurance, railways or public service), their information related to 16,000 males and 2600 females in 102 firms 'carrying on a great variety of businesses scattered throughout the kingdom, and of very different sizes'.

80. *New Survey of London Life and Labour*, vol. viii, *London Industries III*, (London, King, 1934), p. 298 ff.

81. The British Transport Commission gives averages for clerks in the *Annual Staff Census*. The Committee of London Clearing Bankers collected for us and tabulated data for bank employees as at 1 January 1956 and 1 January 1961.
82. See F. D. Klingender, *The Condition of Clerical Labour in Britain* (London: Lawrence, 1925), p. 77.
83. Ibid. p. 67.
84. Bowley and Stamp, *The National Income, 1924*, p. 20.
85. A family would have been excluded if the head of the family were a clerk.
86. From material kindly provided by Cadbury Bros. of Bournville.
87. Published by the Board of Trade. They are described briefly in Appendix C.
88. Made between 1948 and 1950: see *The Foreman: a Study of Supervision in British Industry* (London: Staples Press, 1951).
89. Level B foremen are described in the report as 'the men and women who are probably most generally in mind when the terms "Foreman" or "forewoman" are used . . .'.
90. *Status and Pay of Supervisory Staff* (London: Institute of Personnel Management, 1958).
91. *Civil Service Arbitration Tribunal Award 388.* (London: HMSO, 1960),
92. See Royal Commission on the Civil Service (1953), *Introductory Factual Memorandum on the Civil Service* (London: HMSO, 1954), pp. 75–6.
93. *Report of Committee on Pay, etc. of State Servants*, pp. 27 and 32.
94. The pay scales have been averaged over 20 incremental years.
95. The industries included are:

pottery, bricks, glass, chemicals;
metal manufacture, engineering and shipbuilding;
textiles;
clothing, laundries, dry cleaning;
food, drink, tobacco;
sawmilling and wood products;
paper and printing;
building and contracting;
gas, electricity and water.

96. Table 1.1 shows 10,000 in 1911, 18,000 in 1921, 28,000 in 1931 and 79,000 in 1951.
97. *The Foreman*, (1951).
98. *Department of Employment Gazette*, vol. 86, no. 7 (July 1978), p. 804.
99. Board of Trade, see Appendix C.
100. So called because they manipulate telephones, telegraphs or (as postmen or sorters) letters.
101. Domestic servants include those in private households and in hotels and catering.
102. Board of Trade earnings reports. The weekly average has been multiplied by 52 to give an annual rate to facilitate comparison with classes 1, 2 and 3. Note that at this stage no allowance is made for unemployment or unpaid holidays.

103. E. Cadbury, M. C. Matheson and G. Shann, (London, Fisher Unwin, 1906), p. 119
104. From the Board of Trade earnings and hours reports, *op. cit.*
105. *Women's Work and Wages*, p. 329.
106. This included cash wages, tips, other allowances in cash and the value (estimated at the cost to the employer) of meals and lodging, where provided, and of other allowances in kind.
107. I.e., by Wages Councils (which supplanted Trade Boards in 1948), the Agricultural Wages Boards and the various Catering Wages Boards.
108. In Table 2.27, the 1906 averages for classes 4 to 7 have been raised by 9 per cent to approximate to the level of 1913–14. This is a rough approximation based on Bowley's estimates (*Wages and Income in the United Kingdom since 1860*, pp. 6 and 7).
109. There is a considerable difference between the NES and the population census with regard to occupational classes. From the 1971 census, one gets 43 per cent of women in classes 1 to 3 and 57 in classes 4 to 7 (excluding class 2A from the calculation). The NES for 1978 shows a ratio of 65 : 35 for full-time workers only, and 55·5 : 44·5 if part-time workers are included. Thus it gives a majority to classes 1 to 3.
110. For 1960 and before, see Tables 2.19 and 2.24 above; for 1970, see *British Labour Statistics Year Book 1970*, Table 25, p. 78, and *Department of Employment Gazette* 'Statistical Series', each month, e.g., February 1979, Table 128, p. 210.
111. 1906: Tables 2.19 and 2.24 above; 1978, *New Earnings Survey 1978*, part D, Table 104, p. D43.
112. 1906 and 1960, Tables 2.19, 2.21 and 2.24, above; 1970 and 1978, kindly supplied by the National Union of Railwaymen.

## NOTES TO CHAPTER 3

  1. *Prices and Wages in the United Kingdom, 1914–1920*, Economic and Social History of the World War, British Series (Oxford: Clarendon Press, 1920).
  2. Ibid., p. 98.
  3. When increases were given as cost of living bonuses, they sometimes took the form of equal percentage additions at all levels of pay, on the grounds that loss from rising prices was proportional to income, or they gave more to the poorer than to the richer, on the grounds that the latter could better afford the sacrifice involved. In engineering and building, artisans and labourers generally received the same money increase. In woollen textiles, flat rates were abandoned in June 1917 and replaced by percentage increases.
  4. Government, corporation and public company officials were taxed under Schedule D, all other employees under Schedule E.
  5. £120 was allowed on incomes exceeding £130 but not exceeding £400; £100 on those exceeding £400 but not exceeding £600; and £70 on those exceeding £600 but not exceeding £700. By deducting the estimated numbers in each of these ranges from the total, we get estimates of those exceeding £700. Totals in this group have been extrapolated for the three

missing years to retain their proportion to the numbers in the range £600–£700.

6. See *Ministry of Labour Gazette*, vol. 29, no. 2 (February 1921), p. 64. According to the Ministry's records, in 1919, 6·3 million workers had their hours reduced by an average of 6·4 per week. 'If the number of agricultural labourers, shop assistants and police whose hours have been reduced could be included, the total number would be substantially increased'. See *Ministry of Labour Gazette*, vol. 28, no. 1 (January 1920).

7. Bowley's index.

8. Using the Ministry's figures, this would have left weekly rates about 10s. above the level of 1914, and represented a severe reduction in real rates.

9. These calculations, published monthly in the *Ministry of Labour Gazette*, are not based on reductions or increases in actual wage bills but are calculations of what would happen if changes in negotiated (standard) rates were literally implemented by employers.

10. *Report of the Committee on Pay, etc. of State Servants* (1923), p. 22.

11. Ibid., p. 34

12. Guy Routh, 'Civil Service Pay, 1875 to 1950', *Economica*, n.s., vol. 21, no. 83 (August 1954), p. 201.

13. See *Statistical Abstract for the United Kingdom, 1913 and 1923 to 1936*, Cmd. 5627 (London: HMSO, 1938), p. 54.

14. For those assessed under Schedule D, an adjustment was made by the Inland Revenue to accord the income shown with the assessment for the year concerned instead of with the average for the previous three years.

15. 10,000 in 1923 and nearly 11,000 in 1924. See *18th Abstract of Labour Statistics of the United Kingdom*, Cmd. 2740 (London: HMSO, 1926), pp. 74 and 76.

16. Product price sliding scales operated in coal and steel.

17. The Ministry of Labour took earnings censuses in 1924, 1928, 1931 and 1935 (reported in *Ministry of Labour Gazette*, vols. 34 and 35 (1926–7); vol. 37 (1929); vol. 41 (1933); and vol. 45 (1937).

18. An unemployed employer may seem a contradiction in terms but, as already mentioned, employers and managers were not separately coded in 1931.

19. From the Office Management Association (Institute of Office Management) inquiry, *Clerical Salaries Analysis*, first conducted in 1942.

20. From the Draughtsmen's and Allied Technicians' Association (formerly the Association of Engineering and Shipbuilding Draughtsmen).

21. From this we may approximate the change for various sections. The average for coalminers and for agricultural labourers was about 23 per cent up, which indicates that the overall average must have been pulled down by the sluggish behaviour of non-manual rates and/or those of shop-assistants and domestic servants.

In 1940, non-manual workers earning up to £420 became subject to unemployment insurance, so we do not know exactly how many workers there were whose average earnings would conform to the movement shown in the earnings inquiries. The Ministry of Labour estimated that the 5,550,000 workers about whom details were obtained in the 1938 inquiry represented about 70 per cent of the labour force concerned, so that the labour force would be just under 8 million. For 1940, no such estimate was made, but it was probably not less than a million below the 1938 number. To this, about 1·3 million must be added for coalmining and agriculture.

The total in civil employment in June 1940 was estimated to be 17·8 million. Employers and self-employed may be estimated by interpolation between 1931 and 1951 at 1·5 million, giving an employee population of 16·3 million. Of these, the earnings of 7 million were about 30 per cent above the 1938 level; 1·3 million, 23 per cent above the 1938 level, so that, to reduce the average rise to 14 per cent, the earnings of the other 8 million must have been 1·5 per cent below the 1938 level.

Whether there was an actual reduction in the average of the non-manual industrial employee population or not (and it could have been brought about by the substitution of female for male labour) it does appear that a major income change in favour of manual industrial workers took place between 1938 and 1940.

22. See Table 2.27, p. 120.
23. Arbitration proceedings between the British Medical Association and the Minister of Health, March 1952, reported in Supplement to *The British Medical Journal*, 29 March 1952, p. 129. Between 1949/50 and 1950/1, there was an increase of only 0·8 per cent (1937 = 100, 1950/1 was 189·5 per cent).
24. Table 3.1.
25. See *Report of the Commissioners for the Special Areas in England and Wales 1937*, Cmd. 5595 (H. M. Stationery Office, 1937), p. 30. These were areas of high unemployment designated under the Special Areas Acts.
26. *Ministry of Labour Gazette*, vol. 48, no. 5 (May 1940), p. 128. The analysis relates to males aged eighteen and over.
27. See Central Statistical Office, *National Income and Expenditure, 1961* (London: HMSO, 1961), p. 13.
28. Weekly earnings are those of manual workers covered by the Ministry's earnings census. Salary earnings are those of administrative and technical grades (including employees with professional qualifications) and clerical and analogous grades. The distributive trade is not included. See *Statistics on Incomes, Prices, Employment and Production*, No. 2, September 1962 (London: HMSO), p. 7.
29. This reflects the findings of the Guillebaud Committee on conditions outside the railways: British Transport Commission, etc., *Report of Railway Pay Committee of Inquiry* (London, Special Joint Committee on Machinery of Negotiation for Railway Staff, 1960).
30. See the *Clerical Salaries Analysis* published biennially by the Institute of Office Management. The 1960 report does not include an industrial analysis.
31. Information about earnings is taken from the Inquiries of the Engineering and Allied Employers' National Federation.
32. See *Ministry of Labour Gazette*, vol. 66, no. 5 (May 1958), p. 190, for the first of these analyses.
33. In manufacturing industry, construction, gas, electricity, water, transport and public administration. See the *Department of Employment Gazette*, December 1973, Tables 124 and 125, p. 1319.

34. See *British Labour Statistics Historical Abstract 1886–1968* (London: HMSO, 1971), Table 60, p. 134, for the period January 1963 to June 1968: *Employment and Productivity Gazette*, May 1970, p. 385 for 1969, and *British Labour Statistics Yearbook 1970*, Table 25, pp. 74–8 for 1970.

35. The circumstances are described in National Board for Prices and Incomes Report No. 120, *Pay and Conditions in the Electrical Contracting Industry*, Cmnd. 4097 (London: HMSO, 1969).

36. *Employment and Productivity Gazette*, vol. 78, no. 8 (August 1970), pp. 706–7.

37. Roger Tarling and Frank Wilkinson have helpfully tabulated the various policies and their characteristics, 1948 to 1977, in 'The Social Contract: Post-War Incomes Policies and Their Inflationary Impact', *Cambridge Journal of Economics*, vol. 1, no. 4 (December 1977), pp. 398–9.

38. *Machinery of Prices and Incomes Policy*, Cmnd. 2577, 11 February 1965.

39. *Prices and Incomes Policy*, Cmnd. 2639, April 1965.

40. *Prices and Incomes Standstill*, Cmnd. 3073, July 1966.

41. See the Department of Employment *Time Rates of Wages and Hours of Work*.

42. Report No. 169, Cmnd. 4648 (London: HMSO, April 1971), para. 121, p. 41. Table 7 of the report (p. 162), shows that for building, shipbuilding, engineering, railways and police, time rates for unskilled workers fell relative to those for skilled workers between 1960 and 1970, and, except for building, between 1950 and 1960.

43. See Table 2·28.

44. As we shall see later, there were some signs of a widening dispersion in pay between 1977 and 1978 within each sex as well as between the sexes.

45. It would have been more satisfactory to have been able to take 'shop assistant' as one of the occupations, but unfortunately the change of definition in 1973 breaks the continuity of the series. In Table 3·11, 'Sales' includes all those in CODOT group VIII—Selling. For a review of current literature on this subject, see Peter J. Sloane, *The Earnings Gap between men and Women in Britain: The Current State of Research Knowledge* (SSRC/EOC Joint Panel on Equal Opportunities Research, mimeo.). Sloane writes that 'rough calculations suggest' that incomes policies raised female relative pay by six percentage points between 1970 and 1975, and equal pay legislation or other factors by only two. See also P. J. Sloane (ed.), *Women and Low Pay* (Macmillan, 1979).

46. *A Programme for Controlling Inflation: The First Stage*, Cmnd. 5125 (London: HMSO, November 1972).

47. *The Programme for Controlling Inflation: The Second Stage* Cmnd. 5205 (London: HMSO, January 1973).

48. Ibid., pp. 8–9.

49. *The Price and Pay Code for Stage 3: A Consultative Document* Cmnd. 5444 (London: HMSO, October 1973).

50. See 'Pay Policy: Mr Healey's Statement to the House', *Department of Employment Gazette*, vol. 84, no. 5 (May 1976), pp. 451–2.

51. See *The Attack on Inflation after 31st July 1977*, Cmnd. 6882 (London: HMSO, July 1977).

52. It was now the Ford workers who delivered the *coup de grâce* in a

prolonged strike that ended on 24 November 1978, in a settlement greatly in excess of the official limits.

53. A survey carried out in April–June 1977 showed that vacancies notified to employment offices were about a third of all vacancies. (See *DEP Gazette*, vol. 87, no. 2 [February 1979], p. 137.) Nor, of course, do all the unemployed register at employment offices. The population census of April 1971 recorded as unemployed 852,350 males and 437,470 females, while the DEP recorded 617,700 unemployed males and 112,500 unemployed females. But it is trends rather than absolute numbers in which we are interested here.

## NOTES TO CHAPTER 4

1. The doctrines are identified, dated and explained in Guy Routh, *The Origin of Economic Ideas* (London: Macmillan, 1975).
2. T. R. Malthus, *Principles of Political Economy* (first published 1820) (Oxford: Blackwell, 1951), p. 220.
3. Routh, *Origin of Economic Ideas*, p. 142.
4. *Principles of Economics* (first published 1890), 9th (variorum) edn (London: Macmillan, 1961), vol. i, p. 539.
5. *First Report* (London: HMSO. 1958), section 146, p. 45.
6. *The Inequality of Pay* (Oxford: University Press, 1977), p. 144. A succint account of 'The economist's approach to pay determination' is presented on pp. 10–17.
7. *Wealth of Nations*, bk i, chap. viii, Glasgow edn (Oxford: Clarendon Press, 1976), p. 92.
8. 'Seven Centuries of Building Wages', *Economica*, vol. 22, no. 87 (August 1955), pp. 201–2. See also Phelps Brown, *The Inequality of Pay*, p. 68.
9. 'Wage Flexibility and the Distribution of Labour', *Lloyd's Bank Review*, no. 54, (October 1959). Reprinted in B. J. McCormick and E. Owen Smith (eds.), *The Labour Market*, Penguin Modern Economics (Harmondsworth: Penguin Books, 1968), in which the quotation is on p. 197.
10. Paris, OECD, 1965. The group included Professors Pieter de Wolff of the Central Planning Bureau in the Hague, Sir E. H. Phelps Brown of the London School of Economics, and Lloyd Ulman of Berkeley.
11. Equivalent to the British 'minimum list headings'. See *UN Statistical Papers*, Series M, No. 4 (New York, 1958).
12. Ibid., pp. 117–18.
13. See E. M. Hugh-Jones (ed.), *Wage Structure in Theory and Practice* (Amsterdam: North-Holland Publishing Co., 1966), pp. 180–201, and particularly table 12.
14. 'Britain's Industrial Performance since the War', *Department of Employment Gazette*, vol. 86, no. 5, p. 512 ff.
15. Ibid., p. 516.
16. The Civil Service between 1957 and 1960 maintained the relativities between female clerical officers, clerical assistants and shorthand typists grade I (100 w.p.m. shorthand and 40 w.p.m. typing) and tackled the typist

problem by shuttling typing between London and Brighton and providing clerical officers with typewriters.

17. *Department of Employment Gazette*, vol. 84, no. 8 (August 1976), p. 851 ff. An even more awkward question for the demand-supply hypothesis is why, with deteriorating employment, they should have been given an increase, on average, of 45 per cent between these two years.
18. Data are given each month in the *Department of Employment Gazette*, Statistical Series, Table 101.
19. Ibid., 'Unemployment, Vacancies and Placings by Occupation, Great Britain', (August 1976), vol. LXXXIV, no. 8, p. 851 ff.
20. *Management Matters*, no. 54 (Winter 1976), p. 4.
21. *Wealth of Nations*, Glasgow edn bk i, p. 118.
22. *Essai sur la nature du commerce en général*, ed. Henry Higgs (London: Macmillan, 1931), pp. 21–3.
23. *Wealth of Nations*, Glasgow edn, p. 148.
24. *Principles of Political Economy*, bk 2, chap. xiv, para. 1.
25. J. E. Cairnes, *Some Leading Principles of Political Economy Newly Expounded*, (London: Macmillan, 1874), pp. 64–78.
26. *The Common Sense of Political Economy* (London: Routledge, 1935), p. 334.
27. Ibid., p. 335.
28. Ibid., p. 336.
29. *Principles of Economics*, 8th edn (London: Macmillan, 1920), p. 568.
30. S. M. Lipset and R. Bendix (eds.), *Social Mobility in Industrial Society* (London: Heinemann, 1955), pp. 13–14.
31. Ibid., chap. ii, p. 74.
32. 'What Is a Social Class?', *Journal of Legal and Political Sociology* (1947), p. 21, reprinted in R. Bendix and S. M. Lipset, *Class, Status and Power* (London: Routledge and Kegan Paul, 1954).
33. D. V. Glass (ed.), *Social Mobility in Britain* (London: Routledge and Kegan Paul, 1954), p. 21.
34. 35,000 teachers were produced under the Emergency Training Scheme between 1945 and 1951.
35. The report, based on 941 satisfactorily completed questionnaires, was published in G. Routh, 'The Social Co-ordinates of Design Technicians', *The Draughtsman*, vol. 44, no. 9 (September 1961), p. 7.
36. The Social Survey investigation reported in Glass, *Social Mobility in Britain*, p. 183.
37. Our estimate for the growth in the number of men in the class between 1951 and 1960 was 2·1 per cent compound per year, while in 1960 we estimated there were 480,000 men in the class. *The Registrar General's Decennial Supplement, England and Wales, 1951*, showed a death rate of 0·66 per cent per year in the age group 20–64 for men in socio-economic group 3 (higher administrative, professional and managerial), while about 1·16 per cent would turn 65 and (in the main) retire (*Occupational Mortality*, part 2 of the *Supplement*, vol. 2).
38. *The Wealth of Nations*, Glasgow edn, pp. 92–3.
39. See 'The Scholastic Theory of the Just Wage', appendix to Michael Fogarty, *The Just Wage* (London: Chapman, 1961).

40. A. Lehmkhul, *Theologia Moralis*, 5th edn (Freiburg i. Breisgau, Herder, 1888), vol. i, p. 362, quoted by Fogarty on p. 269.

41. 'An Objective Approach to Pay Differentials', *The New Scientist*, vol. 4, no. 85, (3 July 1958), p. 313. See also Elliott Jaques, *Measurement of Responsibility* (London: Tavistock Publications, 1956).

42. Barbara Wootton, *The Social Foundations of Wage Policy* (London: Allen and Unwin, 1954), p. 162.

43. This was the case in recent disputes about the salaries of Civil Service clerical officers, on the one hand, and postal and telegraph officers on the other, though the model is not often as simple as this. More generally, it happens with Civil Service rates, which by an elaborate process are made to follow rates outside the Civil Service and are thus regarded as a good indicator of what outside rates are doing when these outside rates are themselves revised.

44. See, for example, A. M. Ross, *Trade Union Wage Policy* (Berkeley and Los Angeles: University of California Press, 1948); Paul H. Douglas, *Real Wages in the United States, 1890–1926* (Boston: Houghton Mifflin, 1930); R. Ozanne, 'Impact of Unions on Wage Levels and Income Distribution', *Quarterly Journal of Economics*, vol. 73, no. 2. (May 1959), p. 177; J. E. Maher, 'Union, Non-union Wage Differentials', *American Economic Review*, vol. 46, 3 (June 1956), p. 338.

45. See D. Robinson, 'Wage Differentials over Time', *Bulletin of the Oxford University Institute of Statistics*, vol. 23, no. 4 (November 1961), p. 367.

46. See *Proceedings at a Special Conference between the Engineering and Allied Employers' National Federation, the Amalgamated Engineering Union, the National Union of Foundry Workers and the Engineering Joint Trades Movement, London, 5th November 1940: Wages and Working Conditions* (*London, 1940*).

47. Note that the previous calculation related labourers to the average for all skilled men, while this one relates them to fitters only.

48. The difference between standard rates and earnings.

49. For an explanation of this use of the term 'paradigm', see Thomas S. Kuhn, *The Structure of Scientific Revolutions*, 2nd edn (University of Chicago Press, 1970). The phenomenon that it describes has long been familiar to economists. See, e.g., Joseph Schumpeter, 'Science and Ideology', *American Economic Review*, vol. 39, no. 2 (March 1949), pp. 345–59.

50. In the estimate, that is, of the pursuers. As Falstaff remarked, if we all got our just deserts, who of us would escape a beating?

51. See Routh, *The Origin of Economic Ideas*, p. 46.

52. Ibid., pp. 215–16.

53. These two papers are reprinted in McCormick and Smith, *The Labour Market*.

54. Note that this model depends on the somewhat unlikely assumption that the fewer workers you employ, the higher will be their marginal product, because they will be combined with a higher quantity of capital per worker.

55. Wilfred Brown describes how, if the pay of any group in his factory were to be raised, the agreement of all the other groups would first have to be obtained (*Piecework Abandoned* [London: Heinemann, 1962]). Peter B.

Doeringer and Michael J. Piore encountered the same phenomenon in their researches.

> The separation of wage decisions from those involving adjustment to external conditions reflects the constraints surrounding the internal wage structure. Because the structure is relatively rigid and tightly bound by the exigencies of internal allocation and by customary law, adjustments in the entry wage tend to exert a leverage upon all wages in the enterprise. This makes such adjustments a relatively expensive means of accommodation to market pressure since the marginal costs of adjustment rise more rapidly than the 'supply price' of labor. In addition, most managers, at least in medium and large enterprises, seem to consider wage changes a relatively ineffective means of accommodating to labor scarcities. (*Internal Labor Markets and Manpower Analysis* [Heath Lexington Books, 1971], pp. 97–8.)

56. Sidney and Beatrice Webb observed the 'clinging of each generation to its accustomed livelihood' as 'a primitive bulwark against the innovation of fixing all the conditions of labour by "free competition" among candidates for employment'. (*Industrial Democracy* [London: Longmans, 1897], vol. 2, pp. 696–7.)
57. 'They are apt to express themselves as if they thought that competition actually does, in all cases, whatever it can be shown to be the tendency of competition to do. This is partly intelligible, if we consider that only through the principle of competition has political economy any pretension to the character of a science . . .' (John Stuart Mill, *Principles of Political Economy*, ed. W. J. Ashley [London: Longmans, Green, 1909], p. 242.)
58. J. E. Cairnes, op. cit. pp. 151–2.
59. *Labor Markets and Wage Determination* (University of California Press, 1977), p. 5.
60. Ibid., p. 41. The paper from which I quote was first published in 1950.
61. Guy Routh, 'Mobility of the Inhabitants of an English Town', *Growth and Change*, vol. 5, no. 3 (July 1974), pp. 2–7.
62. These relate to the collective agreements or wages council orders included in the Department of Employment's annual *Changes in Rates of Wages and Hours of Work*. The *Department of Employment Gazette* carries a summary each January. See, e.g., vol. 85, no. 1 (January 1977, p. 40).
63. Aubrey Jones, *The New Inflation* (Harmondsworth and London: Penguin Books and André Deutsch, 1973), p. 19.
64. Ibid., p. 21.
65. 'Inequality, Inequity and Incentive', *Times Higher Education Supplement*, 6 January 1978, p. 13.
66. *Labor Markets and Wage Determination*, pp. 40–1.
67. A. W. Phillips, 'The Relation between Unemployment, and the Rate of Change of Money Wage Rates in the United Kingdom, 1861–1957', *Economica*, vol. XXV, no. 100, (November 1958).
68. And was hailed by a member of parliament as 'the greatest English economist since Keynes', a dubious compliment to pay an Australian.
69. We look back in disgust at the intellectual bankruptcy of British

governments in the 1930s; present-day governments, not only in Britain, will, I fear, be viewed in similar light by future generations.

70. Royal Commission on Trade Unions and Employers' Associations 1965–1968, *Report* (London: HMSO, 1968), para. 1020, p. 262.
71. *The Changing Contours of British Industrial Relations*, to be published by Basil Blackwell in 1980.
72. The study will be published by Martin Robertson in 1980.
73. C. H. Hull (ed.), *The Economic Writings of Sir William Petty* (Cambridge: University Press, 1899), pp. 26 and 32.
74. 'Instead of all the workers being levelled down to low wage standards and all the rich levelled up to fashionable income standards, everybody under a system of equal incomes would find her and his own natural level; but the great would always be those who had done great things, and never the idiots whose mothers had spoiled them and whose fathers had left them a hundred thousand a year; and the little would be persons of small minds and mean characters, and not poor persons who had never had a chance. That is why idiots are always in favor of inequality of income (their only chance of eminence), and the really great in favor of equality.' (*The Intelligent Woman's Guide to Socialism and Capitalism* [London: Constable, 1928], p. 71.)
75. *Wealth of Nations*, Glasgow edn, p. 95.
76. See, e.g., that for 1974, Table 52, p. 124.
77. See K. G. J. C. Knowles and D. J. Robertson, 'Differences between the Wages of Skilled and Unskilled workers, 1880–1950', *Bulletin of the Oxford University Institute of Statistics*, vol. 13, no. 4, (April 1951).
78. See my calculations in 'Interpretations of Pay Structure', *International Journal of Social Economics*, vol. 1, no. 1 (1974), pp. 31–3 (paper presented to the Royal Economic Society Conference on Pay Differentials, 1972).
79. *Principles of Economics*, p. 547.
80. See above p. 79.
81. In Christopher Saunders et al., *Winners and Losers: Pay Patterns in the 1970s* (PEP and Sussex University, 1977), chap. 3.
82. See A. R. Thatcher, 'Year to Year Variations in the Earnings of Individuals', *Journal of the Royal Statistical Society A*, Part 3 (1971), pp. 374–82.
83. Curiously, the initiative went back to the nationally negotiated rates in the pay explosion of 1975 and 1976. I hope some student will take this subject for his doctoral thesis in economic history, economics or industrial relations.
84. The National Board for Prices and Incomes found in 1968 that a quarter of their sample of 6·5 million employees were involved in job evaluation, with the proportion likely to rise to a third in the ensuing few years (Report No. 83). In 1976, the Institute of Personnel Management found that between 70 and 80 per cent of the employees of 213 firms surveyed were covered. In the study to be published in William Brown (ed.), *The Changing Contours of British Industrial Relations* (Oxford: Basil Blackwell, 1980) it was found that job evaluation schemes operated in 43·3 per cent of the establishments employing 55·6 per cent of the manual workers, and 32·1 per cent of the establishments employing 56·2 per cent of the non-manual workers.

85. Peter B. Doeringer and Michael J. Piore, *Internal Labor Markets and Manpower Analysis* (Heath Lexington Books, 1971).
86. Ibid., pp. 1–2.
87. See Derek Robinson (ed.), *Local Labour Markets and Wage Structures* (London: Gower Press, 1970).
88. Ibid., pp. 264–5. Another dimension to these variations has been emphasised by Kenneth Mayhew: the range of earnings within the same plant, of workers doing the same job, that contributes substantially to overall dispersion. ('Earnings Dispersion in Local Labour Markets: Implications for Search Behaviour', *Oxford Bulletin of Economics and Statistics*, vol. 39, no. 2 [May 1977].) He acknowledges the earlier study by H. M. Douty, 'Sources of Occupational Wage and Salary Rate Dispersion within Labor Markets', *Industrial and Labor Relations Review*, October 1961.
89. Ibid., pp. 269–70.
90. D. I. MacKay, D. Boddy, J. Brack, J. A. Diack, N. Jones, *Labour Markets under Different Employment Conditions* (London: Allen and Unwin, 1971).
91. Ibid., p. 391.
92. In *The Impact of Collective Bargaining on Management* (Washington D.C., Brookings Institution, 1960), p. 88.
93. University of Sussex and Institute of Personnel Management, *Salary Exercise, May 1964, Report to Participants* (mimeo.).

## NOTES TO APPENDIX A

1. London: HMSO, 1956.
2. Brief job descriptions are given in *A Dictionary of Occupational Terms*, Ministry of Labour (London: HMSO, 1927).
3. Here defined as a self-employed person whose employment requires the use of sufficient capital to make entry to the employment difficult, for example a self-employed shopkeeper is allocated to occupational class 2A; a self-employed window-cleaner is not.

## NOTES TO APPENDIX C

1. *Report of an Enquiry by the Board of Trade into Earnings and Hours of Labour of Workpeople of the United Kingdom in 1906*, 8 parts, Cd. 4545, 4844, 5086, 5196, 5460, 5814, 6053, 6556 (London: HMSO, 1909–13).
2. *A Compilation of Statistics (Technological, Commercial and General) of the Coal Mining Industry of the United Kingdom* (Cardiff, *The Western Mail*, 1922).
3. W. T. Layton, 'Changes in the Wages of Domestic Servants during Fifty Years', *op. cit.*, *Journal of the Royal Statistical Society*, vol. 71, part 3 (September 1908), p. 515; C. Booth, *Life and Labour of the People in London* (London: Macmillan, 1902); B. S. Rowntree, *Poverty: A Study of Town Life* (London: Macmillan, 1902).
4. 'The Amount and Distribution of Income (Other Than Wages) below the

Tax Exemption limit in the United Kingdom'. The Committee, which collected information from a large number of employers, included Professor Cannan (in the chair), Bowley and Edgeworth.

5. *Census of England and Wales, 1911:* vol. 10, *Occupations and Industries,* Cd. 7018, 7019 (London: HMSO, 1913–14).
6. The comparison is rough, for the trade union figures refer to a limited number of occupations and the National Insurance figures to a limited number of industries. However, engineering, building and woodworking are heavily represented in each.

## NOTES TO APPENDIX D

1. In 1913/14, Schedule E was limited to the salaries of officials of the government, public bodies and public companies. Other employees above the exemption limit were assessed under Schedule D. For 1922/3, all employees were assessed under Schedule E.
2. The 1911 census shows 941.
3. *Annual Report* of the Church Commissioners for England, 1957–58 (London, 1958).
4. *The Stipends and Expenses of the Clergy* (1959).
5. See notes to Table 3.1.
6. That is assuming weights of 5 for numbers at work in towns to 3 in the country.
7. Studies and Reports, series L, No. 1 (Geneva, 1924).
8. Institute of Chemistry *Journal and Proceedings*, Part 3 (1931), p. 197 and Part 2 (1939), p. 207.

## NOTES TO APPENDIX E

1. See Appendix D above.
2. In 1909/10, the Cannan Committee, in 'The Amount of Distribution of Income (Other Than Wages) Below the Income-Tax Exemption Limit in the United Kingdom', calculated that only about 94,000 out of 483,000 clerks were above the income tax exemption level of £160. Thus it is probable that most employees in industry at £200 in 1913/14 were employed in some sort of managerial or managerial/professional capacity.

# Index